T0156107

Practical Amazon EC2, SQS, Kinesis, and S3

A Hands-On Approach to AWS

Sunil Gulabani

Apress®

Practical Amazon EC2, SQS, Kinesis, and S3: A Hands-On Approach to AWS

Sunil Gulabani
Ahmedabad, Gujarat, India

ISBN-13 (pbk): 978-1-4842-2840-1   ISBN-13 (electronic): 978-1-4842-2841-8
DOI 10.1007/978-1-4842-2841-8

Library of Congress Control Number: 2017944280

Cover image designed by Freepik

Managing Director: Welmoed Spahr
Editorial Director: Todd Green
Acquisitions Editor: Celestin Suresh John
Development Editor: Poonam Jain and Laura Berendson
Technical Reviewer: Unmesh Gundecha
Coordinating Editor: Sanchita Mandal
Copy Editor: Ann Dickson
Compositor: SPi Global
Indexer: SPi Global
Artist: SPi Global

Distributed to the book trade worldwide by Springer Science+Business Media New York, 233 Spring Street, 6th Floor, New York, NY 10013. Phone 1-800-SPRINGER, fax (201) 348-4505, e-mail orders-ny@springer-sbm.com, or visit www.springeronline.com. Apress Media, LLC is a California LLC and the sole member (owner) is Springer Science + Business Media Finance Inc (SSBM Finance Inc). SSBM Finance Inc is a **Delaware** corporation.

For information on translations, please e-mail rights@apress.com, or visit http://www.apress.com/rights-permissions.

Apress titles may be purchased in bulk for academic, corporate, or promotional use. eBook versions and licenses are also available for most titles. For more information, reference our Print and eBook Bulk Sales web page at http://www.apress.com/bulk-sales.

Any source code or other supplementary material referenced by the author in this book is available to readers on GitHub via the book's product page, located at www.apress.com/978-1-4842-2840-1. For more detailed information, please visit http://www.apress.com/source-code.

Printed on acid-free paper

The completion of this undertaking could not have been possible without the participation and motivation of so many people I cannot possibly name them all. However, I would like to express deep appreciation and gratitude to the following people:

—My parents for their endless support and love.

—My wife, Priya, for being my constant pillar of strength and for her understanding spirit.

—My family and friends who, in one way or another, shared their support.

Also, I am thankful to the Apress team for giving me the opportunity to author this book.

Above all, I am grateful to the Great Almighty for my well-being, which was necessary to complete this book.

Contents at a Glance

Contents at a Glance

Contents

About the Author

Sunil Gulabani is a software engineer based in India and the author of *Developing RESTFul Web Services with Jersey 2.0* and *Amazon S3 Essentials*. He completed his graduation in commerce from S. M. Patel Institute of Commerce (SMPIC) and obtained his master's degree in computer applications from AES Institute of Computer Studies (AESICS). Sunil presented a paper entitled "Effective Label Matching for Automated Evaluation of Use Case Diagrams" at an IEEE conference on Technology for Education (T4E) held at IIIT Hyderabad, along with Dr. Vinay Vachharajani and Dr. Jyoti Pareek.

Since 2011, Sunil has been working as a software engineer, and he considers himself a cloud-savvy person. He is experienced in developing enterprise solutions using Java Enterprise Edition. He has a keen interest in system architecture and integration, data modeling, relational databases, and mapping with NoSQL for high throughput.

Sunil is interested in writing tech blogs, and he is actively involved in knowledge-sharing communities. You can visit him online at www.sunilgulabani.com and follow him on Twitter at twitter.com/sunil_gulabani. You can also reach Sunil directly at sunil_gulabani@yahoo.com or on LinkedIn at www.linkedin.com/in/sunilgulabani.

About the Technical Reviewer

Unmesh Gundecha has a master's degree in software engineering and over 15 years of experience in Agile software development, cloud computing, test automation, and technical QA. He is an Agile, open source, and DevOps evangelist with a rich experience in a diverse set of tools and technologies. Presently, he is working as an automation architect for a multinational company in Pune, India. Unmesh has also authored *Selenium Testing Tools Cookbook* and *Learning Selenium Testing Tools with Python* (Packt Publishing).

Acknowledgments

First and foremost, I would like to thank God for the good health and knowledge that was necessary to complete this book. In the process of putting this book together, I realized how true this gift of writing is for me.

My wife, Priya. Thanks for not just believing but knowing that I could do this. Because of your constant motivation and love throughout the writing of the book, you have helped me in more ways than anyone else.

Introduction

Practical Amazon EC2, SQS, Kinesis, and S3 introduces Amazon Web Services. It explains how to implement EC2 to run applications, how to use SQS for messaging queuing data from one computer to another, and how to process large streams of data using Kinesis. In this book, I also show how to store files on S3 and access them from anywhere.

First, in the introduction to Amazon Web Services, I will discuss prerequisite setups, such as IAM user and key pair, and local machine setups with tools that will help to implement EC2, SQS, Kinesis, and S3.

Next, I will explain the basics of EC2 and different types of EC2 instances. I will demonstrate how to create EC2 and connect EC2. Furthermore, I will explain SQS and how it is different from traditional MQs. Then I will demonstrate file storage using AWS S3. Finally, I will look at how to process large streams of data using Kinesis.

There are different ways to implement AWS EC2 instances, SQS, Kinesis, and S3. Users can use the method that best suits their project requirements.

I will explore the following:

- **AWS Management Console:** I will focus on the implementation of AWS EC2, SQS, Kinesis, and S3 using the AWS Management Console. I also cover how to configure the attributes from the UI.

- **AWS CLI:** I will explain how to use AWS CLI to implement AWS EC2, SQS, Kinesis, and S3. For using AWS CLI, I will also explain the installation and configuration of AWS CLI on local machines. In addition, I will discuss how to configure the attributes from the AWS CLI.

- **AWS Java SDK:** I will demonstrate how to consume AWS SDK for Java for implementing AWS EC2, SQS, Kinesis, and S3. There are different APIs provided by AWS to perform different actions on the AWS EC2, SQS, Kinesis, and S3. Also, I will provide code snippets and their execution effects on AWS EC2, SQS, Kinesis, and S3, which can be seen on UI.

Furthermore, you will learn how to implement AWS CloudWatch for AWS EC2, SQS, Kinesis, and S3. You will learn how to raise an alarm for EC2, SQS, Kinesis, and S3 when thresholds are reached. (This is used in production environments where services are continuously monitored to see whether they are performing well and that there are no side effects going on pertaining to the services.)

Who Should Read This Book

This book is intended for cloud engineers or developers, software architects, project managers, and users who want to explore Amazon EC2, SQS, Kinesis, and S3. Basic knowledge of Java programming is expected.

CHAPTER 1

■ ■ ■

Getting Started with AWS

In recent years, IT professionals have frequently used the term *cloud computing* to refer to the practice of using remote services to store, manage, and process data. However, the most common term is *Amazon Web Services* (*AWS*). AWS has changed the working methodology of the application/system by providing various services that can be integrated into our applications and systems. It allows developers to focus on the core business logic while services such as infrastructure management, database administration, server management, high availability, cost minimization, and so on, are being handled by AWS.

In this chapter, I will introduce the basics of Amazon Web Services and the prerequisite configurations that will be needed for subsequent chapters.

What Is Amazon Web Services?

Amazon Web Services is a cloud service provider that allows a user to consume different services to ease the application management. AWS provides infrastructure, security, storage, networking, and other services that are useful for application life cycle.

AWS is being exposed as Web Services. This makes it very simple and easy for users to manage the services. It provides services as an on-demand basis. In other words, users can enroll for services according to their requirements or demands for the applications and terminate the services when they are no longer needed.

AWS is located at various geographical locations, also known as *regions*. Users have the choice to select from any of these available geographical locations that they feel will be the most useful in terms of serving the application latency time.

■ **Note** For more information on latency, see `https://en.wikipedia.org/wiki/Latency_(engineering)`.

As AWS is an on-demand service, it uses pay-as-you-go pricing. As a result, you will be charged only for the services you use. AWS also provides detailed monthly billing that helps users to know which services they are consuming the most.

© Sunil Gulabani 2017
S. Gulabani, *Practical Amazon EC2, SQS, Kinesis, and S3*,
DOI 10.1007/978-1-4842-2841-8_1

Sign Up for Amazon Web Services

To have access to AWS, you first need to create an account in Amazon Web Services.

1. Open the URL http://aws.amazon.com in any browser and click Sign In to the Console, as shown in Figure 1-1.

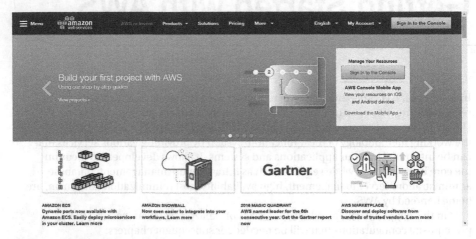

Figure 1-1. *Amazon Web Services landing page*

2. The next page you will see is the sign-in page, where you will select I am a new user. and provide an e-mail address. Then you will click the Sign in using our secure server button, as shown in Figure 1-2.

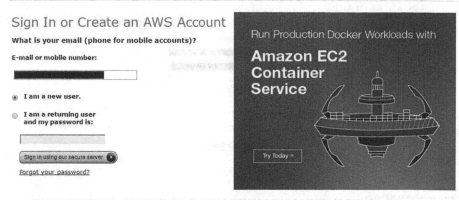

Figure 1-2. Create an AWS account

3.   In the next step, shown in Figure 1-3, you will provide login
      credentials that include your name, e-mail address, and
      password. Using this e-mail address and password, you will be
      able to log in to the AWS Management Console, so make sure
      you remember to save this information in a secure place.

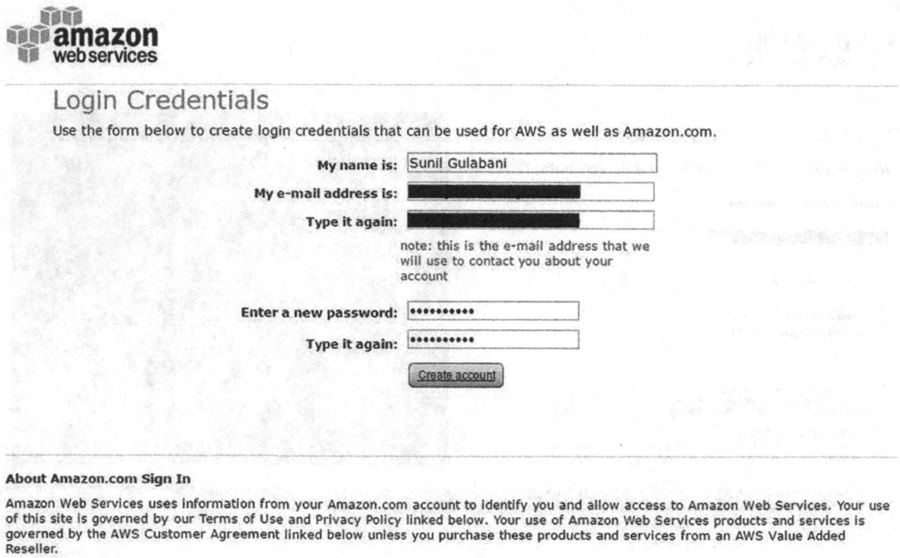

Login Credentials

Use the form below to create login credentials that can be used for AWS as well as Amazon.com.

My name is: Sunil Gulabani

My e-mail address is: ████████████████

Type it again: ████████████████

note: this is the e-mail address that we will use to contact you about your account

Enter a new password: ••••••••••

Type it again: ••••••••••

Create account

About Amazon.com Sign In

Amazon Web Services uses information from your Amazon.com account to identify you and allow access to Amazon Web Services. Your use of this site is governed by our Terms of Use and Privacy Policy linked below. Your use of Amazon Web Services products and services is governed by the AWS Customer Agreement linked below unless you purchase these products and services from an AWS Value Added Reseller.

Figure 1-3. *Login credentials*

4. The next step is to provide contact information to AWS since AWS will generate bills with this name and address, as shown in Figure 1-4.

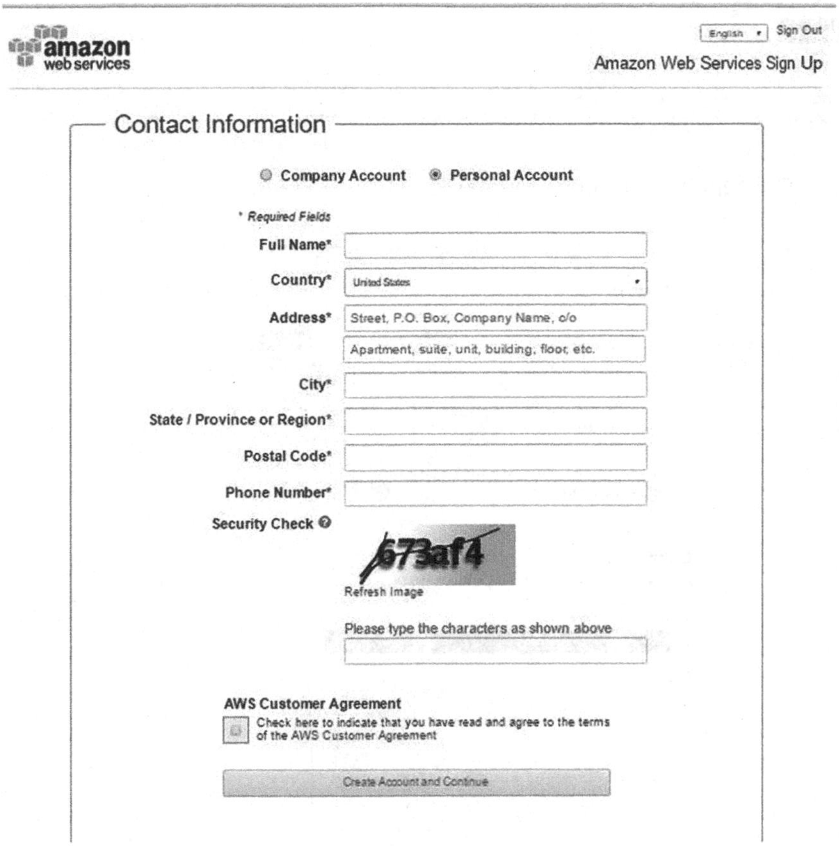

English ▾   Sign Out

Amazon Web Services Sign Up

Contact Information

○ Company Account   ◉ Personal Account

* Required Fields

Full Name*

Country* [United States   ▾]

Address* [Street, P.O. Box, Company Name, c/o]

[Apartment, suite, unit, building, floor, etc.]

City*

State / Province or Region*

Postal Code*

Phone Number*

Security Check ❷

673af4

Refresh Image

Please type the characters as shown above

AWS Customer Agreement

☐ Check here to indicate that you have read and agree to the terms of the AWS Customer Agreement

[Create Account and Continue]

Figure 1-4. *Providing contact information*

5. In the next step, shown in Figure 1-5, you will provide payment information (that is, credit card details) so that AWS can directly charge the monthly billing amount to your credit card account. It is critical to provide this information because without this payment information, users won't be able to consume any services on the AWS Management Console.

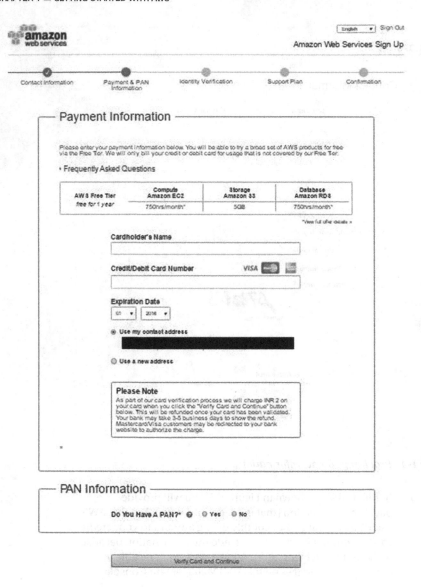

Figure 1-5. *Payment information*

Under Frequently Asked Questions, AWS free tier information is provided. For new users, AWS provides a free usage tier so those users can experiment with AWS services. Only some of the services are available for free by AWS. For more details, please visit https://aws.amazon.com/free.

6. The next step is to verify your identity, as shown in Figure 1-6.
    Here, you will be providing your contact number. When you
    click the Call Me Now button, an automated call is triggered to
    your contact number. Simultaneously, a PIN number will be
    provided to the automated call received.

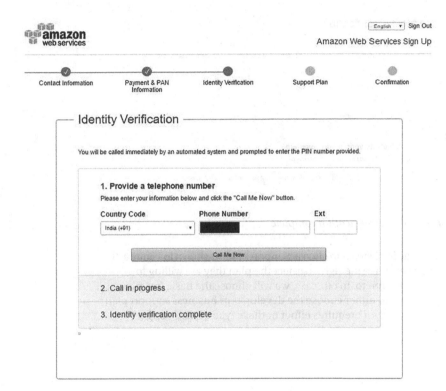

Figure 1-6. Identity verification

7. Once you verify the PIN number via the automated call, you
    can see that your identity verification is complete, as shown in
    Figure 1-7.

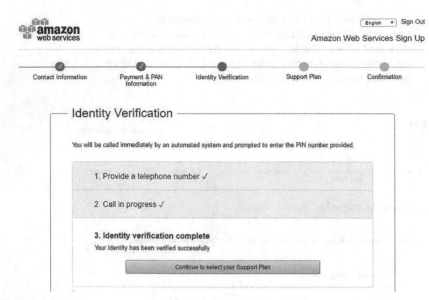

Figure 1-7. *Identity verification complete*

8.   The final step is to choose Support Plan, as shown in Figure 1-8. Users have the right to select the plan they are willing to subscribe to. In our case, we will choose the basic free plan. You can either choose the developer or business support plan if your work requires either of these type of AWS support.

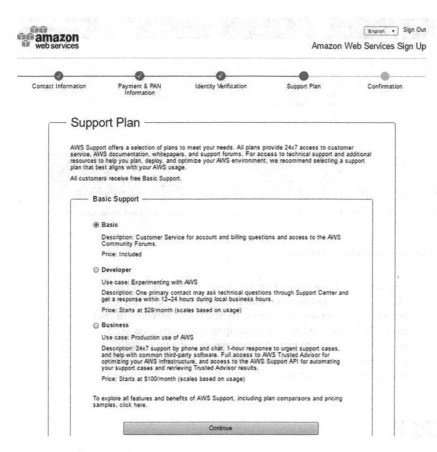

Figure 1-8. *Choose support plan*

As shown in Figure 1-9, you will receive a registration confirmation, which completes the registration process.

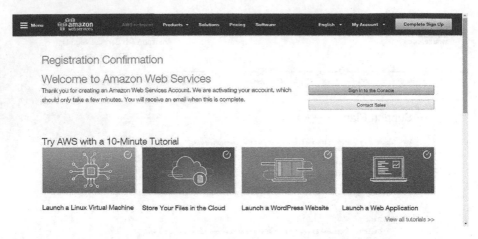

Figure 1-9. Registration confirmation

9. Now that you have created an account on AWS, you will sign in using the credentials that you provided while creating the account. You can see in Figure 1-10 that this time you will click the radio button for I am a returning user and my password is:. This allows you to provide your password. Once you have provided your e-mail and password, click the Sign in using our secure server button.

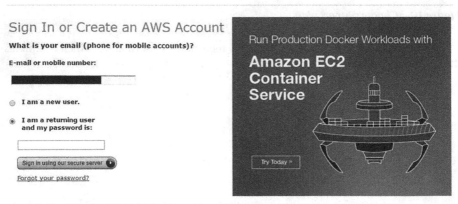

Figure 1-10. Sign-in page for AWS

10.   Once AWS verifies your credentials, you will be redirected to the
       AWS Management Console landing page. (See Figure 1-11.)

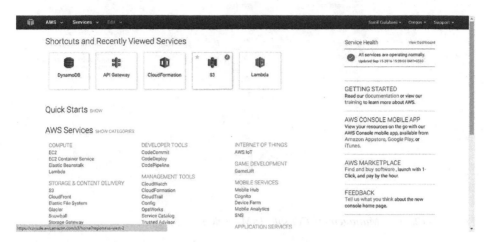

Figure 1-11. *AWS Management Console landing page*

This concludes our explanation of the sign-up and sign-up processes.

Create User and Groups

AWS IAM (Identity and Access Management) helps to control the number of users under
this account that will consume the AWS resources. You can provide authentication and
authorization for new users, which allows them to access AWS limited resources. In
subsequent chapters, we will interact with AWS EC2, SQS, Kinesis, and S3 using SDK. In
order to interact with SDK, we need IAM users' access keys and secret keys.

1.   To create IAM, sign in at `http://aws.amazon.com` and click
      IAM under Security and Identity, as highlighted in Figure 1-12.

11

Figure 1-12. *AWS Management Console, IAM services*

2. The IAM services page will open and allow you to create users, groups, roles, policies, and so on, as shown in Figure 1-13. This enables authorization to access AWS resources.

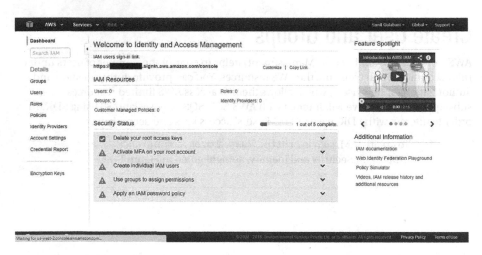

Figure 1-13. *IAM services*

3. Click Users in the menu shown under IAM Resources in Figure 1-13. This will direct you to a page where you can create a new user and display an existing users' list. As of now, we don't have any users created, so it's showing No records found. (See Figure 1-14.)

Figure 1-14. *IAM users screen*

4. The next step is to click the Create New Users button, which will ask you to provide user names and whether you want to generate an access key for each user. This check box should be selected so as to generate an access key and secret key for the user. See Figure 1-15.

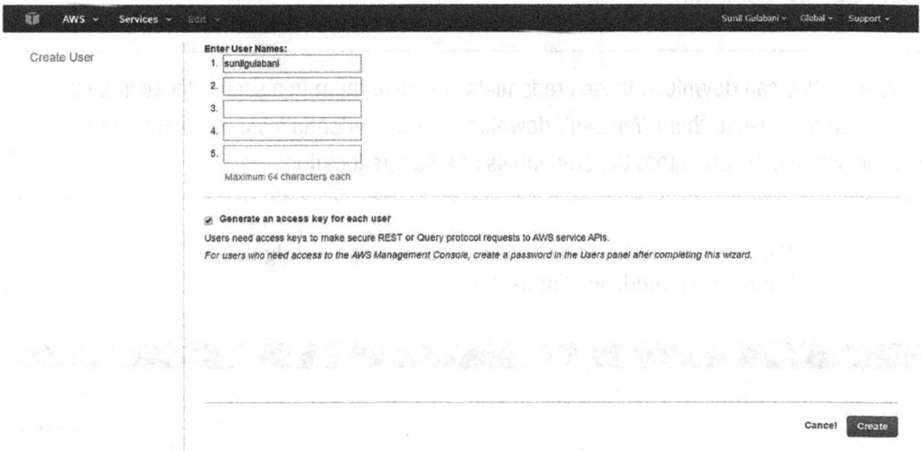

Figure 1-15. *Create user*

5. Clicking the Create User button will create a user and also create security credentials, which have Access Key ID and Secret Access Key (as the check box is selected). See Figure 1-16.

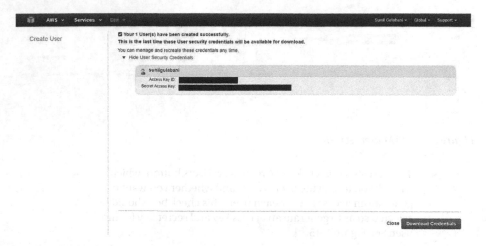

Figure 1-16. *User created*

■ **Note** You can download these credentials and save them in a secure location so that others do not misuse them. You can't download or get credentials once you are off this screen. Be mindful and store the credentials at a secure location.

6. You can see on the users screen that new user sunilgulabani has been created. See Figure 1-17.

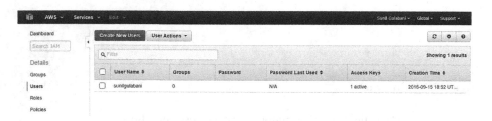

Figure 1-17. *User listing*

7. Now you will create a group that will have full access for AWS EC2, S3, Kinesis, and SQS. To create such a group, click the Groups button in the menu, as shown in Figure 1-18. This will open the Groups screen where you can create new groups and view the list of existing groups.

Figure 1-18. *Groups screen*

8. Click the Create New Group button shown in Figure 1-18. This will open a dialog box for creating a new group, as shown in Figure 1-19.

Figure 1-19. *Create new group*

Creating a new group consists of three steps:

a. Step 1: Group Name. In this step, we will set the group name as "Developers" for our example.

b. Step 2: Attach Policy. Following are a list of policies, and we will select the policies that need to be attached with the group.

- AmazonEC2FullAccess

- AmazonS3FullAccess

- AmazonKinesisFullAccess

- AmazonSQSFullAccess

c. Step 3: Review. In this step, we will review the group name, attach policies, and proceed with creating a group by clicking the Create Group button. See Figure 1-20.

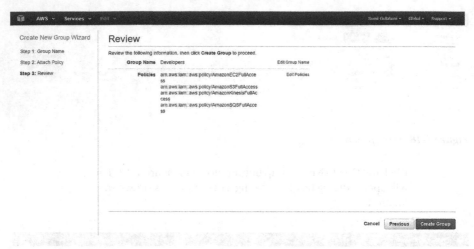

Figure 1-20. *Create group*

9. In Figure 1-20, you can see the listing of the newly created group. Now, we will add users to this group. Select the Developers group and under the Group Actions drop-down list, click the Add Users to Group option. See Figure 1-21.

Figure 1-21. *Add Users to Group menu*

10. Clicking the Add Users to Group button will open the dialog box where we can select the users that are to be added. Select the sunilgulabani user and click the Add Users button. See Figure 1-22.

Figure 1-22. *Add users to group*

Now we have finished creating IAM.

Create Key Pairs

In this section, we will create key pairs that will be used to access the EC2 instance, which will be created in subsequent chapters. This is just a prerequisite so that we have this key pair ready when we need it in the upcoming chapters.

1.   To create a key pair, click EC2, as highlighted in Figure 1-23.

Figure 1-23. *Amazon Management Console (EC2)*

2. This step will direct us to the EC2 dashboard. Here we click Key Pairs, which is highlighted in Figure 1-24.

Figure 1-24. *EC2 dashboard (key pairs)*

3. On the key pairs screen, click Create Key Pair, which will ask
   you for the key pair name. Enter the name and click the Create
   button to create a key pair, as shown in Figure 1-25.

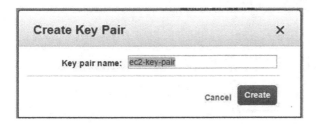

Figure 1-25. *Create Key Pair*

4. Once you click the Create button, a key pair is generated and a
   pem file will be downloaded automatically.

5. Save this pem file in a secure location, as this will be used
   for creating an EC2 instance. You will then log in to the EC2
   instance from our machine.

Install AWS CLI

AWS Command Line Interface (CLI) is one of the ways to access AWS resources. It allows
users to interact with the AWS resources by command prompts, and they can execute the
AWS commands in scripts. We will first install AWS CLI on our (Windows) machine.

1. Go to https://aws.amazon.com/cli/ and find the suitable
   installation file. See Figure 1-26.

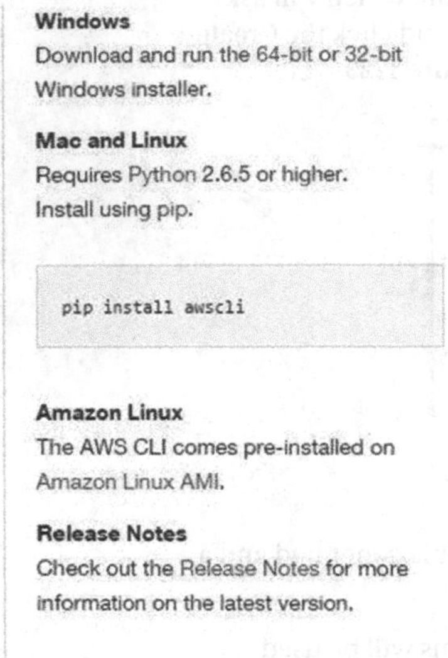

Windows
Download and run the 64-bit or 32-bit
Windows installer.

Mac and Linux
Requires Python 2.6.5 or higher.
Install using pip.

```
pip install awscli
```

Amazon Linux
The AWS CLI comes pre-installed on
Amazon Linux AMI.

Release Notes
Check out the Release Notes for more
information on the latest version.

Figure 1-26. *AWS CLI download*

2. In our case, we downloaded and installed Windows 64-bit.
   For other OS AWS CLI Installation, see
   http://docs.aws.amazon.com/cli/latest/userguide/
   installing.html.

3. Once we have installed AWS CLI, we will verify that AWS CLI
   is installed properly. To verify, open the command prompt
   and type the following command:

   aws --version

This command should return the version of the AWS CLI, as shown in Figure 1-27.

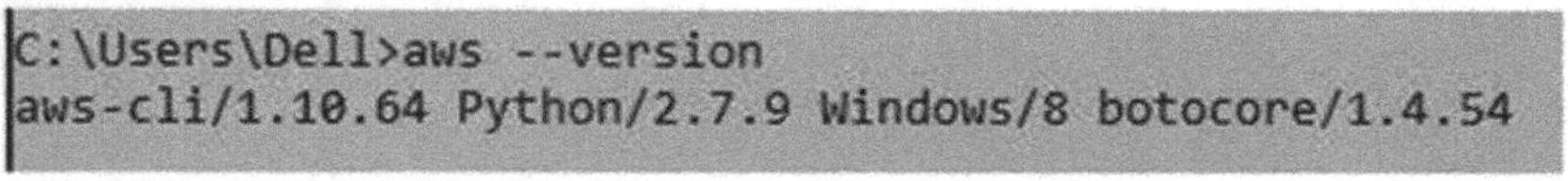

```
C:\Users\Dell>aws --version
aws-cli/1.10.64 Python/2.7.9 Windows/8 botocore/1.4.54
```

Figure 1-27. *AWS CLI version*

The next step is to configure AWS CLI. Open the command prompt and type the
following command:

aws configure

You will be asked for the access key ID, secret access key, default region, and default
output format, as shown in Figure 1-28.

```
C:\Users\Dell>aws configure
AWS Access Key ID [None]: ████████████████
AWS Secret Access Key [None]: ████████████████████████
Default region name [None]: us-west-2
Default output format [None]: json
```

Figure 1-28. AWS CLI configure

4.   You can copy and paste the access key ID and secret access key from the credentials downloaded from the IAM section. Regarding the default region name, you need to set the region name where you want to access AWS resources. For the default output format, the values can be any one of following: JSON, table, or text. The default format is JSON if you don't provide a preference.

Download SSH Client

In subsequent chapter(s), I will use PuTTy SSH Client to connect to the EC2 instances. You can use your choice of SSH Client if you want. To install Putty SSH Client, and PuTTYgen, download the file from www.chiark.greenend.org.uk/~sgtatham/putty/download.html.

or www.putty.org/.

PuTTYgen is used to convert the pem file (which was downloaded after creating key pairs) to a public/private key (ppk) file.

Setup Eclipse

We will use Eclipse software tools to create our application in subsequent chapters.

1.   You can download the eclipse software from https://eclipse.org/home/index.php.

2.   Once you download the Eclipse Installer, you need to select Eclipse IDE for Java EE Developers, as shown in Figure 1-29, and follow the steps to install it.

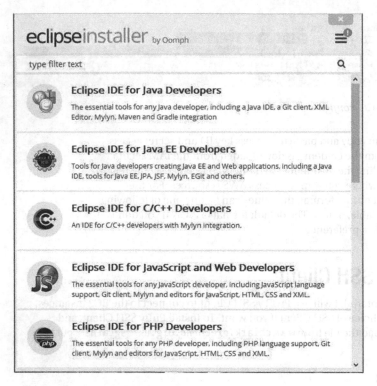

Figure 1-29. *Eclipse Installer*

Summary

Amazon Web Services is one of the leading cloud providers. I have demonstrated how to create IAM, which allows access to AWS resources using SDK or CLI. Also, I have shown how to configure a system to have pre-install software packages.

In Chapter 2, I will guide you through an Elastic Compute Cloud (EC2) instance with AWS Management Console, AWS SDK, and AWS CLI. Also, I will show you how to create a cloud watch alarm on EC2.

CHAPTER 2

■ ■ ■

Hands-on Elastic Compute Cloud

Amazon Elastic Compute Cloud (EC2) provides virtual computing. EC2 can be used for various purposes such as running custom applications, storing files, and so on. Users have a wide variety of operating systems to launch EC2 instances.

In this chapter, we will cover the following topics:

- Introduction to EC2

- Features of EC2

- EC2 Instance Types

- Managing EC2 Using Management Console

- Managing EC2 Using AWS CLI

- Managing EC2 Using AWS SDK (Java)

- Monitoring Using CloudWatch

Introduction to EC2

Amazon EC2 is an elastic virtual server that resides under the AWS cloud environment. It provides scalable computing power for an application. It provides great flexibility for operating systems, memory, CPUs, storage, and so on. Amazon provides EC2 instances for rent to users at a nominal rate. Users can then deploy their software on the EC2 instance.

Amazon has given control to the users to create, start, stop, and terminate the instance at their convenience. Amazon has a variety of Amazon Machine Images (AMIs) available that can be used to create new servers in the cloud. Users can even create their own AMIs from their EC2 instance. EC2 also has the capability to auto-scale the servers up and down based on the load of existing servers in just a few minutes.

Amazon provides different regions to launch the different services. As a result, you can create instances to handle failures at different geographical regions or you can utilize multiregion deployment strategies for your application. Amazon uses the pay-as-you-go concept, which means you only pay for the number of Amazon services you have used.

© Sunil Gulabani 2017   23
S. Gulabani, *Practical Amazon EC2, SQS, Kinesis, and S3*,
DOI 10.1007/978-1-4842-2841-8_2

Features of EC2

The main features of EC2 that play a significant role while using applications include the large number of possible operating systems, elasticity, fault tolerance and latency, pricing, security, and service commitment.

Operating System

Amazon EC2 provides a wide variety of operating systems that can be used to boot the server. Amazon Linux, Debian, SUSE, FreeBSD, CentOS, Red Hat Enterprise Linux, SUSE Linux Enterprise Server, Ubuntu, Windows, and other Linux operating systems are among them.

Elasticity

Amazon EC2 infrastructure is elastic in nature. *Elasticity* means the system manages its resources by provisioning and de-provisioning them without manual intervention and, therefore, manages load dynamically. It has the capability to auto-scale the resources based on the load and configuration created. You can configure the threshold limit when a new EC2 instance needs to be created based on the load on EC2 and terminate EC2 when the load on EC2 is below the threshold limit.

Fault Tolerance and Latency

Amazon EC2 provides flexibility to auto-scale the servers on an as-needed basis. If one instance fails, another instance can be added to serve the purpose. Amazon also provides different availability zones where system architecture is designed in such a way that if a zone in a (region) is down, another zone in the same (region) can serve the request. Moreover, elastic IP can be seamlessly mapped within minutes so that routing to newly created EC2 instances are complete.

Pricing

As previously mentioned, Amazon charges only for the hours consumed. There may be different pricing options available for different capacity instances. Along with EC2, if we also opt for storage, pricing is based on storage type and the amount of data that is being stored in it.

■ **Note**   Amazon provides AWS Free Tier so that you can experiment with certain services at no charge. For more details, visit `https://aws.amazon.com/free/`.

Security

Security is the major concern people have about the cloud. The security provided by EC2 is similar to the traditional firewall. It allows users to manage the accessibility of AWS resources to provide client information such as IP addresses or subnet groups. It is an effective way to manage security on EC2.

Service Commitment

AWS provides the service commitment for its uptime of 99.95%. This means EC2 instances will be up and running for 99.95% of your monthly billing cycle. If this service commitment is not met, users will receive the service credit based on the criteria defined by AWS. For more information, go to `https://aws.amazon.com/ec2/sla/`.

EC2 Instance Types

AWS provides a long list of instance types that users can choose based on their needs. Users' needs vary based on their CPU, memory, storage, and networking capacity. Users choose a specific instance type that suits their application requirement. All instances have a specific price tag that users need to consider while selecting their instance type. In addition, users can configure the scaling behavior to support the instances.

■ **Note** For more information on instances, see `https://aws.amazon.com/ec2/instance-types/`.

Managing EC2 Using Management Console

AWS Management Console is the simplest way to configure AWS resources. All the services have their configuration available on the management console, which makes it easy to manage.

After logging in to the AWS account, click EC2 under the Compute category, as shown in Figure 2-1.

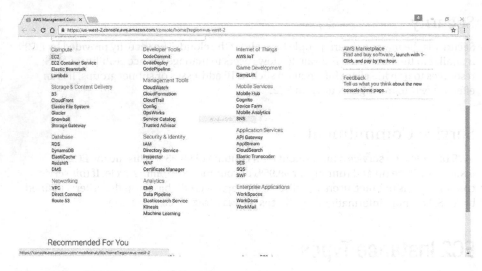

Figure 2-1. *AWS Management Console*

Once you click EC2, you will be navigated to the EC2 dashboard page, as shown in Figure 2-2.

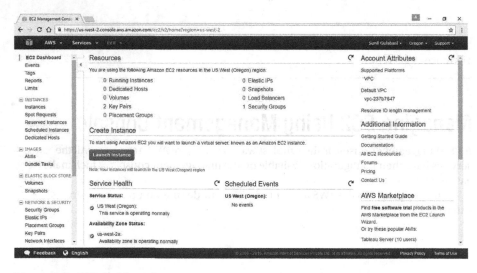

Figure 2-2. *EC2 dashboard page*

The EC2 dashboard page summarizes the services that are used with EC2.

Let's try to achieve the following:

1.   Create a virtual remote Linux machine.

2.   Log in to a virtual remote Linux machine using SSH client
     (See Figure 2-3).

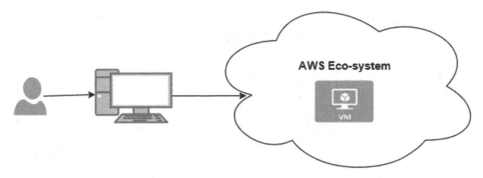

Figure 2-3. *Output*

Now, let's create an EC2 instance. The major steps involved to create an EC2 instance
are as follows:

1.   Create security group

2.   Create key pair

3.   Create EC2 instance

4.   Connect to EC2 instance

Let's look at these steps in detail.

1. Create a Security Group

Security groups work as firewalls for our EC2 instance. They determine what ingress and
egress ports need to be exposed to specific IP addresses so that our application can be
accessible from those IP addresses.

1.   Click Security Groups under the NETWORK & SECURITY
     category on the left-side menu of the EC2 dashboard page.

2.   Click Create Security Group, which opens a window where the
     user will fill in security information, as shown in Figure 2-4.

Create Security Group   ✕

Security group name ⓘ	
Description ⓘ	
VPC ⓘ	vpc-237b7647 (172.31.0.0/16) * ▼

* denotes default VPC

Security group rules:

Inbound Outbound

Type ⓘ	Protocol ⓘ	Port Range ⓘ	Source ⓘ

This security group has no rules

Add Rule

Cancel Create

Figure 2-4. *Create security group*

3. Add an inbound rule for the SSH port. This will be used to connect to the machine from anywhere on Port 22. You can select the source of connection as Custom, Anywhere, or My IP Address from the drop-down list. See Figure 2-5.

Security group rules:

Inbound Outbound

Type ⓘ	Protocol ⓘ	Port Range ⓘ	Source ⓘ		
SSH ▼	TCP	22	Anywhere ▼ 0.0.0.0/0	⟳	✖

Add Rule

Figure 2-5. *Add inbound rule for SSH*

4. Once you have filled in the details, click the Create button. This will create the security group having the SSH port exposed. See Figure 2-6.

Name ▾	Group ID ▴	Group Name ▾	VPC ID ▾	Description ▾
	sg-c8b115b1	Chapter 2	vpc-237b7647	Chapter 2 Security Group

Figure 2-6. *Security group created*

2. Create a Key Pair

Key pairs are used for connecting to EC2 instances. Key pairs need to be stored at a secure location. If key pairs are lost, you won't be able to connect to EC2 instances or recover the key pairs.

1. Click Key Pairs under the NETWORK & SECURITY category in the left-side menu of the EC2 dashboard page.

2. Click the Create Key Pair button, which opens a window where the user has to enter the key pair name, as shown in Figure 2-7.

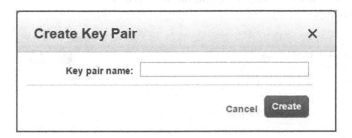

Figure 2-7. Create key pair

3. Click the Create button to create the new key pair. This will automatically download a pem file, which can be used to log in to the EC2 instance to which we will assign this key pair in the next step. See Figure 2-8.

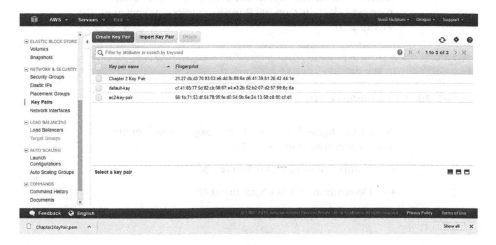

Figure 2-8. Key pair listing and downloaded pem file

3. Create an EC2 Instance

In the following steps, we will configure parameters to launch an EC2 instance:

1. Click Instances under the INSTANCES category in the left-side menu of the EC2 dashboard page.

2. Click Launch Instance on the next page and you will be navigated to the Create Instance Steps page.

    a. Step 1: Choose AMI. Select the AMI from the list that fits your application requirement. For our case, we will select "Red Hat Enterprise Linux 7.2 (HVM), SSD Volume Type - ami-775e4f16," which is eligible for AWS Free Tier. See Figure 2-9.

Figure 2-9. *Choose AMI*

■ **Note**   Make sure to select the correct AMI for your application requirement since you will be charged. If you are eligible for AWS Free Tier, use the free-tier AMIs for this.

---

    b. Step 2: Choose Instance Type. Select the instance type from the list for your application requirements. For our case, we select the General Purpose t2.micro, as shown in Figure 2-10.

Figure 2-10. *Choose instance type*

    c. Step 3: Configure Instance. On this page, we will set the parameters shown in Figure 2-11.

        •   Number of instances to be created

        •   Determining if it is a Spot instance

        •   VPC/subnetting configuration

- IAM role to be assigned to the EC2, which will have access to different AWS resources

- Shutdown behavior—whether to shut down the instance or to terminate the instance

- Enabling termination protection, which will not allow you to terminate the instance unless you disable this property

- Enabling CloudWatch to monitor EC2

- Defining tenancy—determining if location is on shared hardware, dedicated instance, or an instance on a dedicated host

- Executing the shell script command, which is used to pre-initialize some of the software on the machine

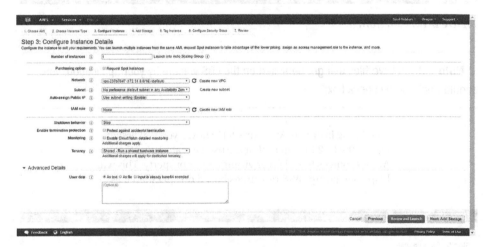

Figure 2-11. *Configure instance details*

    d.   Step 4: Add Storage. You can add the EBS volumes that will be attached to our EC2 instance, as shown in Figure 2-12. One of the most useful parameters here is Delete on Termination. This denotes whether the EBS volume needs to be deleted when the instance gets terminated.

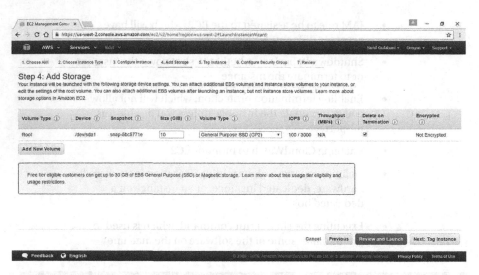

Figure 2-12. *Add storage*

■ **Note** If you have files that get persisted on the EBS volume by your application, you should uncheck the check box.

---

    e.   Step 5: Tag Instance. As Figure 2-13 shows, you can assign tags to the EC2 instances that are used to categorize the AWS resources based on environment or property. This will help us to group AWS resources based on specified tags.

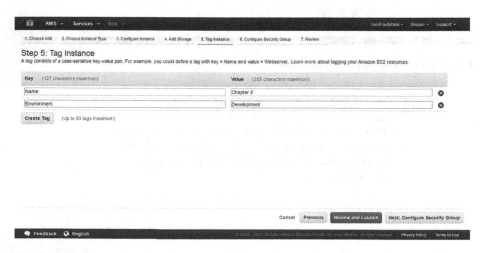

Figure 2-13. *Tag instance*

f.   Step 6: Configure Security Group. This will set the firewall rules used to expose the EC2 instance ports. As Figure 2-14 shows, you can either create a new security group or select from existing security groups. In our case, we will select from the existing security group that we created earlier with name "Chapter 2."

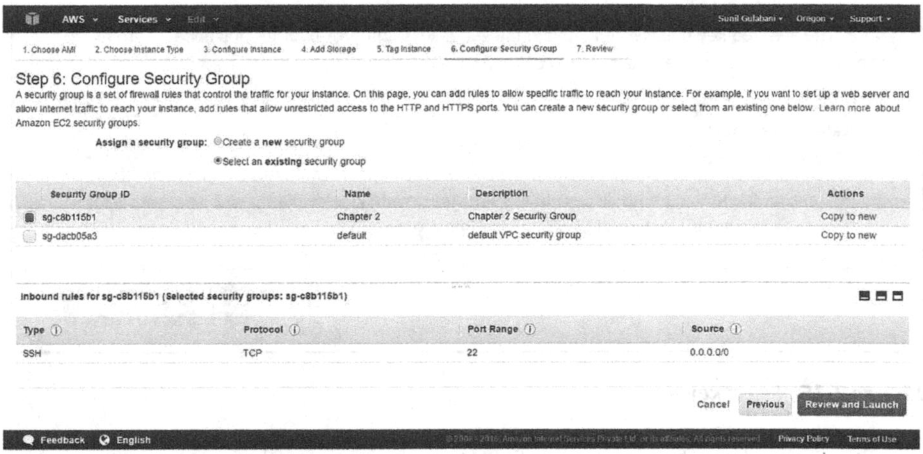

Figure 2-14. *Configure security group*

g.   Step 7: Review. In this step, we will review the configuration and, once we have verified it, click the Launch button. This will ask us to select the key pair. You can either select an existing key pair or create a new one. We will select the key pair we created in the previous section with the name "Chapter 2 Key Pair," as shown in Figure 2-15. After selecting the key pair, acknowledge it by selecting the check box and click the Launch Instances button.

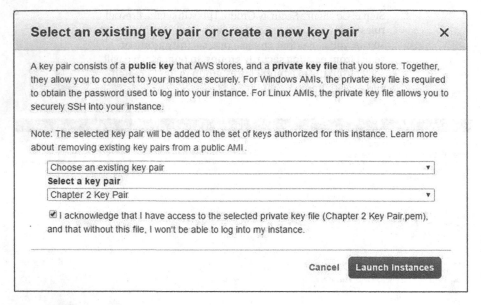

Figure 2-15. *Select key pair*

Step 7 completes the required configuration. You can view the instance status on the Instance page, as shown in Figure 2-16.

Figure 2-16. *Instance status*

4. Verify by Connecting to EC2 Instance

In this step, we will verify connection to EC2 instance by doing the following:

1. Convert EC2 pem file to ppk file. For this, we will use the puttygen.exe, which we installed in Chapter 1.

2. Click the Load button and select the pem file that was downloaded when we created the key pair, as shown in Figure 2-17.

Figure 2-17. *PuTTy Key Generator*

3. Once selected, you can see the private key file is loaded. We will save this using the Save private key option. See Figure 2-18.

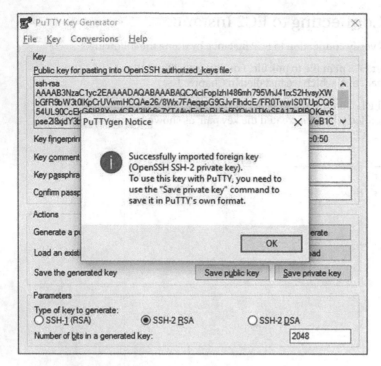

Figure 2-18. Pem file loaded

5. Connect to EC2 Instance

For Windows Users:

1. On the Instance Status page, find the EC2 instance username by clicking the Connect button, as shown in Figure 2-19. In our case, "ec2-user" is the username.

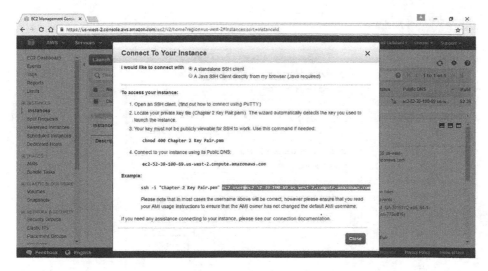

Figure 2-19. *Connect to your instance*

2. Find the public IP for our EC2 instance on the EC2 Instance Details page.

3. We will form the hostname, which has the following format:

USERNAME@INSTANCE_HOST_NAME_OR_PUBLIC_DNS_NAME

So, we have the following for our instance:

ec2-user@52.39.100.69

or

ec2-user@ec2-52-39-100-69.us-west-2.compute.amazonaws.com

4. Open Putty.exe, which we installed in Chapter 1, on your machine. Add the hostname or IP address by pasting the hostname that we formed in the previous step, as shown in Figure 2-20.

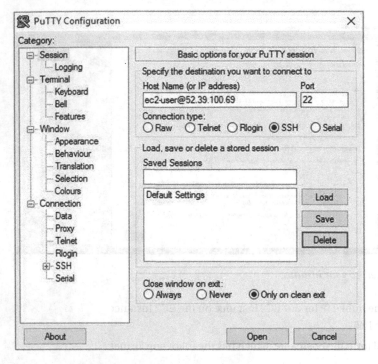

Figure 2-20. *PuTTy configuration—hostname*

5. Add the ppk file to the PuTTy SSH client, which we created in the previous section, as shown in Figure 2-21.

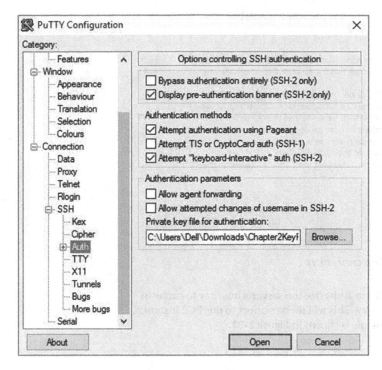

Figure 2-21. *PuTTy configuration—ppk file*

6. Once the configuration is complete, click the Open button. This will authenticate the key pair with your provided hostname. Once authentication is finished, we will get a security alert to cache the host key in the registry, as shown in Figure 2-22.

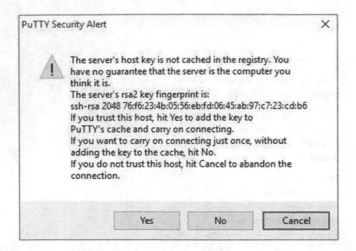

Figure 2-22. *PuTTy security alert*

7. Click Yes to authorize the server's host key to cache in the registry. This will then connect to our EC2 instance. The console is shown in Figure 2-23.

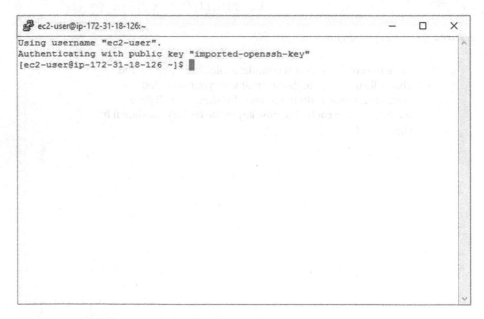

Figure 2-23. *EC2 instance terminal*

We have successfully verified by connecting to the EC2 instance terminal.

■ **Note** To connect to Linux, refer to `http://docs.aws.amazon.com/AWSEC2/latest/UserGuide/AccessingInstancesLinux.html`.

Managing EC2 Using AWS CLI

In Chapter 1, I demonstrated how to install AWS CLI. Now I will show how to use the AWS CLI to manage AWS EC2 instance resources. I will also explain how to create, list, and delete an EC2 instance resource. Following are the services needed to create an EC2 instance:

- Security group
- Key pair
- EC2 instance

To execute the AWS CLI commands, we need to open the command prompt.

Security Group

In this section, we will create, attach an inbound rule to, list, and delete security groups.

1. Create a Security Group

To create a security group, we will execute the following command:

```
>aws ec2 create-security-group --group-name EC2CreationViaAWSCLI
--description "EC2 creation via AWS CLI"
```

■ **Note** For more parameters, see `http://docs.aws.amazon.com/cli/latest/reference/ec2/create-security-group.html`.

---

2. Attach an Inbound Rule to Security Group

Once the security group is created, we will attach the CIDR and port to this newly created security group. In our case, we will attach SSH port (22) and the IP address as 0.0.0.0/0, which means you can access it from anywhere.

■ **Note**   *CIDR* is the acronym for *Classless Inter-Domain Routing*, which is used for assigning IP addresses and IP routing.

```
>aws ec2 authorize-security-group-ingress --group-name EC2CreationViaAWSCLI
--protocol tcp --port 22 --cidr 0.0.0.0/0
```

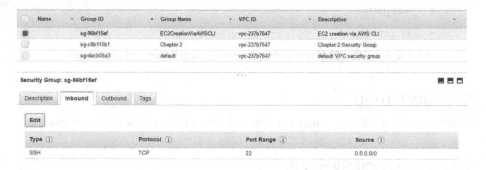

You can verify the details of the security group on the AWS Management Console, as shown in Figure 2-24.

Name	Group ID	Group Name	VPC ID	Description
	sg-96bf15ef	EC2CreationViaAWSCLI	vpc-237b7647	EC2 creation via AWS CLI
	sg-c8b115b1	Chapter 2	vpc-237b7647	Chapter 2 Security Group
	sg-dacb05a3	default	vpc-237b7647	default VPC security group

Security Group: sg-96bf15ef

Description | **Inbound** | Outbound | Tags

Edit

Type ①	Protocol ①	Port Range ①	Source ①
SSH	TCP	22	0.0.0.0/0

Figure 2-24. *Security group listing on AWS Management Console*

■ **Note**   For more parameters, see http://docs.aws.amazon.com/cli/latest/ reference/ec2/authorize-security-group-ingress.html.

3. List the Security Group

To list the security group that we created, we will execute the following command:

```
>aws ec2 describe-security-groups --group-names EC2CreationViaAWSCLI
```

```
C:\Users\Dell>aws ec2 describe-security-groups --group-names EC2CreationViaAWSCLI
{
    "SecurityGroups": [
        {
            "IpPermissionsEgress": [
                {
                    "IpProtocol": "-1",
                    "IpRanges": [
                        {
                            "CidrIp": "0.0.0.0/0"
                        }
                    ],
                    "UserIdGroupPairs": [],
                    "PrefixListIds": []
                }
            ],
            "Description": "EC2 creation via AWS CLI",
            "IpPermissions": [
                {
                    "PrefixListIds": [],
                    "FromPort": 22,
                    "IpRanges": [
                        {
                            "CidrIp": "0.0.0.0/0"
                        }
                    ],
                    "ToPort": 22,
                    "IpProtocol": "tcp",
                    "UserIdGroupPairs": []
                }
            ],
            "GroupName": "EC2CreationViaAWSCLI",
            "VpcId": "vpc-237b7647",
            "OwnerId": "██████████",
            "GroupId": "sg-96bf15ef"
        }
    ]
}
```

To list all the security groups, we will execute the following command:

```
>aws ec2 describe-security-groups
```

■ **Note**   For more parameters, see http://docs.aws.amazon.com/cli/latest/
reference/ec2/describe-security-groups.html.

---

4. Delete Security Group

To delete the security group, execute the following command:

```
>aws ec2 delete-security-group --group-name EC2CreationViaAWSCLI
```

```
C:\Users\Dell>aws ec2 delete-security-group --group-name EC2CreationViaAWSCLI
```

You can also delete the security group based on group id by the following command:

```
>aws ec2 delete-security-group --group-id sg-96bf15ef
```

■ **Note** For more parameters, see http://docs.aws.amazon.com/cli/latest/ reference/ec2/delete-security-group.html.

Key Pair

In this section, we will create, list, delete, and import a key pair.

1. Create a Key Pair

To create a key pair, we will execute the following command:

```
>aws ec2 create-key-pair --key-name EC2CreationViaAWSCLI
```

You can see the response having the "KeyMaterial" element, which we need to store at a secure location in a pem file. You can name this pem file {KeyName}.pem i.e. EC2CreationViaAWSCLI.pem.

■ **Note** For more parameters, see http://docs.aws.amazon.com/cli/latest/ reference/ec2/create-key-pair.html.

---

2. List a Key Pair

To list the key pair that we created, we will execute the following command:

```
>aws ec2 describe-key-pairs --key-name EC2CreationViaAWSCLI
```

```
C:\Users\Dell>aws ec2 describe-key-pairs --key-name EC2CreationViaAWSCLI
{
    "KeyPairs": [
        {
            "KeyName": "EC2CreationViaAWSCLI",
            "KeyFingerprint": "12:b8:3c:d2:79:13:c2:c3:f0:d9:11:7c:5f:6e:da:9c:0f:a3:db:ab"
        }
    ]
}
```

You can also list all the key pairs with following command:

```
>aws ec2 describe-key-pairs
```

```
C:\Users\Dell>aws ec2 describe-key-pairs
{
    "KeyPairs": [
        {
            "KeyName": "Chapter 2 Key Pair",
            "KeyFingerprint": "21:27:db:d3:70:83:03:a6:dd:fb:88:6a:d6:41:39:81:26:42:44:1e"
        },
        {
            "KeyName": "default-key",
            "KeyFingerprint": "cf:41:85:77:5d:82:cb:68:67:a4:e3:2b:52:b2:07:d2:57:99:8c:6a"
        },
        {
            "KeyName": "ec2-key-pair",
            "KeyFingerprint": "56:1b:71:53:4f:54:78:99:fe:d0:54:5b:6e:24:13:58:c8:80:cf:d1"
        },
        {
            "KeyName": "EC2CreationViaAWSCLI",
            "KeyFingerprint": "12:b8:3c:d2:79:13:c2:c3:f0:d9:11:7c:5f:6e:da:9c:0f:a3:db:ab"
        },
        {
            "KeyName": "jenkins-ec2",
            "KeyFingerprint": "42:d9:25:92:6d:42:87:6b:92:34:9c:9a:6b:8b:73:85:15:c4:a2:fd"
        }
    ]
}
```

■ **Note** For more parameters, see http://docs.aws.amazon.com/cli/latest/reference/ec2/describe-key-pairs.html.

3. Delete a Key Pair

To delete the key pair, we will execute following command:

```
>aws ec2 delete-key-pair --key-name EC2CreationViaAWSCLI
```

```
C:\Users\Dell>aws ec2 delete-key-pair --key-name EC2CreationViaAWSCLI
```

■ **Note** For more parameters, see http://docs.aws.amazon.com/cli/latest/
reference/ec2/delete-key-pair.html.

4. Import a Key Pair

There may be cases where you create the SSH key using the RSA encryption technique.
This allows you to provide the public key to AWS instead of AWS providing you the private
key over the network while creating it. This assumes that you have already created the
SSH key and have the public key on your machine. To import the existing public key, we
will execute the following command:

```
>aws ec2 import-key-pair --key-name "AWS-CLI-IMPORTED-KEY" --public-key-
material file://EC2CreationViaAWSCLI.pub
```

```
C:\Users\Dell>aws ec2 import-key-pair --key-name "AWS-CLI-IMPORTED-KEY" --public-key-material file://EC2CreationViaAWSCLI.pub
{
    "KeyName": "AWS-CLI-IMPORTED-KEY",
    "KeyFingerprint": "ca:de:69:c7:25:32:97:2d:95:d5:f7:77:83:4a:cf:68"
}

C:\Users\Dell>aws ec2 describe-key-pairs
{
    "KeyPairs": [
        {
            "KeyName": "AWS-CLI-IMPORTED-KEY",
            "KeyFingerprint": "ca:de:69:c7:25:32:97:2d:95:d5:f7:77:83:4a:cf:68"
        },
        {
            "KeyName": "Chapter 2 Key Pair",
            "KeyFingerprint": "21:27:db:d3:70:83:03:a6:dd:fb:88:6a:d6:41:39:81:26:42:44:1e"
        },
        {
            "KeyName": "default-key",
            "KeyFingerprint": "cf:41:85:77:5d:82:cb:68:67:a4:e3:2b:52:b2:07:d2:57:99:8c:6a"
        },
        {
            "KeyName": "ec2-key-pair",
            "KeyFingerprint": "56:1b:71:53:4f:54:78:99:fe:d0:54:5b:6e:24:13:58:c8:80:cf:d1"
        },
        {
            "KeyName": "jenkins-ec2",
            "KeyFingerprint": "42:d9:25:92:6d:42:87:6b:92:34:9c:9a:6b:8b:73:85:15:c4:a2:fd"
        }
    ]
}
```

■ **Note** For more parameters, see http://docs.aws.amazon.com/cli/latest/
reference/ec2/import-key-pair.html.

EC2 Instance

Next, I will explain how to describe images, select instance types, launch EC2, list EC2
instances, get instance status, create instance tags, and start-stop-terminate instances.

1. Describe Images

To get the AMI ID, we will describe images. This will return the public images and private images that are available. For our case, we will check if redhat linux server image i.e. ami-775e4f16 is available:

```
>aws ec2 describe-images --image-ids ami-775e4f16
```

```
C:\Users\Dell>aws ec2 describe-images --image-ids ami-775e4f16
{
    "Images": [
        {
            "VirtualizationType": "hvm",
            "Name": "RHEL-7.2_HVM_GA-20151112-x86_64-1-Hourly2-GP2",
            "Hypervisor": "xen",
            "SriovNetSupport": "simple",
            "ImageId": "ami-775e4f16",
            "State": "available",
            "BlockDeviceMappings": [
                {
                    "DeviceName": "/dev/sda1",
                    "Ebs": {
                        "DeleteOnTermination": true,
                        "SnapshotId": "snap-5bc5771e",
                        "VolumeSize": 10,
                        "VolumeType": "gp2",
                        "Encrypted": false
                    }
                }
            ],
            "Architecture": "x86_64",
            "ImageLocation": "309956199498/RHEL-7.2_HVM_GA-20151112-x86_64-1-Hourly2-GP2",
            "RootDeviceType": "ebs",
            "OwnerId": "309956199498",
            "RootDeviceName": "/dev/sda1",
            "CreationDate": "2015-11-12T21:09:55.000Z",
            "Public": true,
            "ImageType": "machine",
            "Description": "Provided by Red Hat, Inc."
        }
    ]
}
```

▪ **Note**   For more parameters, see http://docs.aws.amazon.com/cli/latest/reference/ec2/describe-images.html.

2. Select an Instance Type

To select an instance type, you need to find out which instance type suits your application requirements. You can find all the instance types at http://aws.amazon.com/ec2/instance-types.

For our example, we will use the t2.micro instance type.

3. Launch EC2

Now we will launch a new EC2 instance that has one instance count, "EC2CreationViaAWSCLI" key pair, and "EC2CreationViaAWSCLI" security group. First, verify that the key pair and security group are created. If not, execute the command for creating a key pair and security group. Let's launch EC2 instance by executing this command:

```
>aws ec2 run-instances --image-id ami-775e4f16 --instance-type
t2.micro --count 1 --key-name EC2CreationViaAWSCLI --security-groups
EC2CreationViaAWSCLI
```

```
C:\Users\Dell>aws ec2 run-instances --image-id ami-775e4f16 --instance-type t2.micro --count 1 --key-name EC2CreationViaAWSCLI --security-groups EC2CreationViaAWSCLI
{
    "OwnerId": "298147259238",
    "ReservationId": "r-020b567eb3cd51f07",
    "Groups": [],
    "Instances": [
        {
            "Monitoring": {
                "State": "disabled"
            },
            "PublicDnsName": "",
            "RootDeviceType": "ebs",
            "State": {
                "Code": 0,
                "Name": "pending"
            },
            "EbsOptimized": false,
            "LaunchTime": "2016-10-22T08:19:00.000Z",
            "PrivateIpAddress": "172.31.20.152",
            "ProductCodes": [],
            "VpcId": "vpc-237b7647",
            "StateTransitionReason": "",
            "InstanceId": "i-04275d1e63998a3d3",
            "ImageId": "ami-775e4f16",
            "PrivateDnsName": "ip-172-31-28-152.us-west-2.compute.internal",
            "KeyName": "EC2CreationViaAWSCLI",
            "SecurityGroups": [
                {
                    "GroupName": "EC2CreationViaAWSCLI",
                    "GroupId": "sg-60178e19"
                }
            ],
            "ClientToken": "",
            "SubnetId": "subnet-9b3007fc",
            "InstanceType": "t2.micro",
            "NetworkInterfaces": [
                {
                    "Status": "in-use",
                    "MacAddress": "02:c2:9e:62:94:b5",
                    "SourceDestCheck": true,
                    "VpcId": "vpc-237b7647",
                    "Description": ""
```

Executing this run-instance command will initiate the request to launch a new instance with specified configurations. To check if the instance is ready to connect, we will use describer-instance-status along with the instanceId that is generated via run-instances:

```
>aws ec2 describe-instance-status --instance-id i-04275d1e63998a3d3
```

```
C:\Users\Dell>aws ec2 describe-instance-status --instance-id i-04275d1e63998a3d3
{
    "InstanceStatuses": [
        {
            "InstanceId": "i-04275d1e63998a3d3",
            "InstanceState": {
                "Code": 16,
                "Name": "running"
            },
            "AvailabilityZone": "us-west-2a",
            "SystemStatus": {
                "Status": "ok",
                "Details": [
                    {
                        "Status": "passed",
                        "Name": "reachability"
                    }
                ]
            },
            "InstanceStatus": {
                "Status": "ok",
                "Details": [
                    {
                        "Status": "passed",
                        "Name": "reachability"
                    }
                ]
            }
        }
    ]
}
```

You can see that InstanceStatus shows "running" value. Possible values for this include the following:

- pending

- running

- shutting down

- terminated

- stopping

- stopped

To list all instances status, use the following command:

```
>aws ec2 describe-instance-status
```

Once the instance state is running, you can verify that you are able to connect to EC2 instance using the SSH client. Refer to the "Verify by Connecting to EC2 Instance" section.

■ **Note** For more parameters, see http://docs.aws.amazon.com/cli/latest/reference/ec2/describe-instance-status.html.

49

4. List EC2 Instances

To get the EC2 instance details based on the instanceId, use describe-instances:

```
>aws ec2 describe-instances --instance-ids i-04275d1e63998a3d3
```

```
C:\Users\Dell>aws ec2 describe-instances --instance-ids i-04275d1e63998a3d3
{
    "Reservations": [
        {
            "OwnerId": "298147259238",
            "ReservationId": "r-020b567eb3cd51f87",
            "Groups": [],
            "Instances": [
                {
                    "Monitoring": {
                        "State": "disabled"
                    },
                    "PublicDnsName": "ec2-35-160-89-233.us-west-2.compute.amazonaws.com",
                    "State": {
                        "Code": 16,
                        "Name": "running"
                    },
                    "EbsOptimized": false,
                    "LaunchTime": "2016-10-22T08:19:08.000Z",
                    "PublicIpAddress": "35.160.89.233",
                    "PrivateIpAddress": "172.31.28.152",
                    "ProductCodes": [],
                    "VpcId": "vpc-237b7647",
                    "StateTransitionReason": "",
                    "InstanceId": "i-04275d1e63998a3d3",
                    "ImageId": "ami-775e4f16",
                    "PrivateDnsName": "ip-172-31-28-152.us-west-2.compute.internal",
                    "KeyName": "EC2CreationViaAWSCLI",
                    "SecurityGroups": [
                        {
                            "GroupName": "EC2CreationViaAWSCLI",
                            "GroupId": "sg-60178e19"
                        }
                    ],
                    "ClientToken": "",
                    "SubnetId": "subnet-983007fc",
                    "InstanceType": "t2.micro",
                    "NetworkInterfaces": [
                        {
                            "Status": "in-use",
                            "MacAddress": "02:c2:9e:62:94:b5",
                            "SourceDestCheck": true,
                            "VpcId": "vpc-237b7647",
```

To get all EC2 instances details, use describe-instances without providing any filters:

```
>aws ec2 describe-instances
```

■ **Note**   For more parameters, see http://docs.aws.amazon.com/cli/latest/reference/ec2/describe-instances.html.

---

5. Get Instance Status

To get the instance status that we created, execute the following command:

```
>aws ec2 describe-instance-status --instance-id i-0f6ed7e30cf57f488
```

```
C:\Users\Dell>aws ec2 describe-instance-status --instance-id i-0f6ed7e30cf57f488
{
    "InstanceStatuses": [
        {
            "InstanceId": "i-0f6ed7e30cf57f488",
            "InstanceState": {
                "Code": 16,
                "Name": "running"
            },
            "AvailabilityZone": "us-west-2b",
            "SystemStatus": {
                "Status": "initializing",
                "Details": [
                    {
                        "Status": "initializing",
                        "Name": "reachability"
                    }
                ]
            },
            "InstanceStatus": {
                "Status": "initializing",
                "Details": [
                    {
                        "Status": "initializing",
                        "Name": "reachability"
                    }
                ]
            }
        }
    ]
}
```

You can see that the InstanceStatus tag has the value "initializing," which denotes that the instance is created but it is initializing. Once the initialization process is complete, the instance status will be reflected as "ok." Now, the instance has been initialized successfully.

To get the instance status of all the EC2 instances available under the user account, use the following command:

```
>aws ec2 describe-instance-status
```

■ **Note** For more parameters, see http://docs.aws.amazon.com/cli/latest/reference/ec2/describe-instance-status.html.

6. Assign Instance Tags

To assign tags to EC2 instances, execute the following command:

```
>aws ec2 create-tags --resources i-0f6ed7e30cf57f488 --tags
Key=Chapter,Value=2 Key=Environment,Value=Production
```

```
C:\Users\Dell>aws ec2 create-tags --resources i-0f6ed7e30cf57f488 --tags Key=Chapter,Value=2 Key=Environment,Value=Production
C:\Users\Dell>
```

■ **Note** For more parameters, see http://docs.aws.amazon.com/cli/latest/
reference/ec2/create-tags.html.

To describe the tags that are assigned to an EC2 instance, execute the following
command:

```
>aws ec2 describe-tags --filters "Name=resource-id,Values=i-
0f6ed7e30cf57f488"
```

```
C:\Users\Dell>aws ec2 describe-tags --filters "Name=resource-id,Values=i-0f6ed7e30cf57f488"
{
    "Tags": [
        {
            "ResourceType": "instance",
            "ResourceId": "i-0f6ed7e30cf57f488",
            "Value": "2",
            "Key": "Chapter"
        },
        {
            "ResourceType": "instance",
            "ResourceId": "i-0f6ed7e30cf57f488",
            "Value": "Production",
            "Key": "Environment"
        }
    ]
}
```

■ **Note** For more parameters, see http://docs.aws.amazon.com/cli/latest/
reference/ec2/describe-tags.html.

To delete the tags for an EC2 instance, execute the following command:

```
>aws ec2 delete-tags --resources i-0f6ed7e30cf57f488 --tags
Key=Chapter,Value=2
```

```
C:\Users\Dell>aws ec2 delete-tags --resources i-0f6ed7e30cf57f488 --tags Key=Chapter,Value=2

C:\Users\Dell>aws ec2 describe-tags --filters "Name=resource-id,Values=i-0f6ed7e30cf57f488"
{
    "Tags": [
        {
            "ResourceType": "instance",
            "ResourceId": "i-0f6ed7e30cf57f488",
            "Value": "Production",
            "Key": "Environment"
        }
    ]
}
```

Here, in delete-tags, we have provided both the key and value. However, it's optional to provide value for the Value element. If we provide the value, it becomes mandatory that both the key and value should match the actual tags and only then can it delete the tags. The following command can be used when to delete the tag based only on the key:

```
>aws ec2 delete-tags --resources i-0f6ed7e30cf57f488 --tags
Key=Chapter,Value=
```

■ **Note** For more parameters, see http://docs.aws.amazon.com/cli/latest/ reference/ec2/delete-tags.html.

7. Start-Stop-Terminate Instance

You may require your instance to start-stop manually. First of all, stop your instance using the following command:

```
>aws ec2 stop-instances --instance-ids i-0f6ed7e30cf57f488
```

```
C:\Users\Dell>aws ec2 stop-instances --instance-ids i-0f6ed7e30cf57f488
{
    "StoppingInstances": [
        {
            "InstanceId": "i-0f6ed7e30cf57f488",
            "CurrentState": {
                "Code": 64,
                "Name": "stopping"
            },
            "PreviousState": {
                "Code": 16,
                "Name": "running"
            }
        }
    ]
}

C:\Users\Dell>aws ec2 stop-instances --instance-ids i-0f6ed7e30cf57f488
{
    "StoppingInstances": [
        {
            "InstanceId": "i-0f6ed7e30cf57f488",
            "CurrentState": {
                "Code": 80,
                "Name": "stopped"
            },
            "PreviousState": {
                "Code": 80,
                "Name": "stopped"
            }
        }
    ]
}
```

You can see that CurrentState is stopped now. The time it takes to stop the instances may vary depending on the processes that are running on the EC2 instances.

■ **Note**   For more parameters, see `http://docs.aws.amazon.com/cli/latest/` `reference/ec2/stop-instances.html`.

To start the instance, execute the following command:

```
>aws ec2 start-instances --instance-ids i-0f6ed7e30cf57f488
```

```
C:\Users\Dell>aws ec2 start-instances --instance-ids i-0f6ed7e30cf57f488
{
    "StartingInstances": [
        {
            "InstanceId": "i-0f6ed7e30cf57f488",
            "CurrentState": {
                "Code": 0,
                "Name": "pending"
            },
            "PreviousState": {
                "Code": 80,
                "Name": "stopped"
            }
        }
    ]
}
C:\Users\Dell>aws ec2 start-instances --instance-ids i-0f6ed7e30cf57f488
{
    "StartingInstances": [
        {
            "InstanceId": "i-0f6ed7e30cf57f488",
            "CurrentState": {
                "Code": 16,
                "Name": "running"
            },
            "PreviousState": {
                "Code": 16,
                "Name": "running"
            }
        }
    ]
}
```

In this case, the CurrentState should be running.

■ **Note**   For more parameters, see `http://docs.aws.amazon.com/cli/latest/` `reference/ec2/start-instances.html`.

To terminate the instance, execute the following command:

```
>aws ec2 terminate-instances --instance-ids i-05bdea264ee46c415
```

```
C:\Users\Dell>aws ec2 terminate-instances --instance-ids i-05bdea264ee46c415
{
    "TerminatingInstances": [
        {
            "InstanceId": "i-05bdea264ee46c415",
            "CurrentState": {
                "Code": 48,
                "Name": "terminated"
            },
            "PreviousState": {
                "Code": 48,
                "Name": "terminated"
            }
        }
    ]
}
```

You can provide multiple Instance IDs that you need to terminate. In this case, the CurrentState should be terminated.

■ **Note**   For more parameters, see http://docs.aws.amazon.com/cli/latest/ reference/ec2/terminate-instances.html.

Managing EC2 Using AWS SDK (Java)

AWS SDK helps to manage the AWS resources using different platform APIs. For our case, I will discuss Java APIs to manage AWS resources. I will show how to create, list, and delete an EC2 instance resource:

- Create AWSCredentials object
- Security group
- Key pair
- EC2 instance

Create AWSCredentials Object

To connect with AWS for Java using SDK, you need to provide the AWS credentials. There are various ways to provide AWS credentials: Default Credential Provider, Specify Credential Provider or Provider Chain, Provide Access Key, and Secret Key.

1. Default Credential Provider

This is the default provider when we don't provide any parameters while creating an AWS service client. `DefaultAWSCredentialsProviderChain` is the class that will be used to create the AWS credentials. This class will find the credentials in the following order:

- **Environment Variables:** This technique uses the `EnvironmentVariableCredentialsProvider` class that fetches values for `AWS_ACCESS_KEY_ID` and `AWS_SECRET_ACCESS_KEY`.

- **System Properties:** This technique is used to find the values for `aws.accessKeyId` and `aws.secretKey` in Java system properties.

- **Credentials Property File:** A default credentials property file can be loaded to get these credentials. This property file resides under `C:\Users\{USER}\.aws\credentials` or `~/.aws/credentials`. This path differs based on the operating system.

- **Instance Profile Credentials:** Instance profile credentials are attached with the EC2. When your application is deployed on EC2 and wants to interact with the AWS resources, you can assign the instance role to our EC2. This way you eradicate the need to manage the AWS credentials explicitly. While creating the service client, you will use the `InstanceProfileCredentialsProvider` class.

For our case, we will use `ProfileCredentialsProvider`, which comes under the "Configuration Property File" topic. In the credentials file, there may be different profiles that have `aws_access_key_id` and `aws_secret_access_key`. We have added the sunilgulabani profile under the credentials file. So, to create AWSCredentials object, you will use the following:

```
AWSCredentials credentials =
    new ProfileCredentialsProvider("sunilgulabani").getCredentials();
```

2. Specify Credential Provider or Provider Chain

There are different providers you can use to create the AWSCredentials object. You can use any of the provider classes that are mentioned under the "All Known Implementing Class" at `http://docs.aws.amazon.com/AWSJavaSDK/latest/javadoc/com/amazonaws/auth/AWSCredentialsProvider.html`.

You can even create your own class by doing the following:

- Implementing `AWSCredentialsProvider` interface

- Sub-classing the `AWSCredentialsProviderChain` class

3. Provide Access Key and Secret Key Explicitly

There may be cases when we need to explicitly pass the access key ID and secret access key to create an AWSCredentials object. To create an AWSCredentials object, we will use the following:

```
AWSCredentials credentials =
    new BasicAWSCredentials("access_key_id", "secret_access_key");
```

Security Groups

This section covers the following topics: creating a security group, attaching an inbound rule to a security group, listing a security group, and deleting a security group.

1. Create a Security Group

To create a security group, use the createSecurityGroup method under the AmazonEC2Client class:

```
private final static String SECURITY_GROUP_NAME =
    "EC2CreationViaAWSJavaSDK";
private final static String SECURITY_GROUP_DESCRIPTION =
    "EC2 creation via AWS java sdk";

createSecurityGroup(SECURITY_GROUP_NAME, SECURITY_GROUP_DESCRIPTION);

public String createSecurityGroup(String groupName, String groupDescription) {
    CreateSecurityGroupRequest securityGroupRequest =
        new CreateSecurityGroupRequest();

    securityGroupRequest.withGroupName(groupName);

    securityGroupRequest.withDescription(groupDescription);

    CreateSecurityGroupResult response =
        amazonEC2Client.createSecurityGroup(securityGroupRequest);

    return response.getGroupId();
}
```

```
{
  "groupId": "sg-72fc1015",
  "sdkResponseMetadata": {
    "metadata": {
      "AWS_REQUEST_ID": "0cce459f-6f51-4ae5-9dce-264cb419de3a"
    }
  },
  "sdkHttpMetadata": {
    "httpHeaders": {
      "Transfer-Encoding": "chunked",
      "Server": "AmazonEC2",
      "Vary": "Accept-Encoding",
      "Date": "Sat, 12 Nov 2016 13:50:08 GMT",
      "Content-Type": "text/xml;charset\u003dUTF-8"
    },
    "httpStatusCode": 200
  }
}
```

2. Attach an Inbound Rule to Security Group

To assign an inbound rule, use the authorizeSecurityGroupIngress method under the AmazonEC2Client class:

assignSSHConnectionAccessToSecurityGroup(SECURITY_GROUP_NAME);

```
public void assignSSHConnectionAccessToSecurityGroup(String groupName) {
    AuthorizeSecurityGroupIngressRequest request =
        new AuthorizeSecurityGroupIngressRequest();

    request.withGroupName(groupName);

    IpPermission ipPermission = createIpPermission();

    request.withIpPermissions(ipPermission);

    AuthorizeSecurityGroupIngressResult response =
        amazonEC2Client.authorizeSecurityGroupIngress(request);
}

private IpPermission createIpPermission() {
    IpPermission ipPermission = new IpPermission();

    ipPermission.withIpProtocol("tcp");
```

```
    ipPermission.withFromPort(22);

    ipPermission.withToPort(22);

    ipPermission.withIpRanges("0.0.0.0/0");

    return ipPermission;
}
```

```
{
  "sdkResponseMetadata": {
    "metadata": {
      "AWS_REQUEST_ID": "713627d5-e0d7-40a0-9473-17c1f7ef5526"
    }
  },
  "sdkHttpMetadata": {
    "httpHeaders": {
      "Transfer-Encoding": "chunked",
      "Server": "AmazonEC2",
      "Vary": "Accept-Encoding",
      "Date": "Sat, 12 Nov 2016 13:50:08 GMT",
      "Content-Type": "text/xml;charset\u003dUTF-8"
    },
    "httpStatusCode": 200
  }
}
```

3. List a Security Group

To list a security group, use the describeSecurityGroups method under the
AmazonEC2Client class:

describeSecurityGroups(securityGroupId);

```
public void describeSecurityGroups(String securityGroupId) {
    DescribeSecurityGroupsRequest request =
        new DescribeSecurityGroupsRequest();

    request.setGroupIds(Arrays.asList(securityGroupId));

    DescribeSecurityGroupsResult response =
        amazonEC2Client.describeSecurityGroups();
}
```

59

```
{
  "securityGroups": [
    {
      "ownerId": "██████████",
      "groupName": "default",
      "groupId": "sg-52977b35",
      "description": "default VPC security group",
      "ipPermissions": [
        {
          "ipProtocol": "-1",
          "userIdGroupPairs": [
            {
              "userId": "██████████",
              "groupId": "sg-52977b35"
            }
          ]
        }
      ],
      "ipPermissionsEgress": [
        {
          "ipProtocol": "-1",
          "ipRanges": [
            "0.0.0.0/0"
          ]
        }
      ],
      "vpcId": "vpc-1eb5677a"
    }
  ],
  "sdkResponseMetadata": {
    "metadata": {
      "AWS_REQUEST_ID": "72209902-7712-452c-8f2a-6caeb3ee2bda"
    }
  },
  "sdkHttpMetadata": {
    "httpHeaders": {
      "Transfer-Encoding": "chunked",
      "Server": "AmazonEC2",
      "Vary": "Accept-Encoding",
      "Date": "Sat, 12 Nov 2016 14:01:39 GMT",
      "Content-Type": "text/xml;charset\u003dUTF-8"
    },
    "httpStatusCode": 200
  }
}
```

4. Delete a Security Group

To delete a security group, use the deleteSecurityGroup method under the AmazonEC2Client class:

deleteSecurityGroupBasedOnGroupName(SECURITY_GROUP_NAME);

```
public void deleteSecurityGroupBasedOnGroupName(String groupName) {

    DeleteSecurityGroupRequest request = new DeleteSecurityGroupRequest();

    request.setGroupName(groupName);

    DeleteSecurityGroupResult response =
        amazonEC2Client.deleteSecurityGroup(request);
}
```

```
{
  "sdkResponseMetadata": {
    "metadata": {
      "AWS_REQUEST_ID": "01671e2d-bc25-4783-ba48-6f2fc758a974"
    }
  },
  "sdkHttpMetadata": {
    "httpHeaders": {
      "Transfer-Encoding": "chunked",
      "Server": "AmazonEC2",
      "Vary": "Accept-Encoding",
      "Date": "Sat, 12 Nov 2016 13:50:10 GMT",
      "Content-Type": "text/xml;charset\u003dUTF-8"
    },
    "httpStatusCode": 200
  }
}
```

You can delete a security group based on groupId:

deleteSecurityGroupBasedOnGroupId(securityGroupId);

```
public void deleteSecurityGroupBasedOnGroupId(String groupId) {
    DeleteSecurityGroupRequest request = new DeleteSecurityGroupRequest();

    request.setGroupId(groupId);

    DeleteSecurityGroupResult response =
        amazonEC2Client.deleteSecurityGroup(request);
}
```

```
{
  "sdkResponseMetadata": {
    "metadata": {
      "AWS_REQUEST_ID": "da6dc3bc-6039-477c-9295-b970d99ebbc0"
    }
  },
  "sdkHttpMetadata": {
    "httpHeaders": {
      "Transfer-Encoding": "chunked",
      "Server": "AmazonEC2",
      "Vary": "Accept-Encoding",
      "Date": "Sat, 12 Nov 2016 14:06:16 GMT",
      "Content-Type": "text/xml;charset\u003dUTF-8"
    },
    "httpStatusCode": 200
  }
}
```

Key Pair

In this section, I will discuss how to create a key pair, list a key pair, delete a key pair, and import a key pair.

1. Create a Key Pair

To create a key pair, use createKeyPair under the AmazonEC2Client class:

```
private final static String KEY_PAIR_NAME = "EC2CreationViaAWSJavaSDK";

createKeyPair(KEY_PAIR_NAME);

public void createKeyPair(String keyName) {
    CreateKeyPairRequest request = new CreateKeyPairRequest();

    request.withKeyName(keyName);

    CreateKeyPairResult response = amazonEC2Client.createKeyPair(request);

    KeyPair keyPair = response.getKeyPair();

    String privateKey = keyPair.getKeyMaterial();

    fileOperations.saveFile(keyName + "_keypair.pem", privateKey);
}
```

```
{
  "keyPair": {
    "keyName": "EC2CreationViaAWSJavaSDK",
    "keyFingerprint": "1b:e2:a3:31:8f:15:c5:db:31:ef:87:71:58:18:53:4b:bb:0e:4a:93",
    "keyMaterial": "-----BEGIN RSA PRIVATE KEY-----\nMIIEowIBAAKCAQEAmJ4NRZeYySAjn7bgqz/8jaU2p0iCchIoUC+b4twHOF/JBhJ3BlezA4mgf9OE\nDcikwirnWhrulKlnYsI3NK1YGG7pAf10JEv/hvJN84WqwPEY"
  },
  "sdkResponseMetadata": {
    "metadata": {
      "AWS_REQUEST_ID": "7e0fea3b-8613-432c-b461-1fefa3014dd5"
    }
  },
  "sdkHttpMetadata": {
    "httpHeaders": {
      "Transfer-Encoding": "chunked",
      "Server": "AmazonEC2",
      "Vary": "Accept-Encoding",
      "Date": "Sat, 12 Nov 2016 13:39:12 GMT",
      "Content-Type": "text/xml;charset\u003dUTF-8"
    },
    "httpStatusCode": 200
  }
}
```

2. List a Key Pair

To list a key pair, use the describeKeyPairs method under the AmazonEC2Client class:

```
describeKeyPairs(KEY_PAIR_NAME);

public void describeKeyPairs(String keyName) {
    DescribeKeyPairsRequest request = new DescribeKeyPairsRequest();

    if(!StringUtils.isNullOrEmpty(keyName)) {
        List<String> searchCriteria = new ArrayList<String>();
        searchCriteria.add(keyName);
        request.setKeyNames(searchCriteria);
    }

    DescribeKeyPairsResult response = amazonEC2Client.describeKeyPairs(request);
}
```

```
{
    "keyPairs": [
        {
            "keyName": "EC2CreationViaAWSJavaSDK",
            "keyFingerprint": "1b:e2:a3:31:8f:15:c5:db:31:ef:87:71:58:18:53:4b:bb:0e:4a:93"
        }
    ],
    "sdkResponseMetadata": {
        "metadata": {
            "AWS_REQUEST_ID": "a4b151f9-f0ee-4c43-972e-3ea0b2ddce1a"
        }
    },
    "sdkHttpMetadata": {
        "httpHeaders": {
            "Transfer-Encoding": "chunked",
            "Server": "AmazonEC2",
            "Vary": "Accept-Encoding",
            "Date": "Sat, 12 Nov 2016 13:39:14 GMT",
            "Content-Type": "text/xml;charset\u003dUTF-8"
        },
        "httpStatusCode": 200
    }
}
```

To list all key pairs, we use the following code:

describeKeyPairs(null);

```
{
  "keyPairs": [
    {
      "keyName": "EC2CreationViaAWSJavaSDK",
      "keyFingerprint": "1b:e2:a3:31:8f:15:c5:db:31:ef:87:71:58:18:53:4b:bb:0e:4a:93"
    }
  ],
  "sdkResponseMetadata": {
    "metadata": {
      "AWS_REQUEST_ID": "d3235e0b-e5ab-40af-aafb-f1975022a664"
    }
  },
  "sdkHttpMetadata": {
    "httpHeaders": {
      "Transfer-Encoding": "chunked",
      "Server": "AmazonEC2",
      "Vary": "Accept-Encoding",
      "Date": "Sat, 12 Nov 2016 13:39:13 GMT",
      "Content-Type": "text/xml;charset\u003dUTF-8"
    },
    "httpStatusCode": 200
  }
}
```

3. Delete a Key Pair

To delete a key pair, use the deleteKeyPair method under the AmazonEC2Client class:

deleteKeyPair(KEY_PAIR_NAME);

```
public void deleteKeyPair(String keyName) {

    DeleteKeyPairRequest request = new DeleteKeyPairRequest();

    request.setKeyName(keyName);

    DeleteKeyPairResult response = amazonEC2Client.deleteKeyPair(request);
}
```

```
{
   "sdkResponseMetadata": {
      "metadata": {
         "AWS_REQUEST_ID": "4203383d-5872-45cc-8249-0d7eb335ca43"
      }
   },
   "sdkHttpMetadata": {
      "httpHeaders": {
         "Transfer-Encoding": "chunked",
         "Server": "AmazonEC2",
         "Vary": "Accept-Encoding",
         "Date": "Sat, 12 Nov 2016 13:39:16 GMT",
         "Content-Type": "text/xml;charset\u003dUTF-8"
      },
      "httpStatusCode": 200
   }
}
```

4. Import a Key Pair

To import a key pair to AWS, use the importKeyPair method under the AmazonEC2Client class:

```
importKeyPair(
        "AWS-JAVA-SDK-IMPORTED-KEY",
        "C:\\Users\\Dell\\EC2CreationViaAWSCLI.pub");

public void importKeyPair(String keyName, String publicKeyFilePath) {

    ImportKeyPairRequest request = new ImportKeyPairRequest();

    request.setKeyName(keyName);

    request.setPublicKeyMaterial(fileOperations.readFile(publicKeyFilePath));

    ImportKeyPairResult response = amazonEC2Client.importKeyPair(request);
}
```

```
{
  "keyName": "AWS-CLI-IMPORTED-KEY",
  "keyFingerprint": "ca:de:69:c7:25:32:97:2d:95:d5:f7:77:83:4a:cf:68",
  "sdkResponseMetadata": {
    "metadata": {
      "AWS_REQUEST_ID": "6f2fd04a-8489-41ef-835d-c740503c9407"
    }
  },
  "sdkHttpMetadata": {
    "httpHeaders": {
      "Transfer-Encoding": "chunked",
      "Server": "AmazonEC2",
      "Vary": "Accept-Encoding",
      "Date": "Sat, 12 Nov 2016 13:39:16 GMT",
      "Content-Type": "text/xml;charset\u003dUTF-8"
    },
    "httpStatusCode": 200
  }
}
```

EC2 Instance

In this section, I will explain how to get the AMI ID, select an instance type, launch EC2, list EC2 instances, get instance status, assign instance tags, and start-stop-terminate an instance.

1. Get the AMI ID

To get the AMI ID, we will describe the image. This will return the public images and private images that are available to us. We will check that redhatlinux server image, that is, ami-775e4f16 is available:

```
describeImageIds("ami-775e4f16");

public void describeImageIds(String imageId) {
    DescribeImagesRequest request = new DescribeImagesRequest();
    if(!StringUtils.isNullOrEmpty(imageId)) {
        request.withImageIds(imageId);
    }
    DescribeImagesResult response = amazonEC2Client.describeImages(request);
}
```

```
{
  "images": [
    {
      "imageId": "ami-775e4f16",
      "imageLocation": "309956199498/RHEL-7.2_HVM_GA-20151112-x86_64-1-Hourly2-GP2",
      "state": "available",
      "ownerId": "309956199498",
      "creationDate": "2015-11-12T21:09:55.000Z",
      "publicValue": true,
      "architecture": "x86_64",
      "imageType": "machine",
      "sriovNetSupport": "simple",
      "name": "RHEL-7.2_HVM_GA-20151112-x86_64-1-Hourly2-GP2",
      "description": "Provided by Red Hat, Inc.",
      "rootDeviceType": "ebs",
      "rootDeviceName": "/dev/sda1",
      "blockDeviceMappings": [
        {
          "deviceName": "/dev/sda1",
          "ebs": {
            "snapshotId": "snap-5bc5771e",
            "volumeSize": 10,
            "deleteOnTermination": true,
            "volumeType": "gp2",
            "encrypted": false
          }
        }
      ],
      "virtualizationType": "hvm",
      "hypervisor": "xen"
    }
  ],
  "sdkResponseMetadata": {
    "metadata": {
      "AWS_REQUEST_ID": "56a58c68-3553-4066-928e-b08322dac106"
    }
  },
  "sdkHttpMetadata": {
    "httpHeaders": {
      "Transfer-Encoding": "chunked",
      "Server": "AmazonEC2",
      "Vary": "Accept-Encoding",
      "Date": "Sun, 13 Nov 2016 04:38:51 GMT",
      "Content-Type": "text/xml;charset\u003dUTF-8"
    },
    "httpStatusCode": 200
  }
}
```

2. Select an Instance Type

To select the instance type, you need to find out which instance type suits your application requirements. You can find all the instance types at http://aws.amazon.com/ec2/instance-types.

For our example, we will use the t2.micro instance type.

3. Launch EC2

Now we will launch a new EC2 instance that has one instance count, "EC2CreationViaAWSJavaSDK" key pair, and "EC2CreationViaAWSJavaSDK" security group. First, verify that the key pair and security group are created. If not, you can execute the code for creating key pair and security group.

Use the following code to launch an EC2 instance:

```
private final static String AMI = "ami-775e4f16";
private final static InstanceType INSTANCE_TYPE = InstanceType.T2Micro;
private final static int MIN_INSTANCE_COUNT = 1;
private final static int MAX_INSTANCE_COUNT = 1;
private final static String KEY_PAIR_NAME = "EC2CreationViaAWSJavaSDK";
private final static String SECURITY_GROUP_NAME =
    "EC2CreationViaAWSJavaSDK";

String instanceId = launchInstance(AMI, INSTANCE_TYPE,
                                   MIN_INSTANCE_COUNT, MAX_INSTANCE_COUNT,
                                   KEY_PAIR_NAME, SECURITY_GROUP_NAME);
public String launchInstance(String ami, InstanceType instanceType,
                       int minInstanceCount, int maxInstanceCount,
                       String keyPairName, String securityGroupName) {

    RunInstancesRequest request = new RunInstancesRequest();

    request.setImageId(ami);

    request.setInstanceType(instanceType);

    request.setKeyName(keyPairName);

    List<String> securityGroups = new ArrayList<String>();

    securityGroups.add(securityGroupName);

    request.setSecurityGroups(securityGroups);

    request.setMinCount(minInstanceCount);

    request.setMaxCount(maxInstanceCount);

    RunInstancesResult response = amazonEC2Client.runInstances(request);

    return getInstanceId();
}
```

```
{
  "reservation": {
    "reservationId": "r-e5e9243d",
    "ownerId": "254393510377",
    "groups": [],
    "instances": {
      {
        "instanceId": "i-fac9596e",
        "imageId": "ami-775e4f16",
        "state": {
          "code": 0,
          "name": "pending"
        },
        "privateDnsName": "ip-172-31-20-198.us-west-2.compute.internal",
        "publicDnsName": "",
        "stateTransitionReason": "",
        "keyName": "EC2CreationViaAWSJavaSDK",
        "amiLaunchIndex": 0,
        "instanceType": "t2.micro",
        "launchTime": "Nov 16, 2016 4:51:50 PM",
        "placement": {
          "availabilityZone": "us-west-2a",
          "groupName": "",
          "tenancy": "default"
        },
        "monitoring": {
          "state": "disabled"
        },
        "subnetId": "subnet-d610c5a1",
        "vpcId": "vpc-ca538caf",
        "privateIpAddress": "172.31.20.198",
        "stateReason": {
          "code": "pending",
          "message": "pending"
        },
        "architecture": "x86_64",
        "rootDeviceType": "ebs",
        "rootDeviceName": "/dev/sda1",
        "virtualizationType": "hvm",
        "clientToken": "4aa2b15e-5ab1-46e7-82f5-da8ca436b80f",
        "securityGroups": [
          {
            "groupName": "EC2CreationViaAWSJavaSDK",
            "groupId": "sg-461e4f3f"
          }
        ],
        "sourceDestCheck": true,
        "hypervisor": "xen",
        "networkInterfaces": [
          {
            "networkInterfaceId": "eni-087c9748",
            "subnetId": "subnet-d610c5a1",
            "vpcId": "vpc-ca538caf",
            "description": "",
            "ownerId": "254393510377",
            "status": "in-use",
            "macAddress": "06:e1:c8:3b:de:31",
            "privateIpAddress": "172.31.20.198",
            "privateDnsName": "ip-172-31-20-198.us-west-2.compute.internal",
            "sourceDestCheck": true,
            "groups": [
              {
                "groupName": "EC2CreationViaAWSJavaSDK",
                "groupId": "sg-461e4f3f"
              }
```

```
        },
        "attachment": {
            "attachmentId": "eni-attach-3f850bb5",
            "deviceIndex": 0,
            "status": "attaching",
            "attachTime": "Nov 16, 2016 4:51:50 PM",
            "deleteOnTermination": true
        },
        "privateIpAddresses": [
            {
                "privateIpAddress": "172.31.20.198",
                "privateDnsName": "ip-172-31-20-198.us-west-2.compute.internal",
                "primary": true
            }
        ]
        }
    },
    "ebsOptimized": false

    }
  ],
  "groupNames": []
},
"sdkResponseMetadata": {
    "metadata": {
        "AWS_REQUEST_ID": "b079e19b-1042-4e9d-8027-1b0ccbe8236d"
    }
},
"sdkHttpMetadata": {
    "httpHeaders": {
        "Transfer-Encoding": "chunked",
        "Server": "AmazonEC2",
        "Vary": "Accept-Encoding",
        "Date": "Wed, 16 Nov 2016 11:21:50 GMT",
        "Content-Type": "text/xml;charset\u003dUTF-8"
    },
    "httpStatusCode": 200
}
```

Executing this run-instance command will initiate the request to launch a new instance with specified configurations. To check the status that the instance is ready to connect, we will use the describeInstanceStatus method along with the instance ID that is generated via runInstances method:

```
describeInstanceStatus(instanceId);
```

```
public void describeInstanceStatus(String instanceId) {

    DescribeInstanceStatusRequest request =
        new DescribeInstanceStatusRequest();

    request.setInstanceIds(Arrays.asList(instanceId));

    DescribeInstanceStatusResult response =
        amazonEC2Client.describeInstanceStatus(request);
}
```

You can now pass the instanceId parameter that we received from `launchInstance()` method:

```
{
  "instanceStatuses": [
    {
      "instanceId": "i-fac9596e",
      "availabilityZone": "us-west-2a",
      "instanceState": {
        "code": 16,
        "name": "running"
      },
      "systemStatus": {
        "status": "ok",
        "details": [
          {
            "name": "reachability",
            "status": "passed"
          }
        ]
      },
      "instanceStatus": {
        "status": "ok",
        "details": [
          {
            "name": "reachability",
            "status": "passed"
          }
        ]
      }
    }
  ],
  "sdkResponseMetadata": {
    "metadata": {
      "AWS_REQUEST_ID": "3f556bae-00c0-4897-900d-5919980b1cfe"
    }
  },
  "sdkHttpMetadata": {
    "httpHeaders": {
      "Transfer-Encoding": "chunked",
      "Server": "AmazonEC2",
      "Vary": "Accept-Encoding",
      "Date": "Wed, 16 Nov 2016 11:36:39 GMT",
      "Content-Type": "text/xml;charset\u003dUTF-8"
    },
    "httpStatusCode": 200
  }
}
```

You can see that InstanceStatus shows "running" value. Possible values for this are the following:

- pending
- running
- shutting down
- terminated
- stopping
- stopped

To list all instances status, use the following command:

```
describeInstanceStatus(null);
```

Once the instance state is running, you can verify that you are able to connect to the EC2 instance using SSH client. Refer to the "Verify by Connecting to EC2 Instance" section.

4. List EC2 Instances

To get the EC2 instance details based on the instanceId, use describe-instances:

```
describeInstances(instanceId);

public List<String> describeInstances(String instanceId) {
    List<String> instanceIdList = new ArrayList<String>();

    DescribeInstancesRequest request = new DescribeInstancesRequest();

    if(!StringUtils.isNullOrEmpty(instanceId)) {
        request.setInstanceIds(Arrays.asList(instanceId));
    }

    DescribeInstancesResult response =
        amazonEC2Client.describeInstances(request);

    if(response!=null && response.getReservations()!=null &&
        !response.getReservations().isEmpty()) {

        for(Reservation reservation: response.getReservations()) {

            List<Instance> instances = reservation.getInstances();
```

```java
            if(instances!=null && !instances.isEmpty()) {
                for(Instance instance: instances) {
                    instanceIdList.add(instance.getInstanceId());
                }
            }
        }
    }
    return instanceIdList;
}
```

```
{
 "reservations": [
   {
    "reservationId": "r-e5e9243d",
    "ownerId": "254393510377",
    "groups": [],
    "instances": [
      {
       "instanceId": "i-fac9596e",
       "imageId": "ami-775e4f16",
       "state": {
         "code": 16,
         "name": "running"
       },
       "privateDnsName": "ip-172-31-20-198.us-west-2.compute.internal",
       "publicDnsName": "ec2-35-160-135-172.us-west-2.compute.amazonaws.com",
       "stateTransitionReason": "",
       "keyName": "EC2CreationViaAWSJavaSDK",
       "amiLaunchIndex": 0,
       "instanceType": "t2.micro",
       "launchTime": "Nov 16, 2016 4:51:50 PM",
       "placement": {
         "availabilityZone": "us-west-2a",
         "groupName": "",
         "tenancy": "default"
       },
       "monitoring": {
         "state": "disabled"
       },
       "subnetId": "subnet-d610c5a1",
       "vpcId": "vpc-ca538caf",
       "privateIpAddress": "172.31.20.198",
       "publicIpAddress": "35.160.135.172",
       "architecture": "x86_64",
       "rootDeviceType": "ebs",
       "rootDeviceName": "/dev/sda1",
       "blockDeviceMappings": [
         {
           "deviceName": "/dev/sda1",
           "ebs": {
             "volumeId": "vol-d7ae8a63",
             "status": "attached",
             "attachTime": "Nov 16, 2016 4:51:51 PM",
             "deleteOnTermination": true
           }
         }
       ],
       "virtualizationType": "hvm",
       "clientToken": "4aa2b15e-5ab1-46e7-82f5-da8ca436b80f",
       "securityGroups": [
         {
           "groupName": "EC2CreationViaAWSJavaSDK",
           "groupId": "sg-461e4f3f"
         }
       ],
```

```
        "sourceDestCheck": true,
        "hypervisor": "xen",
        "networkInterfaces": [
            {
                "networkInterfaceId": "eni-087c9748",
                "subnetId": "subnet-d610c5a1",
                "vpcId": "vpc-ca538caf",
                "description": "",
                "ownerId": "254393510377",
                "status": "in-use",
                "macAddress": "06:e1:c8:3b:de:31",
                "privateIpAddress": "172.31.20.198",
                "privateDnsName": "ip-172-31-20-198.us-west-2.compute.internal",
                "sourceDestCheck": true,
                "groups": [
                    {
                        "groupName": "EC2CreationViaAWSJavaSDK",
                        "groupId": "sg-461e4f3f"
                    }
                ],
                "attachment": {
                    "attachmentId": "eni-attach-3f850bb5",
                    "deviceIndex": 0,
                    "status": "attached",
                    "attachTime": "Nov 16, 2016 4:51:50 PM",
                    "deleteOnTermination": true
                },
                "association": {
                    "publicIp": "35.160.135.172",
                    "publicDnsName": "ec2-35-160-135-172.us-west-2.compute.amazonaws.com",
                    "ipOwnerId": "amazon"
                },
                "privateIpAddresses": [
                    {
                        "privateIpAddress": "172.31.20.198",
                        "privateDnsName": "ip-172-31-20-198.us-west-2.compute.internal",
                        "primary": true,
                        "association": {
                            "publicIp": "35.160.135.172",
                            "publicDnsName": "ec2-35-160-135-172.us-west-2.compute.amazonaws.com",
                            "ipOwnerId": "amazon"
                        }
                    }
                ]
            }
        ],
        "ebsOptimized": false
    }
],
"groupNames": []
}
],
"sdkResponseMetadata": {
    "metadata": {
        "AWS_REQUEST_ID": "697865d0-e162-4e61-a8a1-698316966a25"
    }
},
"sdkHttpMetadata": {
    "httpHeaders": {
        "Transfer-Encoding": "chunked",
        "Server": "AmazonEC2",
        "Vary": "Accept-Encoding",
        "Date": "Wed, 16 Nov 2016 11:37:00 GMT",
        "Content-Type": "text/xml;charset\u003dUTF-8"
    },
    "httpStatusCode": 200
}
}
```

To get all EC2 instances details, use describeInstances without providing any criteria:

```
describeInstances(null);
```

5. Get an Instance Status

To get the instance status that we created, we will execute the following code:

```
describeInstanceStatus(instanceId);
```

```
public void describeInstanceStatus(String instanceId) {
    DescribeInstanceStatusRequest request =
        new DescribeInstanceStatusRequest();

    request.setInstanceIds(Arrays.asList(instanceId));

    DescribeInstanceStatusResult response =
        amazonEC2Client.describeInstanceStatus(request);
}
```

We will pass the `instanceId` parameter that we received from the `launchInstance()` method:

```
{
  "instanceStatuses": [
    {
      "instanceId": "i-fac9596e",
      "availabilityZone": "us-west-2a",
      "instanceState": {
        "code": 16,
        "name": "running"
      },
      "systemStatus": {
        "status": "ok",
        "details": [
          {
            "name": "reachability",
            "status": "passed"
          }
        ]
      },
      "instanceStatus": {
        "status": "ok",
        "details": [
          {
            "name": "reachability",
            "status": "passed"
          }
        ]
      }
    }
  ],
  "sdkResponseMetadata": {
    "metadata": {
      "AWS_REQUEST_ID": "3f556bae-00c0-4897-900d-5919980b1cfe"
    }
  },
  "sdkHttpMetadata": {
    "httpHeaders": {
      "Transfer-Encoding": "chunked",
      "Server": "AmazonEC2",
      "Vary": "Accept-Encoding",
      "Date": "Wed, 16 Nov 2016 11:36:39 GMT",
      "Content-Type": "text/xml;charset\u003dUTF-8"
    },
    "httpStatusCode": 200
  }
}
```

You can see that the InstanceStatus tag has the value "initializing," which denotes that the instance is created but it is initializing. Once the initialization process is complete, the InstanceStatus will be reflected as "ok"; the instance has been initialized successfully.

To get the instance status of all the EC2 instances available under the user account, use the following code:

```
describeInstanceStatus(null);
```

6. Instance Tags

To assign tags to an EC2 instance, execute the following code:

```
List<Tag> tags = new ArrayList<Tag>();
tags.add(createTag("Chapter", "2"));
tags.add(createTag("Environment", "Production"));

assignTagToEC2(instanceId, tags);

private static Tag createTag(String key, String value) {
    Tag tag = new Tag();

    tag.setKey(key);

    tag.setValue(value);

    return tag;
}

public void assignTagToEC2(String instanceId, List<Tag> tags) {
    CreateTagsRequest request = new CreateTagsRequest();

    request.setResources(Arrays.asList(instanceId));

    request.setTags(tags);

    CreateTagsResult response = amazonEC2Client.createTags(request);
}
```

```
{
  "sdkResponseMetadata": {
    "metadata": {
      "AWS_REQUEST_ID": "da06f194-b032-4738-a873-07817e52ae36"
    }
  },
  "sdkHttpMetadata": {
    "httpHeaders": {
      "Transfer-Encoding": "chunked",
      "Server": "AmazonEC2",
      "Vary": "Accept-Encoding",
      "Date": "Wed, 16 Nov 2016 11:51:51 GMT",
      "Content-Type": "text/xml;charset\u003dUTF-8"
    },
    "httpStatusCode": 200
  }
}
```

To describe the tags that are assigned to an EC2 instance, execute the following code:

```
describeTags(instanceId);

public void describeTags(String instanceId) {
    DescribeTagsRequest request = new DescribeTagsRequest();

    Filter filter = new Filter("resource-id", Arrays.asList(instanceId));

    request.setFilters(Arrays.asList(filter));

    DescribeTagsResult response = amazonEC2Client.describeTags(request);
}
```

```
{
  "tags": [
    {
      "resourceId": "i-fac9596e",
      "resourceType": "instance",
      "key": "Chapter",
      "value": "2"
    },
    {
      "resourceId": "i-fac9596e",
      "resourceType": "instance",
      "key": "Environment",
      "value": "Production"
    }
  ],
  "sdkResponseMetadata": {
    "metadata": {
      "AWS_REQUEST_ID": "de6178c8-0520-4ee0-8c6d-6fa3b0a05590"
    }
  },
  "sdkHttpMetadata": {
    "httpHeaders": {
      "Transfer-Encoding": "chunked",
      "Server": "AmazonEC2",
      "Vary": "Accept-Encoding",
      "Date": "Wed, 16 Nov 2016 11:52:29 GMT",
      "Content-Type": "text/xml;charset\u003dUTF-8"
    },
    "httpStatusCode": 200
  }
}
```

To delete the tags for an EC2 Instance, execute the following code:

```
List<Tag> deleteTags = new ArrayList<Tag>();
deleteTags.add(createTag("Chapter", "2"));

deleteTags(instanceId, deleteTags);

public void deleteTags(String instanceId, List<Tag> tags) {
    DeleteTagsRequest request = new DeleteTagsRequest();

    request.setResources(Arrays.asList(instanceId));

    request.setTags(tags);

    DeleteTagsResult response = amazonEC2Client.deleteTags(request);
}
```

```
{
  "sdkResponseMetadata": {
    "metadata": {
      "AWS_REQUEST_ID": "8c1a05df-445d-4761-90a2-dac6ca7ff203"
    }
  },
  "sdkHttpMetadata": {
    "httpHeaders": {
      "Transfer-Encoding": "chunked",
      "Server": "AmazonEC2",
      "Vary": "Accept-Encoding",
      "Date": "Wed, 16 Nov 2016 11:53:09 GMT",
      "Content-Type": "text/xml;charset\u003dUTF-8"
    },
    "httpStatusCode": 200
  }
}
```

Here in deleteTags, we have provided the both the key and value. However, it's optional to provide the value for the Value element. If you provide the value, it becomes mandatory that both the key and value match the actual tags and only then can it delete the tags. The following code can be used when you want to delete tag based on the key only:

```
deleteTags.add(createTag("Chapter", ""));
```

7. Start-Stop-Terminate Instance

You may require your instance to start-stop-terminate manually. First of all, stop your instance using the following code:

```
stopInstance(instanceId);

public void stopInstance (String instanceId) {
    StopInstancesRequest request = new StopInstancesRequest();

    request.setInstanceIds(Arrays.asList(instanceId));

    StopInstancesResult response = amazonEC2Client.stopInstances(request);
}
```

```
{
  "stoppingInstances": [
    {
      "instanceId": "i-fac9596e",
      "currentState": {
        "code": 64,
        "name": "stopping"
      },
      "previousState": {
        "code": 16,
        "name": "running"
      }
    }
  ],
  "sdkResponseMetadata": {
    "metadata": {
      "AWS_REQUEST_ID": "3f426b52-1a59-438d-976a-c82763cccc08"
    }
  },
  "sdkHttpMetadata": {
    "httpHeaders": {
      "Transfer-Encoding": "chunked",
      "Server": "AmazonEC2",
      "Vary": "Accept-Encoding",
      "Date": "Wed, 16 Nov 2016 11:54:03 GMT",
      "Content-Type": "text/xml;charset\u003dUTF-8"
    },
    "httpStatusCode": 200
  }
}
```

You can see that currentState is stopped now. The times to stop the instances may vary depending on the processes that are running on the EC2 instances.

To start the instance, execute the following code:

```
startInstance(instanceId);

public void startInstance(String instanceId) {

    StartInstancesRequest request = new StartInstancesRequest();

    request.setInstanceIds(Arrays.asList(instanceId));

    StartInstancesResult response = amazonEC2Client.startInstances(request);
}
```

```
{
  "startingInstances": [
    {
      "instanceId": "i-fac9596e",
      "currentState": {
        "code": 0,
        "name": "pending"
      },
      "previousState": {
        "code": 80,
        "name": "stopped"
      }
    }
  ],
  "sdkResponseMetadata": {
    "metadata": {
      "AWS_REQUEST_ID": "2bdd1e7e-5604-4725-8b11-100e19422d0d"
    }
  },
  "sdkHttpMetadata": {
    "httpHeaders": {
      "Transfer-Encoding": "chunked",
      "Server": "AmazonEC2",
      "Vary": "Accept-Encoding",
      "Date": "Wed, 16 Nov 2016 12:00:30 GMT",
      "Content-Type": "text/xml;charset\u003dUTF-8"
    },
    "httpStatusCode": 200
  }
}
```

Once the process is completed successfully, the currentState should appear as running.

To terminate the instance, execute the following code:

```
terminateInstance(instanceId);

public void terminateInstance (String instanceId) {
    TerminateInstancesRequest request = new TerminateInstancesRequest();

    request.setInstanceIds(Arrays.asList(instanceId));

    TerminateInstancesResult response =
        amazonEC2Client.terminateInstances(request);
}
```

```
{
  "terminatingInstances": [
    {
      "instanceId": "i-fac9596e",
      "currentState": {
        "code": 32,
        "name": "shutting-down"
      },
      "previousState": {
        "code": 16,
        "name": "running"
      }
    }
  ],
  "sdkResponseMetadata": {
    "metadata": {
      "AWS_REQUEST_ID": "c5c24edb-dab4-4d70-ae58-25202e156f2f"
    }
  },
  "sdkHttpMetadata": {
    "httpHeaders": {
      "Transfer-Encoding": "chunked",
      "Server": "AmazonEC2",
      "Vary": "Accept-Encoding",
      "Date": "Wed, 16 Nov 2016 12:08:24 GMT",
      "Content-Type": "text/xml;charset\u003dUTF-8"
    },
    "httpStatusCode": 200
  }
}
```

Once the process is successfully completed, the currentState should be terminated.

Monitoring Using CloudWatch

Monitoring is an important aspect in software or application life cycle. CloudWatch enables us to automate the monitoring of the instances based on several metrics available. You can configure the metrics threshold limits for our instances. You can create the CloudWatch alarm either using the EC2 Management Console or the CloudWatch Console.

Create an Alarm Using the EC2 Management Console

You can create an alarm from the EC2 Management Console as follows:

1. Go to the EC2 Management Console and select "Instances" from the menu.

2. Select the instance for which you want to create alarm.

3. Select "Monitoring" tab.

4. Click the Create Alarm button (See Figure 2-25).

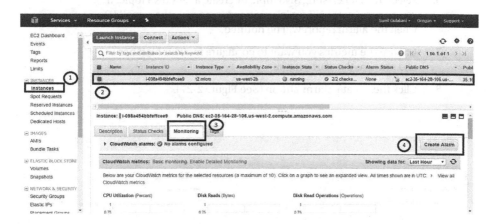

Figure 2-25. *CloudWatch alarm using EC2 Management Console*

5. The Create Alarm window will be displayed, as shown in Figure 2-26.

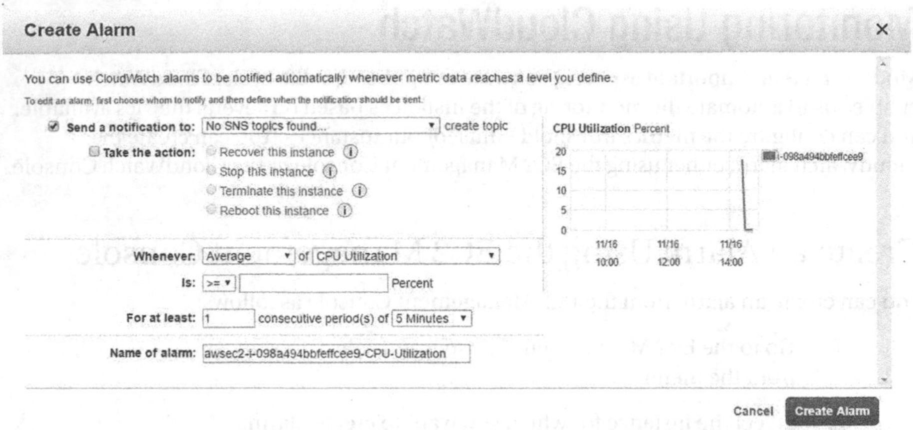

Create Alarm ✕

You can use CloudWatch alarms to be notified automatically whenever metric data reaches a level you define.
To edit an alarm, first choose whom to notify and then define when the notification should be sent.

☑ **Send a notification to:** No SNS topics found... ▼ create topic

☐ **Take the action:** ○ Recover this instance ⓘ
○ Stop this instance ⓘ
○ Terminate this instance ⓘ
○ Reboot this instance ⓘ

Whenever: Average ▼ of CPU Utilization ▼

Is: >= ▼ [   ] Percent

For at least: 1 consecutive period(s) of 5 Minutes ▼

Name of alarm: awsec2-i-098a494bbfeffcee9-CPU-Utilization

CPU Utilization Percent

20
15
10
5
0
11/16   11/16   11/16
10:00   12:00   14:00

■ i-098a494bbfeffcee9

Cancel   Create Alarm

***Figure 2-26.** Create alarm window*

6. Select from an existing SNS topic or create a new SNS topic. If you create a new SNS topic, you need to provide the e-mail ID when the alarm report will be notified.

7. Choose the metrics you want to configure for your instance and provide the alarm name.

8. Click the Create Alarm button (See Figure 2-27).

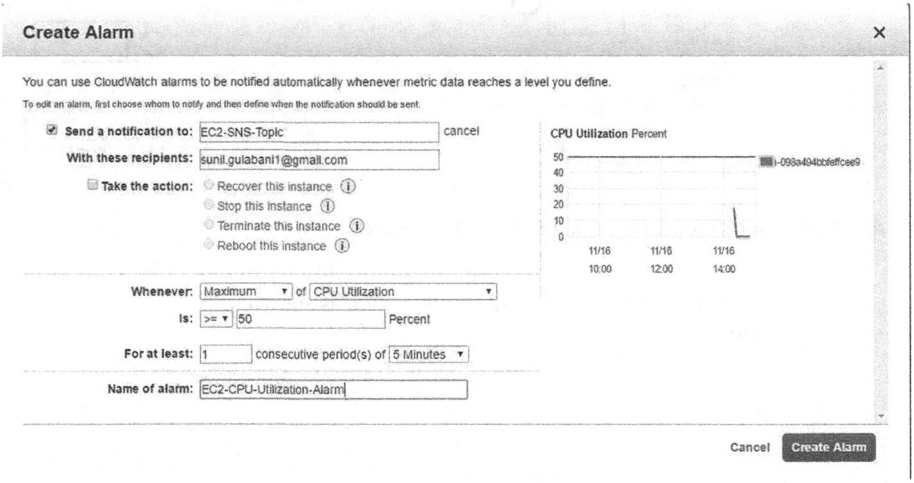

Create Alarm ✕

You can use CloudWatch alarms to be notified automatically whenever metric data reaches a level you define.
To edit an alarm, first choose whom to notify and then define when the notification should be sent.

☑ **Send a notification to:** EC2-SNS-Topic cancel

With these recipients: sunil.gulabani1@gmail.com

☐ **Take the action:** ○ Recover this instance ⓘ
○ Stop this instance ⓘ
○ Terminate this instance ⓘ
○ Reboot this instance ⓘ

Whenever: Maximum ▼ of CPU Utilization ▼

Is: >= ▼ 50 Percent

For at least: 1 consecutive period(s) of 5 Minutes ▼

Name of alarm: EC2-CPU-Utilization-Alarm

CPU Utilization Percent

50
40
30
20
10
0
11/16   11/16   11/16
10:00   12:00   14:00

■ i-098a494bbfeffcee9

Cancel   Create Alarm

***Figure 2-27.** Create alarm with new SNS topic and metrics*

84

The alarm will be created successfully (See Figure 2-28).

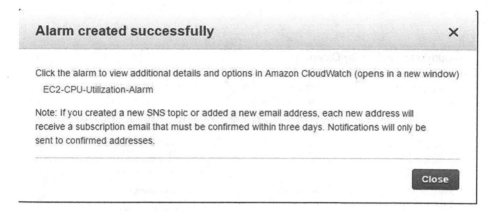

Figure 2-28. *Alarm created successfully*

Create an Alarm Using the CloudWatch Management Console

You can create an alarm from the CloudWatch Management Console using the following steps:

1. Go to the CloudWatch Management Console and select Alarms from the menu.

2. Click Create Alarm (See Figure 2-29).

Figure 2-29. *CloudWatch Console*

3. Create an alarm window to be displayed in two steps:

   a. Select metric.

   b. Select the Per-Instance Metrics under EC2 Metrics (See Figure 2-30).

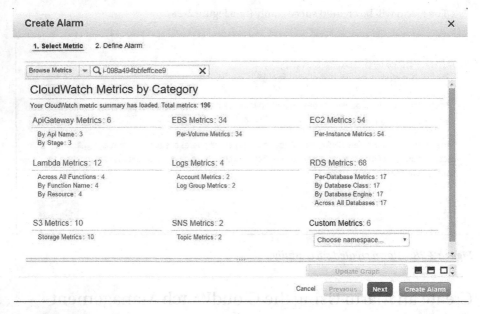

Figure 2-30. *Create an alarm using CloudWatch Console*

     c.   Search for the EC2 instance based on the instance ID and select the metrics. Click the Next button, as shown in Figure 2-31.

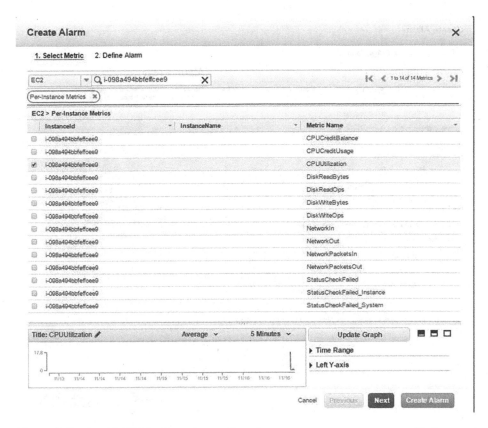

Figure 2-31. Search EC2 instance for creating alarm

    d.   Define the alarm.

    e.   Provide the name and description for the alarm.

    f.   Provide threshold limits.

    g.   Select the appropriate actions and advance options for notification, auto-scaling action, and EC2 Action.

    h.   Click Create Alarm (See Figure 2-32).

Create Alarm ✕

1. Select Metric   **2. Define Alarm**

Alarm Threshold

Provide the details and threshold for your alarm. Use the graph on the right to help set the appropriate threshold.

Name: [EC2-Alarm-CloudWatch]

Description: [EC2-Alarm-CloudWatch]

Whenever: CPUUtilization

is: [>= ▾] [50]

for: [1] consecutive period(s)

Actions

Define what actions are taken when your alarm changes state.

Notification   Delete

Whenever this alarm: [State is ALARM   ▾]

Send notification to: [EC2-SNS-Topic   ▾] New list Enter list ❶

Email list: [sunil.gulabani1@gmail.com]

[+ Notification] [+ AutoScaling Action] [+ EC2 Action]

Alarm Preview

This alarm will trigger when the blue line goes up to or above the red line for a duration of 5 minutes

CPUUtilization >= 50

60
50
40
30
20
10
0
        11/16   11/16   11/16
        13:00   14:00   15:00

Namespace: AWS/EC2

InstanceId: [i-098a494bbfeffcee9]

Metric Name: [CPUUtilization]

Period: [5 Minutes ▾]

Statistic: [Average ▾]

Cancel   **Previous**   Next   **Create Alarm**

Figure 2-32. *Define alarm*

The alarm created successfully (See Figure 2-33).

✔ Your alarm EC2-Alarm-CloudWatch has been saved.   ✕

Figure 2-33. *Alarm created successfully*

Finally, we have completed creating the alarm on our EC2 instance. Whenever the threshold limit on the EC2 instance is achieved, the receipt e-mail address will be notified.

Summary

In this chapter, I have discussed how to create EC2 instances and connect using the SSH client (PuTTy). Moreover, I explained how to configure a security group so that you can connect to an EC2 instance and key pair that is used to authorize login to the EC2 instance. Lastly, I demonstrated how to configure an alarm on an EC2 instance that will be triggered when the threshold limit is crossed.

In Chapter 3, I will show how to configure SQS and how to implement SQS producer and consumer applications.

CHAPTER 3

■ ■ ■

Hands-on Simple Queue Service (SQS)

Queuing service is communication among distributed applications. Generally, you have queuing service where you need asynchronous processes to be carried out. The purpose of queuing service is to transport data from origin applications and allow destination applications to read messages and process further.

In this chapter, I will cover the following topics:

- Messaging Queuing Service

- Introduction of AWS SQS

- Features of SQS

- Using AWS Management Console

- Using AWS CLI

- Using AWS SDK—Java

- Monitoring Using CloudWatch

What Is Messaging Queuing Service?

Messaging queuing service provides different applications to transfer messages. The queuing service follows the producer/consumer paradigm. Producer applications are responsible for sending messages to the queue and consumer applications are responsible for reading messages from the queue. Consumer applications can read messages from the queue at any time; it is not mandatory to have connection established to the queue when the producer sends messages. Whenever the consumer application is connected, it reads the messages from the queuing service. The queuing service will add the messages in sequential order.

Messaging queuing service is asynchronous communication. A queuing service is used when you don't have to respond back to the request immediately. Applications can add messages to the queuing service and the consumer application can process it at a later stage. There may be cases where the request is taking time to process, so the producer application will add the message to the queue. (See Figure 3-1.)

© Sunil Gulabani 2017
S. Gulabani, *Practical Amazon EC2, SQS, Kinesis, and S3*,
DOI 10.1007/978-1-4842-2841-8_3

Figure 3-1. *Message queuing service*

Introduction of AWS SQS

AWS Simple Queue Service (SQS) is a distributed queuing service application where you can add and read messages over the Internet. Amazon manages AWS SQS and only charges users for what they have consumed. AWS SQS is a highly scalable solution that allows applications to add and read messages, which makes decoupling the application components efficient. AWS SQS can be accessed via Web Services API and AWS SDK, which is available for different programming languages.

AWS SQS provide two types of queues:

1. Standard Queue

Standard queue is the default queue type supported by AWS SQS. It doesn't restrict the number of transactions per second, and it ensures that messages are delivered at least once. This type of queue is used when there aren't any critical events that need to be processed by consumer applications since there may be duplicate messages that need to be handled in the application. (See Figure 3-2.)

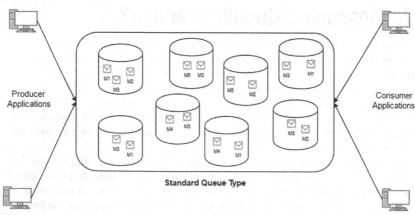

Figure 3-2. *Standard queue type*

2. FIFO Queue

A FIFO (first in, first out) queue maintains order for delivery of messages. The name of the queue should have the suffix ".fifo". It restricts 300 transactions per second and ensures that messages are delivered exactly once. This type of queue should be used when there is a defined series of steps to be performed so that unordered messages are not received for processing in consumer applications. (See Figure 3-3.)

Figure 3-3. *FIFO queue type*

Features of SQS

Following are the main features of SQS that play a significant role in applications:

- **High Availability:** AWS SQS provides high availability for sending and receiving messages as they are stored on distributed servers.

- **Authentication:** To access the queue, permission is necessary at the queue level. The users can access the queue based on AWS IAM.

- **Visible Timeout:** When a consumer reads a message from the queue, it hides the message that is being processed so that no other consumer processes it.

- **Delay Messages:** Delay of messages can be configured at the queue level as well as at the message level while sending messages.

- **Cost:** AWS charges only for the API requests that are made to SQS so there are no fixed costs attached with AWS SQS.

Using AWS Management Console

AWS Management Console can be used to manage SQS. It provides an easy way to configure SQS. To configure SQS, log in to AWS Console. Under the All Services category, click SQS, as highlighted in Figure 3-4.

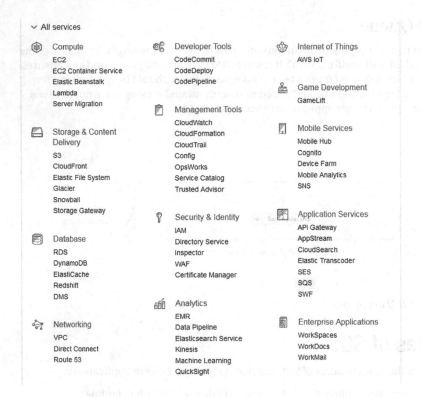

Figure 3-4. AWS Management Console

1. Create Queue

Creating a queue is the first step in using AWS SQS. When you open AWS SQS Console, you are redirected to the Create New Queue screen. If you aren't, click the Create New Queue button, which will redirect you to the screen shown in Figure 3-5.

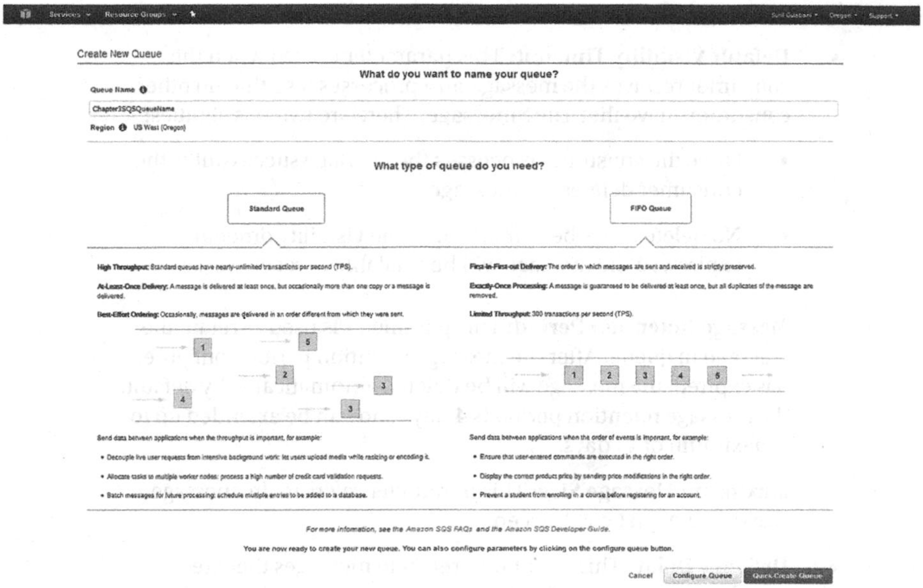

Figure 3-5. *Create queue*

You will provide the queue name and select the queue type that you prefer to use in your project. As previously mentioned, if you select "FIFO queue" as the queue type, you need to add the suffix ".fifo" to your queue name. If you want to create a queue with default parameters, you can click the Quick-Create Queue button. Otherwise, if you need to configure queue parameters, click the Configure Queue button. (See Figure 3-6.)

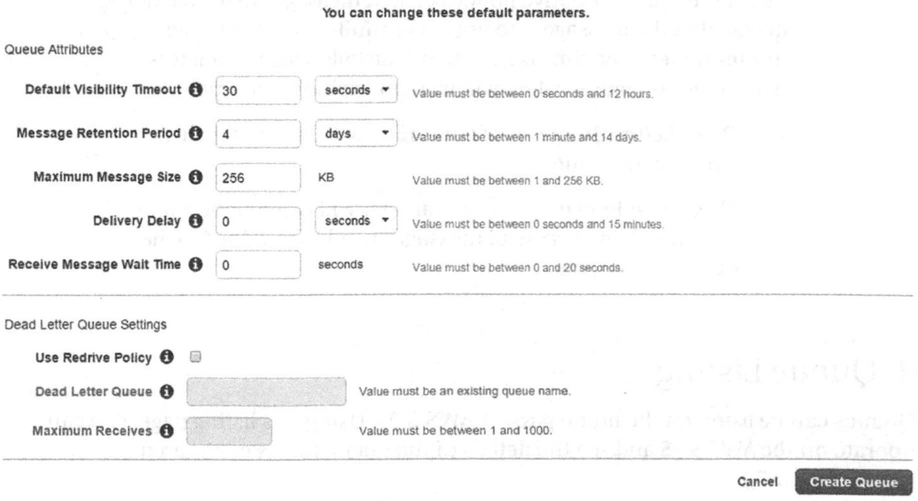

Figure 3-6. *Configure queue*

Following are the queue attributes:

- **Default Visibility Timeout:** This parameter is used when the consumer receives the message and processes it so that no other consumers have that same message. There are two possibilities:

  - Once the consumer processes the message successfully, the consumer deletes the message.

  - No delete call is been made until the visibility timeout expires, so the message will be available to receive a call.

- **Message Retention Period:** This parameter is used to retain the message in queue. After the message retention period configured has expired, the message will be deleted automatically. By default, the message retention period is 4 days and can be extended up to a maximum of 14 days.

- **Maximum Message Size:** This parameter refers to the message size that the queue will accept.

- **Delivery Delay:** This parameter refers to messages that are invisible to consumers for that specific time. The value can be between 0 and 15 minutes.

- **Receive Message Wait Time:** This parameter will be used for long polling. It will help to reduce the cost of using SQS. By default, the short polling is configured in AWS SQS. This will enable the receive message request to query all servers and provide respective responses.

- **Use Redrive Policy:** This parameter enables configuration of dead letter queue. Redrive policy will add messages to dead letter queue after the messages are not successfully processed when maximum received time is specified. The following parameters need to be configured when you want to enable redrive policy:

  - **Dead Letter Queue:** This parameter will contain the dead letter queue name.

  - **Maximum Receives:** This parameter will contain the count after which unsuccessful messages need to be added to the dead letter queue.

2. Queue Listing

Queues can be listed on the home page of AWS SQS. Using this listing page, you can operate on the AWS SQS and see the details of the queue that is configured. (See Figure 3-7.)

Figure 3-7. *Queue listing*

3. Configure Queue Permission

When you create a queue, by default only the queue owner can have access to the queue. If you need to provide queue access to another user, you also need to provide the necessary permission.

1. Select the queue from the listing and click the Permissions tab. (See Figure 3-8.)

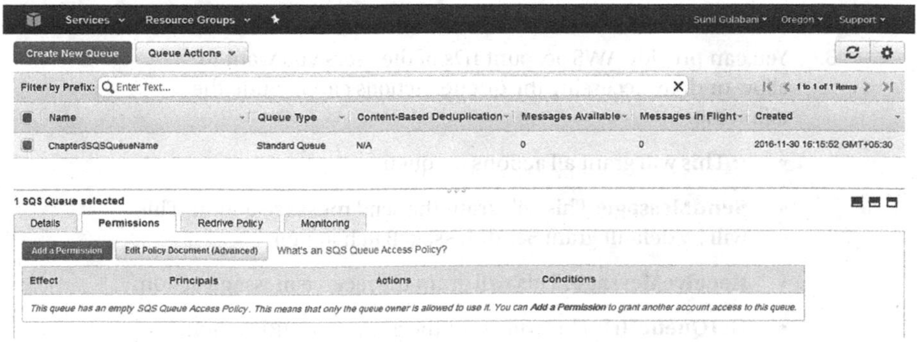

Figure 3-8. *Queue permissions*

2. This will show the permissions provided to queue. To add permission, click the Add Permission button. (See Figure 3-9.)

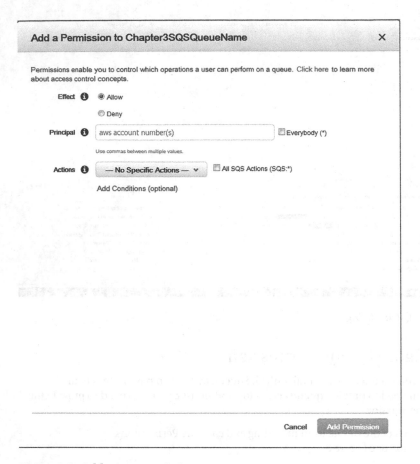

Figure 3-9. *Add queue permissions*

3. You can provide AWS account IDs of the users you want to allow or deny accessing the queue. Actions can include the following:

- ***:** This will grant all actions on queue.

- **SendMessage**: This will grant the send message action. This will by default grant SendMessageBatch action.

- **ReceiveMessage**: This will grant the receive message action.

- **GetQueueUrl**: This will grant the get queue URL action.

- **GetQueueAttributes**: This will grant the get queue attributes action.

- **DeleteMessage**: This will grant the delete message action. This will by default grant the DeleteMessageBatch action.

- **ChangeMessageVisibility**: This will grant the change message visibility action.

Once you have finished providing AWS account IDs and selected necessary actions, click the Add Permission button. This will create the permission as you can see in Figure 3-10.

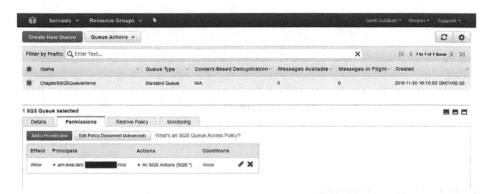

Figure 3-10. *Queue permissions added*

4. If you want to edit the permission and edit using policy document, click the Edit Policy Document (Advanced) button. This will open the Edit Policy Document window showing policy for the permissions you provided in the last step. Here you can edit the policy to provide permissions to respective AWS user IDs, actions, and resources (SQS). (See Figure 3-11.)

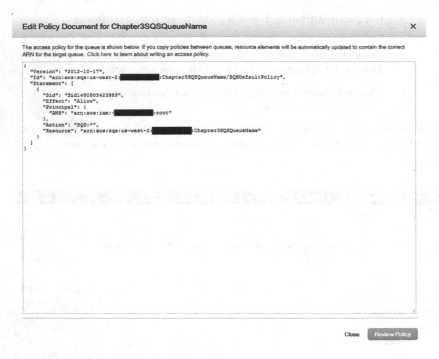

Figure 3-11. *Edit queue permissions*

4. Configure Dead Letter Queue

A dead letter queue is used when messages from source queues have not been consumed successfully.

To configure a dead letter queue, select the queue from the listing and right-click it, which will show the options menu. You can also click Queue Actions and select the Configure Queue menu.(See Figure 3-12.)

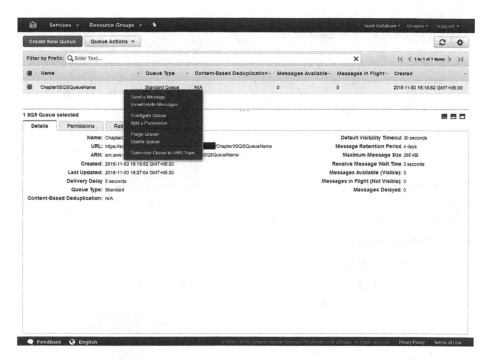

Figure 3-12. *Queue options*

This will open the Configure Queue window, as shown in Figure 3-13.

Configure Chapter3SQSQueueName ✕

Queue Settings

Default Visibility Timeout ℹ	30	seconds ▾	Value must be between 0 seconds and 12 hours.
Message Retention Period ℹ	4	days ▾	Value must be between 1 minute and 14 days.
Maximum Message Size ℹ	256	KB	Value must be between 1 and 256 KB.
Delivery Delay ℹ	0	seconds ▾	Value must be between 0 seconds and 15 minutes.
Receive Message Wait Time ℹ	0	seconds	Value must be between 0 and 20 seconds.

Dead Letter Queue Settings

Use Redrive Policy ℹ	☐	
Dead Letter Queue ℹ		Value must be an existing queue name.
Maximum Receives ℹ		Value must be between 1 and 1000.

Cancel   **Save Changes**

Figure 3-13. *Configure queue*

Here you need to enable the check box for "Use Redrive Policy," and you need a dead letter queue that you will create first and then come back to this screen again.

Now you will create the queue that will be used as a dead letter queue. It is mandatory that the queue type for the source queue and the dead letter queue are the same. Figure 3-14 shows the queue that we created with the name "Chapter3SQSDeadLetterQueue."

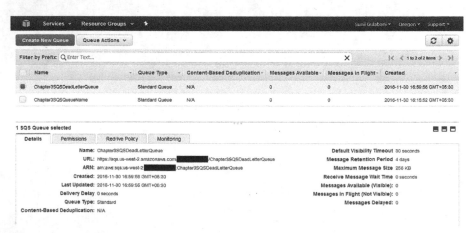

Figure 3-14. *Create dead letter queue*

Open the Configure Queue screen and select the check box for Use Redrive Policy. This will enable the input boxes for Dead Letter Queue and Maximum Receives fields. Enter the dead letter queue name as "Chapter3SQSDeadLetterQueue" and maximum receives as "10." After you have input this information, click the Save Changes button. (See Figure 3-15.)

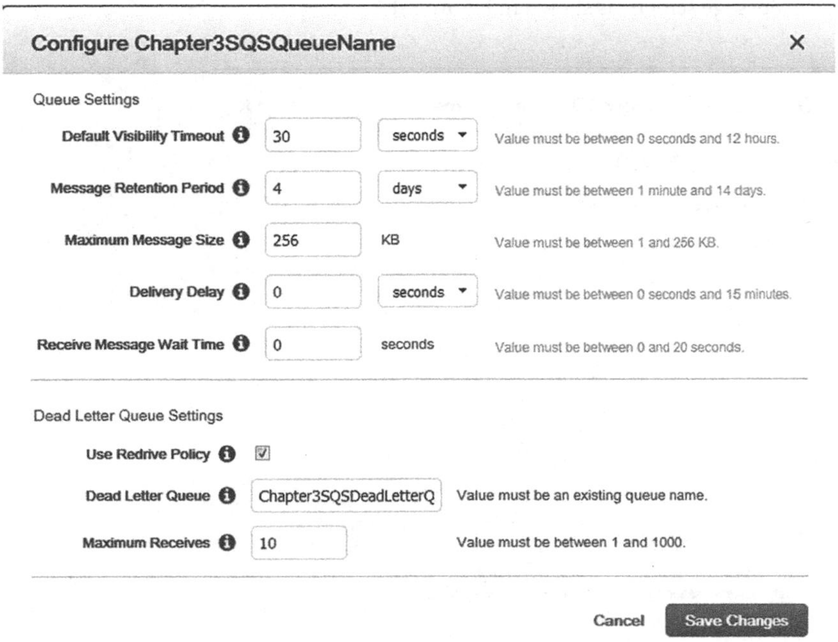

Figure 3-15. *Configure dead letter queue to source queue*

The redrive policy that we configured can be viewed under the Redrive Policy tab, as shown in Figure 3-16.

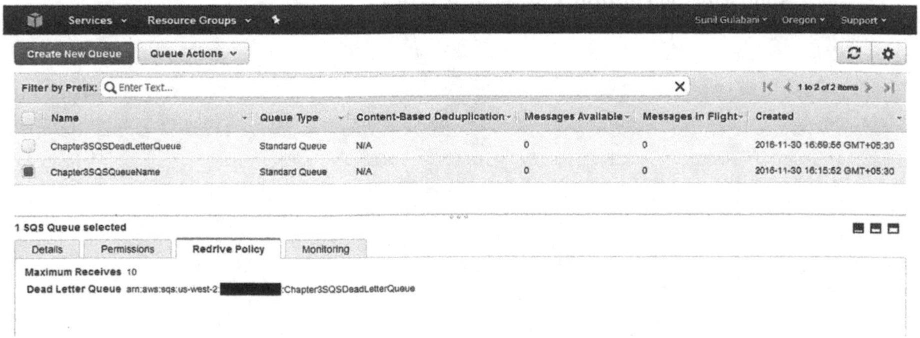

Figure 3-16. *Redrive policy tab*

5. Send Message

The Send a Message button is used to deliver messages to the queue.

1. To send a message, choose the queue, right-click, and select Send a Message from menu. This will open the Send a Message screen, as shown in Figure 3-17.

Figure 3-17. *Send a Message screen*

2. We added the message body "Hello World!!!" and clicked the Send Message button. (See Figure 3-18.)

Figure 3-18. *Send message success*

3. The message is successfully sent and you can see the message identifier and MD5 of the body in the success screen.

■ **Note**   For more details on MD5, see https://en.wikipedia.org/wiki/MD5.

4. On closing the success screen, you can check on the queue listing that message is sent to and see that the "Messages Available" count is shown as 1, as shown in Figure 3-19. Once the message gets consumed, this count will decrease.

Chapter3SQSQueueName	Standard Queue	N/A	1	0	2016-11-30 16:15:52 GMT+05:30

Figure 3-19. *Queue listing with unread message*

5. To send a message along with the message attributes, select the queue, right-click it, and click Send a Message from the menu, as shown in Figure 3-20.

Figure 3-20. *Send a message with message attributes—1*

6. Add message body as "Hello World with Message Attributes" and click the Message Attributes tab. Now add name, type, and value and click the Add Attribute button. This will add to list of message attributes. Once done, click the Send Message button, as shown in Figure 3-21.

Figure 3-21. *Send message with message attributes—2*

6. Receive Message

Receive Message will retrieve messages from the queue. You can provide the maximum number of messages to retrieve from the queue and the polling time in seconds to determine if any messages are available.

1. To receive messages, select the queue, right-click it, and click View/Delete Messages from the menu, as shown in Figure 3-22.

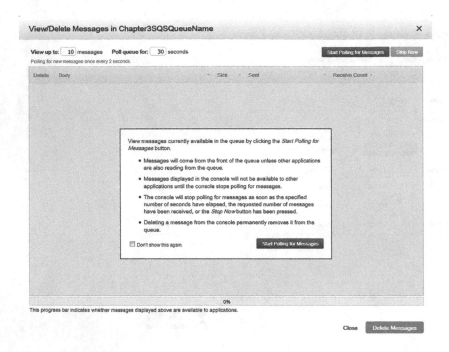

Figure 3-22. Receive message

2. Configure the parameters and click Start Polling for Messages. This action will retrieve messages from the queue. You can explicitly stop the polling or wait for the polling to complete. (See Figure 3-23.)

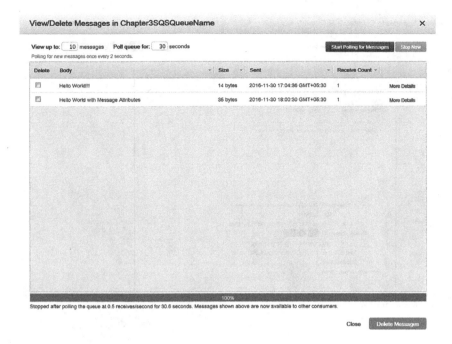

Figure 3-23. *Receive message listing*

3. You can see the two messages have been retrieved. These are the messages we sent in the Send Message section. To view the message attributes, click the More Details link on each message listed. (See Figure 3-24.)

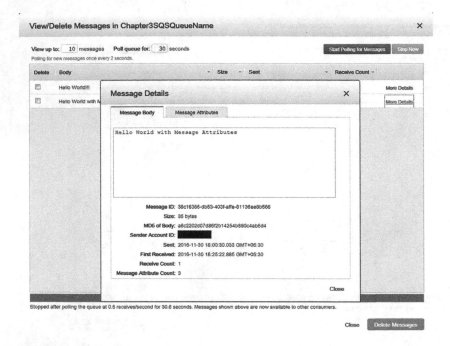

Figure 3-24. *Received message—more details—1*

4. Find the message body that we have sent and click the Message Attributes tab to see the message attributes that we sent. (See Figure 3-25.)

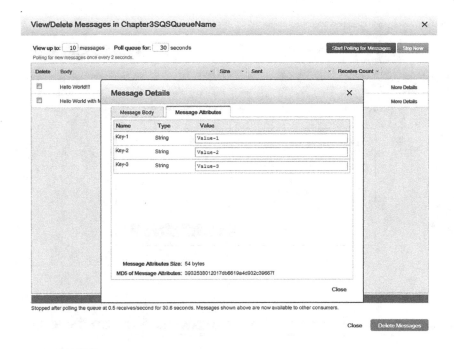

Figure 3-25. *Received message—more details—2*

7. Delete Message

Delete Message will remove messages from the queue. SQS doesn't remove messages automatically when you retrieve messages. You explicitly need to delete messages.

1. When you receive messages, select the check boxes of messages to delete and click the Delete Messages button. This will prompt for confirmation to delete the messages.

2. Click the Yes, Delete Checked Messages button. (See Figure 3-26.)

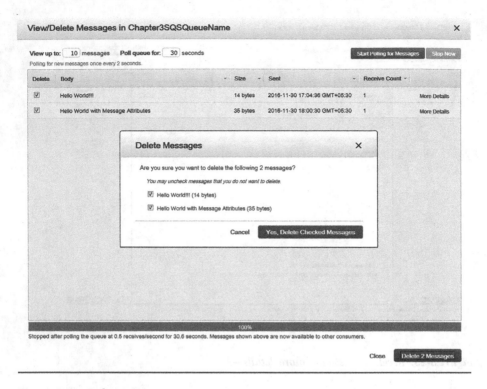

Figure 3-26. *Delete message*

8. Purge Queue

Purge Queue will delete all messages that are available in the queue. Once you purge the queue, deleted messages can't be retrieved. The deletion process takes nearly 60 seconds.

    1.   To purge the queue, select the queue, right-click it, and click "Purge Queue" from the menu. This will prompt for confirmation. (See Figure 3-27.)

Figure 3-27. *Purge queues*

2.   Click the Yes, Purge Queue button, and this will purge the queued messages. You can see the success screen in Figure 3-28.

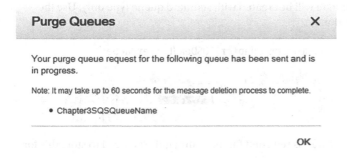

Figure 3-28. *Purge queues success*

9. Delete Queue

Delete Queue will delete the queue regardless if the queue is empty or not. The deletion process takes nearly 60 seconds.

1.   Select the queue, right-click the queue you want to delete, and click Delete Queue from the menu.

2.   Click the Yes, Delete Queue button, and it will delete the queue, as shown in Figure 3-29.

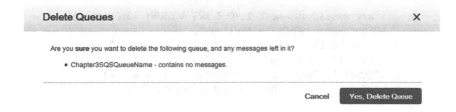

Figure 3-29. *Delete queues*

Using AWS CLI

In Chapter 1, I explained how to install AWS CLI. Now I will demonstrate how to use AWS CLI to manage AWS SQS.

111

create-queue

To create a queue, you need to pass the queue name. The queue name should be unique under the same account. You can create a FIFO queue by providing the `FifoQueue` attribute; otherwise, the queue will be created with standard queue type only. Use the following code to create a queue:

```
>aws sqs create-queue --queue-name Chapter3SQSDeadLetterQueue
```

```
C:\Users\Dell>aws sqs create-queue --queue-name Chapter3SQSDeadLetterQueue
{
    "QueueUrl": "https://us-west-2.queue.amazonaws.com/██████████/Chapter3SQSDeadLetterQueue"
}
```

You can see that `"QueueUrl"` is returned for the command. You need to store this for our future use.

To create a queue with specific attributes, add `--attributes` to the command:

```
>aws sqs create-queue --queue-name Chapter3SQSQueueName --attributes
file://C:/Users/Dell/create-queue-attributes.json
```

The created file `create-queue-attributes.json` contains the attribute's name and value in JSON format:

```
{
    "DelaySeconds": "0",
    "MaximumMessageSize": "262144",
    "MessageRetentionPeriod": "1209600",
    "ReceiveMessageWaitTimeSeconds": "0",
    "VisibilityTimeout": "30",
    "Policy": "{\"Version\": \"2012-10-17\", \"Id\":
                \"arn:aws:sqs:us-west-2:YOUR_AWS_ACCOUNT_ID:Chapter3
                SQSQueueName/SQSDefaultPolicy\",
                \"Statement\": [{\"Sid\": \"Sid1465389499769\",
                \"Effect\": \"Allow\",\"Principal\": \"*\",\"Action\":
                \"SQS:*\",\"Resource\": \"arn:aws:sqs:us-west-2:
                YOUR_AWS_ACCOUNT_ID:Chapter3SQSQueueName\"}]}"

}
```

```
C:\Users\Dell>aws sqs create-queue --queue-name Chapter3SQSQueueName --attributes file://C:/Users/Dell/create-queue-attributes.json
{
    "QueueUrl": "https://us-west-2.queue.amazonaws.com/██████████/Chapter3SQSQueueName"
}
```

You can also pass the attributes in key-value pair form separated by a comma (,):

```
key1=value,key2=value2 ...
```

```
>aws sqs create-queue --queue-name Chapter3SQSQueueName --attributes
DelaySeconds=0,MaximumMessageSize=262144
```

■ **Note**   For more parameters in detail, refer to `http://docs.amazonaws.cn/cli/` `latest/reference/sqs/create-queue.html`.

get-queue-url

Using the get-queue-url command, you will be able to get the URL of an existing queue:

```
>aws sqs get-queue-url --queue-name Chapter3SQSQueueName
```

```
C:\Users\Dell>aws sqs get-queue-url --queue-name Chapter3SQSQueueName
{
    "QueueUrl": "https://us-west-2.queue.amazonaws.com/          /Chapter3SQSQueueName"
}
```

If you need a queue URL that was created using a different account, you can pass the account ID in the request:

```
>aws sqs get-queue-url --queue-name Chapter3SQSQueueName --queue-owner-aws-
account-id 1234567890
```

```
C:\Users\Dell>aws sqs get-queue-url --queue-name Chapter3SQSQueueName --queue-owner-aws-account-id
{
    "QueueUrl": "https://us-west-2.queue.amazonaws.com/          /Chapter3SQSQueueName"
}
```

Replace the 1234567890 with an actual AWS account ID using the queue that was created. Make sure the queue has been granted the necessary permission to access it.

■ **Note**   For more parameters in detail, refer to `http://docs.amazonaws.cn/cli/` `latest/reference/sqs/get-queue-url.html`.

add-permission

This command provides access to the queue. By default, the queue owner has all controls to a queue. If different users need to access the queue, permission must be provided to them.

```
>aws sqs add-permission --queue-url https://us-west-2.queue.
amazonaws.com/YOUR_AWS_ACCOUNT_ID/Chapter3SQSQueueName --label
Chapter3SQSPermission --aws-account-ids YOUR_AWS_ACCOUNT_ID --actions
"SendMessage" "ReceiveMessage" "DeleteMessage" "ChangeMessageVisibility"
"GetQueueAttributes" "GetQueueUrl"
```

```
C:\Users\Dell>aws sqs add-permission --queue-url https://us-west-2.queue.amazonaws.com/███████/Chapter3SQSQueueName --label Chapter3SQSPermission --aws-account-ids
███████ --actions "SendMessage" "ReceiveMessage" "DeleteMessage" "ChangeMessageVisibility" "GetQueueAttributes" "GetQueueUrl"
C:\Users\Dell>
```

You can provide a list of account IDs and different queue actions to grant access. There won't be any output for this request. To provide all actions available, you can also provide "*":

```
>aws sqs add-permission --queue-url https://us-west-2.queue.amazonaws.com/
YOUR_AWS_ACCOUNT_ID/Chapter3SQSQueueName --label Chapter3SQSAllPermission
--aws-account-ids YOUR_AWS_ACCOUNT_ID --actions "*"
```

```
C:\Users\Dell>aws sqs add-permission --queue-url https://us-west-2.queue.amazonaws.com/███████/Chapter3SQSQueueName --label Chapter3SQSAllPermission --aws-account-
ids ███████ --actions "*"
C:\Users\Dell>
```

■ **Note**   For more parameters in detail, refer to http://docs.amazonaws.cn/cli/
latest/reference/sqs/add-permission.html.

---

remove-permission

This command will remove the permission from the queue based on the label provided in the request:

```
>aws sqs remove-permission --queue-url https://us-west-2.queue.amazonaws.
com/YOUR_AWS_ACCOUNT_ID/Chapter3SQSQueueName --label Chapter3SQSPermission
```

```
C:\Users\Dell>aws sqs remove-permission --queue-url https://us-west-2.queue.amazonaws.com/███████/Chapter3SQSQueueName --label Chapter3SQSPermission
C:\Users\Dell>
```

There won't be any output for this request. The "get-queue-attributes" section shows how to get the list of permissions.

■ **Note**   For more parameters in detail, refer to http://docs.amazonaws.cn/cli/
latest/reference/sqs/remove-permission.html.

---

set-queue-attributes

The set-queue-attributes command sets the queue attributes values. You can provide attributes either in key value form separated by a comma (,) or in a JSON format:

```
>aws sqs set-queue-attributes --queue-url https://us-west-2.queue.amazonaws.
com/YOUR_AWS_ACCOUNT_ID/Chapter3SQSQueueName --attributes DelaySeconds=0,Max
imumMessageSize=262144,MessageRetentionPeriod=1209600
```

```
C:\Users\Dell>aws sqs set-queue-attributes --queue-url https://us-west-2.queue.amazonaws.com/            /Chapter3SQSQueueName --attributes DelaySeconds=0,MaximumMessag
eSize=262144,MessageRetentionPeriod=1209600
C:\Users\Dell>
```

When queue attributes are changed, it takes 60 seconds to go into effect. The MessageRetentionPeriod attribute may take 15 minutes to go into effect:

```
>aws sqs set-queue-attributes --queue-url https://us-west-2.queue.amazonaws.
com/YOUR_AWS_ACCOUNT_ID/Chapter3SQSQueueName --attributes file://C:/Users/
Dell/set-queue-attributes.json
```

File:set-queue-attributes.json

```
{
    "DelaySeconds": "0",
    "MaximumMessageSize": "262144",
    "MessageRetentionPeriod": "1209600",
    "ReceiveMessageWaitTimeSeconds": "0",
    "VisibilityTimeout": "30",
    "Policy": "{\"Version\": \"2012-10-17\", \"Id\":
              \"arn:aws:sqs:us-west-2:YOUR_AWS_ACCOUNT_
              ID:Chapter3SQSQueueName/SQSDefaultPolicy\",
              \"Statement\": [{\"Sid\": \"Sid1465389499769\",\"Effect\":
              \"Allow\",\"Principal\": \"*\",\"Action\":\"SQS:*\",
              \"Resource\": \"arn:aws:sqs:us-west-2:YOUR_AWS_ACCOUNT_
              ID:Chapter3SQSQueueName\"}]}",
    "RedrivePolicy": "{\"maxReceiveCount\":\"10\",
                     \"deadLetterTargetArn\":\"arn:aws:sqs:
                     us-west-2:YOUR_AWS_ACCOUNT_ID:Chapter3SQSDeadLetter
                     Queue\"}"
}
```

```
C:\Users\Dell>aws sqs set-queue-attributes --queue-url https://us-west-2.queue.amazonaws.com/            /Chapter3SQSQueueName --attributes file://C:/Users/Dell/set-que
ue-attributes.json
C:\Users\Dell>
```

■ **Note**   For more parameters in detail, refer to http://docs.amazonaws.cn/cli/
latest/reference/sqs/set-queue-attributes.html.

get-queue-attributes

The get-queue-attributes command provides the queue attributes:

```
>aws sqs get-queue-attributes --queue-url https://us-west-2.queue.amazonaws.
com/YOUR_AWS_ACCOUNT_ID/Chapter3SQSQueueName --attribute-names All
```

To only get specific attributes, you can pass the attribute name in the request:

```
>aws sqs get-queue-attributes --queue-url https://us-west-2.queue.
amazonaws.com/YOUR_AWS_ACCOUNT_ID/Chapter3SQSQueueName --attribute-
names "DelaySeconds" "MaximumMessageSize" "MessageRetentionPeriod"
"ReceiveMessageWaitTimeSeconds" "VisibilityTimeout"
```

> ■ **Note** For more parameters in detail, refer to http://docs.amazonaws.cn/cli/
> latest/reference/sqs/get-queue-attributes.html.

list-queues

The list-queues command provides the list of all queues available:

```
>aws sqs list-queues
```

The maximum number of queues returned is 1000. If you want to search a queue based on the prefix, use the following command:

```
>aws sqs list-queues --queue-name-prefix Chapter3SQSDead
```

```
C:\Users\Dell>aws sqs list-queues --queue-name-prefix Chapter3SQSDead
{
    "QueueUrls": [
        "https://us-west-2.queue.amazonaws.com/███████████/Chapter3SQSDeadLetterQueue"
    ]
}
```

■ **Note**   For more parameters in detail, refer to `http://docs.amazonaws.cn/cli/` `latest/reference/sqs/list-queues.html`.

list-dead-letter-source-queues

This command provides a list of source queues whose RedrivePolicy has been configured with this dead letter queue:

```
>aws sqs list-dead-letter-source-queues --queue-url https://us-west-2.queue.
amazonaws.com/YOUR_AWS_ACCOUNT_ID/Chapter3SQSDeadLetterQueue
```

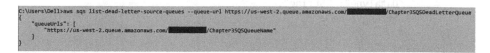

Figure 3-30. List Dead Letter Source Queues

■ **Note**   For more parameters in detail, refer to `http://docs.amazonaws.cn/cli/` `latest/reference/sqs/list-dead-letter-source-queues.html`.

send-message

This will send message to a queue.

```
>aws sqs send-message --queue-url https://us-west-2.queue.amazonaws.com/
YOUR_AWS_ACCOUNT_ID/Chapter3SQSQueueName --message-body "Hello AWS SQS!!!"
```

```
C:\Users\Dell>aws sqs send-message --queue-url https://us-west-2.queue.amazonaws.com/███████/Chapter3SQSQueueName --message-body "Hello AWS SQS!!!"
{
    "MD5OfMessageBody": "2b28033cefe61c780b9e9245b13746e5",
    "MessageId": "33a82a07-310e-4587-a800-8f05e123db59"
}
```

You can also delay the message by n seconds by using --delay-seconds parameter as:

```
>aws sqs send-message --queue-url https://us-west-2.queue.amazonaws.com/
YOUR_AWS_ACCOUNT_ID/Chapter3SQSQueueName --message-body "Hello AWS SQS!!!"
--delay-seconds 10
```

C:\Users\Dell>aws sqs send-message --queue-url https://us-west-2.queue.amazonaws.com/▮▮▮▮/Chapter3SQSQueueName --message-body "Hello AWS SQS!!!" --delay-seconds
10
{
    "MD5OfMessageBody": "2b28033cefe61c780b9e9245b13746e5",
    "MessageId": "8c0c0583-7022-4527-a64d-0c4857a9a76d"
}

■ **Note**   This delay second parameter won't be applicable on FIFO queue types. To apply delay, you need to configure it at queue level instead of at a message level.

You can also add attributes having different data type while sending messages:

```
>aws sqs send-message --queue-url https://us-west-2.queue.amazonaws.com/
YOUR_AWS_ACCOUNT_ID/Chapter3SQSQueueName --message-body "Hello AWS SQS!!!"
--message-attributes file://C:/Users/Dell/send-message-attributes.json
```

File: send-message-attributes.json

```json
{
    "Chapter": {
            "DataType": "String",
            "StringValue": "2"
    },
    "Environment": {
            "DataType": "Binary",
            "BinaryValue": "Production!"
    }
}
```

C:\Users\Dell>aws sqs send-message --queue-url https://us-west-2.queue.amazonaws.com/▮▮▮▮/Chapter3SQSQueueName --message-body "Hello AWS SQS!!!" --message-attri
butes file://C:/Users/Dell/send-message-attributes.json
{
    "MD5OfMessageBody": "2b28033cefe61c780b9e9245b13746e5",
    "MD5OfMessageAttributes": "9382fb20bda3d66f814315861c3a9d8a",
    "MessageId": "069562d6-0458-4f85-bcc3-da526dc8c603"
}

■ **Note**   For more parameters in detail, refer to http://docs.amazonaws.cn/cli/ latest/reference/sqs/send-message.html.

send-message-batch

This command enables sending messages in batches. The maximum number of messages that can be sent is 10 messages per batch:

```
>aws sqs send-message-batch --queue-url https://us-west-2.queue.amazonaws.
com/YOUR_AWS_ACCOUNT_ID/Chapter3SQSQueueName --entries file://C:/Users/Dell/
send-message-batch.json
```

File: send-message-batch.json

```
[{
        "Id": "Message-1",
        "MessageBody": "Hello AWS SQS 1!!!",
        "DelaySeconds": 10
}, {
        "Id": "Message-2",
        "MessageBody": "Hello AWS SQS 2!!!",
        "DelaySeconds": 10,
        "MessageAttributes": {
                "Chapter": {
                        "DataType": "String",
                        "StringValue": "2"
                },
                "Environment": {
                        "DataType": "Binary",
                        "BinaryValue": "Production!"
                }
        }
}]
```

You can also pass message lists inline. Different messages are separated by a space, and each message has several properties such as Id, MessageBody, DelaySeconds, and MessageAttributes:

```
>aws sqs send-message-batch --queue-url https://us-west-2.queue.amazonaws.com/
YOUR_AWS_ACCOUNT_ID/Chapter3SQSQueueName --entries Id=Message-1,MessageBody=
"Hello AWS SQS 1!!!",DelaySeconds=10 Id=Message-2,MessageBody="Hello AWS SQS
2!!!",DelaySeconds=10,MessageAttributes={Chapter={StringValue=2,DataType=String},
Environment={StringValue="Production!",DataType=String}
```

```
C:\Users\Dell>aws sqs send-message-batch --queue-url https://us-west-2.queue.amazonaws.com/███████████/Chapter3SQSQueueName --entries Id=Message-1,MessageBody="Hello A
WS SQS 1!!!",DelaySeconds=10 Id=Message-2,MessageBody="Hello AWS SQS 2!!!",DelaySeconds=10,MessageAttributes={Chapter={StringValue=2,DataType=String},Environment={Strin
gValue="Production!",DataType=String}}
    "Successful": [
        {
            "MD5OfMessageBody": "5abd88291eedc31eca114724eeb9b4fb",
            "Id": "Message-1",
            "MessageId": "0e50b41f-e5a3-4b42-a572-8ca076f10046"
        },
        {
            "MD5OfMessageBody": "d125d47167169da7c8957ed64c5a1242",
            "MD5OfMessageAttributes": "9aa9fc90b5895929ae0d0c2c7c21475f",
            "Id": "Message-2",
            "MessageId": "57ebbefd-ca7d-4059-a9fa-3065ecf569e4"
        }
    ]
}
```

> ■ **Note** For more parameters in detail, refer to http://docs.amazonaws.cn/cli/latest/reference/sqs/send-message-batch.html.

receive-message

This command receives messages from a queue. The maximum number of messages that can be received per request is 10 and the maximum number of default messages is 1:

```
>aws sqs receive-message --queue-url https://us-west-2.queue.amazonaws.
com/YOUR_AWS_ACCOUNT_ID/Chapter3SQSQueueName --max-number-of-messages 10
--visibility-timeout 20 --wait-time-seconds 10
```

```
C:\Users\Dell>aws sqs receive-message --queue-url https://us-west-2.queue.amazonaws.com/███████████/Chapter3SQSQueueName --max-number-of-messages 10 --visibility-timeo
ut 20 --wait-time-seconds 10
    "Messages": [
        {
            "Body": "Hello AWS SQS 1!!!",
            "ReceiptHandle": "AQEBuhE5t0xyrwLaCBHQvrx1wZ29tZxlH5F1FgXztxG1A4smHsInp9GXvz4hFhnfRWakK//g8A&Cv3v6N0LSARfWLT2PwJvc6OnnhHQOImogpbKNy8ky8KwLYQWP2gu3x+mEuPg8Wx
NZQXm61vm4jMmZSouN9mC7k1pf3T81Bkbp/cy8FtHcLQ1WAVHTuhyOYmkqKt2AFh2K41fBK2fGWIugtwgWbi6Vn1LsUUgUXHAcPpeT76RvS+5hhW243zi2pauH4mE2kOVpbu9GtwZvLiT2CLcxxBXfjbtZ8cWJzG7OnRprnH
+liSXT1DouFRHIe/jWzssMAPGQW5SUP8C0B4thmOWshFkmkzDxtnBXZqWDCeatsg12jR/8vF6/TTHkPkeLOEW3Km3KSMgWPXyqsAFV+A==",
            "MD5OfBody": "5abd88291eedc31eca114724eeb9b4fb",
            "MessageId": "df3f472f-dec3-4bf8-b0ec-4a2435b7c006"
        },
        {
            "Body": "Hello AWS SQS 2!!!",
            "ReceiptHandle": "AQEBq60Cu7pX0w5V1f7nmfW/dRfo76CQgxnZ29F/T19zkn440wqzjy9KzRufDcWFpO4VwMDsJjysx/FIqAqUv2etj+OV2O0qoZ1Lv4eZHdkmyEqM4Hy2wgRXhjI/2RQ5B/+fA67uml
70rQSm87fI6rzbH7zivEv6t7L74b7HuNrq/HbTCPD6gncVnutGWDrOSdqaC9B1tjcYisQWl2T2xV2t8kHDaA0l/rYgWGn34uStgLyRm4aSm3wLPvSBn2mg8j2wTSyMhiI11YeAMExb0OxjJMOfLxo9gVfDSHwPZAnVUnFktxc
DRLHEqlp8LBNvkZ/6fwK2Y1SA8H+T3jzLcRD9OFlCvB6PuLFhIel37Q1QkNEl2wnKP0Oe9C/X/2HgNaXnVlou+IF1dkv0Dr3zH0vG60g==",
            "MD5OfBody": "d125d47167169da7c8957ed64c5a1242",
            "MessageId": "082e80fe-a0e8-41f4-89cc-f54cbcf7b91c"
        }
    ]
}
```

The visibility timeout parameter hides the message for a number of seconds specified by other requests. The wait-time seconds parameter waits for the specified time to receive messages from the queue.

> ■ **Note** For more parameters in detail, refer to http://docs.amazonaws.cn/cli/latest/reference/sqs/receive-message.html.

delete-message

This command deletes messages from the queue. You need to pass the receipt handle of the message received:

```
>aws sqs delete-message --queue-url https://us-west-2.queue.amazonaws.
com/YOUR_AWS_ACCOUNT_ID/Chapter3SQSQueueName --receipt-handle
AQEBwhE5tOxyrwLaCBMQv......gWPXyqsAFV+A==
```

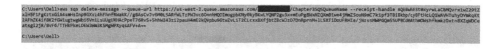

There won't be any output for this request.

■ **Note** For more parameters in detail, refer to `http://docs.amazonaws.cn/cli/latest/reference/sqs/delete-message.html`.

---

delete-message-batch

The delete-message-batch command deletes the messages in a batch of 10 messages. Each deleted message will have a response in output:

```
>aws sqs delete-message-batch --queue-url https://us-west-2.queue.amazonaws.
com/YOUR_AWS_ACCOUNT_ID/Chapter3SQSQueueName --entries Id=082e80fe-a0e8-
41f4-89cc-f54cbcf7b91c,ReceiptHandle=AQEBxXGsIlusZ.....C3bX6gSDQ==
```

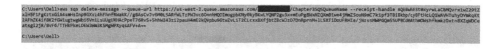

You can also pass the entries in JSON format:

```
>aws sqs delete-message-batch --queue-url https://us-west-2.queue.amazonaws.
com/YOUR_AWS_ACCOUNT_ID/Chapter3SQSQueueName --entries file://C:/Users/Dell/
delete-message-batch.json
```

File: delete-message-batch.json

```
[{
        "Id": "082e80fe-a0e8-41f4-89cc-f54cbcf7b91c",
        "ReceiptHandle": "AQEBxXGsIlusZ........+C3bX6gSDQ=="
},
{
        "Id": "1234-a0e8-41f4-89cc-f54cbcf7b91c",
        "ReceiptHandle": "123aasdasda........+C3bX6gSDQ=="
}]
```

C:\Users\Dell>aws sqs delete-message-batch --queue-url https://us-west-2.queue.amazonaws.com/▉▉▉▉▉/Chapter3SQSQueueName --entries file://C:/Users/Dell/delete-message-batch.json
    "Successful": [
        {
            "Id": "082e80fe-a0e8-41f4-89cc-f54cbcf7b91c"
        }
    ],
    "Failed": [
        {
            "Message": "The input receipt handle \"123aasdasda+/RVdgWR2zJjRVG9caSeuISlEQihbhzon80JzjzVU3vMG7JMQ6xhFVAzJrLgIRRDNZFyQqOHUcwNBAWVEsifGSUw+gDqyfCZcAmPF3YcH3
t1QBH2YJ975///A8SGeC8aB55BvUA0+qqBPs9kcuqIY39QYISNAVGRtM/kvS1bsSEhOO2bpf1jaAQlJMykEj35gyqn6+aE3nt2v1ct4uOaQRfNKyzURRKBuNeglO3kzJT2Ql6vu+uPbwjxfiLXZr6FG97qJ4YbAyorVHTepcz
XyRLBPy1QaXkIzzWdvB8lZ6QeO/lnCHeqkzKOdRWOhIq2OsPuYa9emhvpPNdVnvSuM8glXWV2ZZmOOIATkkzKWt7SWe7YZCno+FQ/yTC2ubhE+c0V+C3bX6gSDQ==\" is not a valid receipt handle.",
            "SenderFault": true,
            "Code": "ReceiptHandleIsInvalid",
            "Id": "1234-a0e8-41f4-89cc-f54cbcf7b91c"
        }
    ]
}

In the previous command, we provided one valid and one invalid message ID and receipt handle in JSON file, so in output we received one successful and one failed message.

■ **Note** For more parameters in detail refer: http://docs.amazonaws.cn/cli/latest/reference/sqs/delete-message-batch.html.

---

change-message-visibility

This command will change the message's visibility timeout for a specified number of seconds. The maximum timeout you can configure is 0 to 43,200 seconds (that is, 12 hours).

```
>aws sqs change-message-visibility --queue-url https://us-west-2.queue.
amazonaws.com/YOUR_AWS_ACCOUNT_ID/Chapter3SQSQueueName --receipt-handle
AQEBIvyCtihBCvEBNdhd........zYgGHQ4ytgoM7aDqXTdQjkkywA== --visibility-
timeout 12000
```

C:\Users\Dell>aws sqs change-message-visibility --queue-url https://us-west-2.queue.amazonaws.com/▉▉▉▉▉/Chapter3SQSQueueName --receipt-handle AQEBIvyCtihBCvEBNdh
dX9Cn6sKMIO6Doa3xm6qny7tlvmpTaID/PnuOH2DKyichH1+ZQG/ZxsaOEgGA/PzkLS6cVN8VQTYwmj+UYK2nXjEkRP2wyhGNJ+FKU33/+0FmN+YOGzgpAp7CFXx9rb7gsxScHrQyOpYYPlHoAmLOM1JC3eo9qxe4mdq3GA8
jNgSr8y+trlldswBZe0I/hTqVC4I4dzyUAsovW9RxRVDvPmhvijyQUoZqacXDMaxb/GHvL8wlDwx6KS9oyVqb7o3ah2oXIaulcIfVV4ETBvpKEAvVEFKd4YRAF+CkimgTfmgW6DvvuwIRO84gnQCbu+A2ZX7DOCFufzuMsZw
6EC4cj1A7kKRH+otI/uo8SqJLasna/zYgGHQ4ytgoM7aDqXTdQjkkywA== --visibility-timeout 12000
C:\Users\Dell>

■ **Note** For more parameters in detail, refer to http://docs.amazonaws.cn/cli/ latest/reference/sqs/change-message-visibility.html.

change-message-visibility-batch

The change-message-visibility-batch command changes the message's visibility in a batch of 10 messages. Each change visibility message will have a response in output:

```
>aws sqs change-message-visibility-batch --queue-url https://us-west-2.
queue.amazonaws.com/YOUR_AWS_ACCOUNT_ID/Chapter3SQSQueueName --entries
Id=c7f18324-8d89-4030-a7ef-18cfac9dbdf4,ReceiptHandle=AQEBIvyCtihBCvE
BN........./zYgGHQ4ytgoM7aDqXTdQjkkywA==,VisibilityTimeout=12000 Id=39af20fb-
a99a-43d9-8e38-f25a3d898522,ReceiptHandle=AQEBFQ4u9w6k0Syd7WzAn........+Inyn
JzPv42ykTOnmgvfQ==,VisibilityTimeout=12000
```

You can also pass the entries in JSON format:

```
>aws sqs change-message-visibility-batch --queue-url https://us-west-2.
queue.amazonaws.com/YOUR_AWS_ACCOUNT_ID/Chapter3SQSQueueName --entries
file://C:/Users/Dell/change-message-visibility-batch.json
```

File: change-message-visibility-batch.json

```
[{
        "Id": "c7f18324-8d89-4030-a7ef-18cfac9dbdf4",
        "ReceiptHandle": "AQEBIvyCtihBCvEB........4ytgoM7aDqXTdQjkkywA==",
        "VisibilityTimeout": 12000
}, {
        "Id": "39af20fb-a99a-43d9-8e38-f25a3d898522",
        "ReceiptHandle": "AQEBFQ4u9w6k0V7........InynJzPv42ykTOnmgvfQ==",
        "VisibilityTimeout": 12000
}]
```

```
C:\Users\Dell>aws sqs change-message-visibility-batch --queue-url https://us-west-2.queue.amazonaws.com/          /Chapter3SQSQueueName --entries file://C:/Users/Dell
/change-message-visibility-batch.json
{
    "Successful": [
        {
            "Id": "c7f18324-8d89-4030-a7ef-18cfac9dbdf4"
        },
        {
            "Id": "39af20fb-a99a-43d9-8e38-f25a3d898522"
        }
    ]
}
```

■ **Note**   For more parameters in detail, refer to `http://docs.amazonaws.cn/cli/`
`latest/reference/sqs/change-message-visibility-batch.html`.

purge-queue

This command deletes all the messages available in the queue. Once messages are
deleted, they can't be recalled back. The delete process may take 60 seconds:

```
>aws sqs purge-queue --queue-urlhttps://us-west-2.queue.amazonaws.com/YOUR_
AWS_ACCOUNT_ID/Chapter3SQSQueueName
```

```
C:\Users\Dell>aws sqs purge-queue --queue-url https://us-west-2.queue.amazonaws.com/          /Chapter3SQSQueueName
C:\Users\Dell>
```

There won't be any output for this request.

■ **Note**   For more parameters in detail, refer to `http://docs.amazonaws.cn/cli/`
`latest/reference/sqs/purge-queue.html`.

delete-queue

The delete-queue command deletes the queue whether the queue contains messages or
not. You can't recall messages after they have been deleted. The delete process may take
60 seconds.

```
>aws sqs delete-queue --queue-url https://us-west-2.queue.amazonaws.com/
YOUR_AWS_ACCOUNT_ID/Chapter3SQSQueueName
```

```
C:\Users\Dell>aws sqs delete-queue --queue-url https://us-west-2.queue.amazonaws.com/          /Chapter3SQSQueueName
C:\Users\Dell>
```

There won't be any output for this request.

■ **Note** For more parameters in detail, refer to `http://docs.amazonaws.cn/cli/latest/reference/sqs/delete-queue.html`.

Using AWS SDK—Java

In this section, I will discuss how to use AWS Java SDK to manage AWS SQS. First, you will need to create AmazonSQSClient.

To create AmazonSQSClient, you first need to create the AWSCredentials using either of the credential provider mechanisms. In our case, we will use ProfileCredentialsProvider:

```
AWSCredentials credentials =
    new ProfileCredentialsProvider("sunilgulabani").getCredentials();

AmazonSQS amazonSQSClient = new AmazonSQSClient(credentials);
```

This will load the `sunilgulabani` profile's access key and secret key via the credentials file.

Create Queue

To create a queue using SDK, call the `createQueue` method of AmazonSQSClient:

```
private static final String DEAD_LETTER_QUEUE_NAME =
    "Chapter3SQSDeadLetterQueue";

createQueue(DEAD_LETTER_QUEUE_NAME);

public String createQueue(String queueName) {
    CreateQueueRequest request = new CreateQueueRequest(queueName);

    CreateQueueResult response = amazonSQSClient.createQueue(request);

    return response.getQueueUrl();
}
```

```
{
  "queueUrl": "https://sqs.us-west-2.amazonaws.com/██████████/Chapter3SQSDeadLetterQueue",
  "sdkResponseMetadata": {
    "metadata": {
      "AWS_REQUEST_ID": "3f95ac27-eac2-527f-93b1-fc9dfece966b"
    }
  },
  "sdkHttpMetadata": {
    "httpHeaders": {
      "Server": "Server",
      "Connection": "keep-alive",
      "x-amzn-RequestId": "3f95ac27-eac2-527f-93b1-fc9dfece966b",
      "Content-Length": "346",
      "Date": "Thu, 01 Dec 2016 12:04:28 GMT",
      "Content-Type": "text/xml"
    },
    "httpStatusCode": 200
  }
}
```

In response, you will get "queueUrl".

Create Queue with Attributes

To create a queue with attributes, add the attributes using CreateQueueRequest's addAttributesEntry method:

```
private static final String QUEUE_NAME = "Chapter3SQSQueueName";

createQueueWithAttributes(QUEUE_NAME);

public String createQueueWithAttributes(String queueName) {
    String queueNameTargetARN = "arn:aws:sqs:" + region.getName() + ":" +
                                awsUserAccountId + ":" + queueName;

    String queueNameDefaultPolicyId =
        queueNameTargetARN + "/SQSDefaultPolicy";

    CreateQueueRequest request = new CreateQueueRequest(queueName);

    request.addAttributesEntry("DelaySeconds", "0");

    request.addAttributesEntry("MaximumMessageSize", "262144");

    request.addAttributesEntry("MessageRetentionPeriod", "1209600");

    request.addAttributesEntry("ReceiveMessageWaitTimeSeconds", "0");

    request.addAttributesEntry("VisibilityTimeout", "30");

    request.addAttributesEntry("Policy", "{" +
                        "\"Version\": \"2012-10-17\"," +
                        "\"Id\": \"" + queueNameDefaultPolicyId + "\"," +
```

```
                    "\"Statement\": [" +
                    " {" +
                    " \"Sid\": \"Sid1465389499769\"," +
                    " \"Effect\": \"Allow\"," +
                    " \"Principal\": \"*\"," +
                    " \"Action\": \"SQS:*\"," +
                    " \"Resource\": \"" + queueNameTargetARN + "\"" +
                    " }" +
                    "]}");

        CreateQueueResult response = amazonSQSClient.createQueue(request);

        return response.getQueueUrl();
}
```

```
{
  "queueUrl": "https://sqs.us-west-2.amazonaws.com/███████/Chapter3SQSQueueName",
  "sdkResponseMetadata": {
    "metadata": {
      "AWS_REQUEST_ID": "b3c607bc-2025-5358-9b2f-57063428774c"
    }
  },
  "sdkHttpMetadata": {
    "httpHeaders": {
      "Server": "Server",
      "Connection": "keep-alive",
      "x-amzn-RequestId": "b3c607bc-2025-5358-9b2f-57063428774c",
      "Content-Length": "340",
      "Date": "Thu, 01 Dec 2016 12:04:29 GMT",
      "Content-Type": "text/xml"
    },
    "httpStatusCode": 200
  }
}
```

In response, you will get "queueUrl".

Get Queue URL

To get the queue URL, use the getQueueUrl method of AmazonSQSClient:

```
getQueueUrl(QUEUE_NAME);

public String getQueueUrl(String queueName) {

    GetQueueUrlResult response = amazonSQSClient.getQueueUrl(queueName);

    return response.getQueueUrl();
}
```

```
{
  "queueUrl": "https://sqs.us-west-2.amazonaws.com/▇▇▇▇▇▇▇/Chapter3SQSQueueName",
  "sdkResponseMetadata": {
    "metadata": {
      "AWS_REQUEST_ID": "d17bfa85-b4e3-5a46-8486-aa3fa0eede52"
    }
  },
  "sdkHttpMetadata": {
    "httpHeaders": {
      "Server": "Server",
      "Connection": "keep-alive",
      "x-amzn-RequestId": "d17bfa85-b4e3-5a46-8486-aa3fa0eede52",
      "Content-Length": "340",
      "Date": "Thu, 01 Dec 2016 12:04:29 GMT",
      "Content-Type": "text/xml"
    },
    "httpStatusCode": 200
  }
}
```

In response, you will get "queueUrl".

Add Permissions

To add permissions, use the addPermission method of AmazonSQSClient:

```
addPermission(queueUrl);

public void addPermission(String queueUrl) {

    AddPermissionRequest request = new AddPermissionRequest();

    request.setQueueUrl(queueUrl);

    request.setActions(getActions());

    request.setAWSAccountIds(getAWSAccountIds());

    request.setLabel("Chapter3SQSPermission");

    AddPermissionResult response = amazonSQSClient.addPermission(request);

}

private List<String> getAWSAccountIds() {
    List<String> awsAccountIdsList = new ArrayList<String>();

    awsAccountIdsList.add(awsUserAccountId);

    return awsAccountIdsList;
}

private List<String> getActions() {
    List<String> actionsList = new ArrayList<String>();
```

```
//  actionsList.add("*");
    actionsList.add("SendMessage");
    actionsList.add("ReceiveMessage");
    actionsList.add("DeleteMessage");
    actionsList.add("ChangeMessageVisibility");
    actionsList.add("GetQueueAttributes");
    actionsList.add("GetQueueUrl");

    return actionsList;
}
```

Along with the queue URL, you also need to provide a permission label name (AWS User ID) to whomever you want to assign permissions as well as what actions (permissions) you need to assign. These will be added to the AddPermissionRequest object:

```
{
  "sdkResponseMetadata": {
    "metadata": {
      "AWS_REQUEST_ID": "89de635b-ff28-5987-a019-33e1eb256d93"
    }
  },
  "sdkHttpMetadata": {
    "httpHeaders": {
      "Server": "Server",
      "Connection": "keep-alive",
      "x-amzn-RequestId": "89de635b-ff28-5987-a019-33e1eb256d93",
      "Content-Length": "215",
      "Date": "Thu, 01 Dec 2016 12:04:29 GMT",
      "Content-Type": "text/xml"
    },
    "httpStatusCode": 200
  }
}
```

There won't be any parameter in response specific to adding permission apart from httpStatusCode, which will be used to identify whether the request was successful or not.

Remove Permissions

To remove permissions from the queue, you need the label name of permission, which is assigned on queue. To remove permissions, use the removePermission method of AmazonSQSClient:

```
removePermission(queueUrl);

public void removePermission(String queueUrl) {

    RemovePermissionRequest request =
        new RemovePermissionRequest(queueUrl, "Chapter3SQSPermission");
```

```
        RemovePermissionResult response =
            amazonSQSClient.removePermission(request);
}
```

```
{
  "sdkResponseMetadata": {
    "metadata": {
      "AWS_REQUEST_ID": "88b037c4-6ca3-5442-8e10-677e78adb056"
    }
  },
  "sdkHttpMetadata": {
    "httpHeaders": {
      "Server": "Server",
      "Connection": "keep-alive",
      "x-amzn-RequestId": "88b037c4-6ca3-5442-8e10-677e78adb056",
      "Content-Length": "221",
      "Date": "Thu, 01 Dec 2016 12:04:30 GMT",
      "Content-Type": "text/xml"
    },
    "httpStatusCode": 200
  }
}
```

There won't be any parameters in response specific to removing permissions apart from httpStatusCode, which will be used to identify whether the request was successful or not.

Set Queue Attributes

To set queue attributes, you need to create queue attributes first, which will be in the form of a key-value pair. Using the setQueueAttributes method of AmazonSQSClient, set the queue attributes:

```
setQueueAttributes(queueUrl, DEAD_LETTER_QUEUE_NAME);

public void setQueueAttributes(String queueUrl, String deadLetterQueueName) {
    SetQueueAttributesRequest request = new SetQueueAttributesRequest(
                                    queueUrl,
                                    createQueueAttributes(
                                        getNameFromUrl(queueUrl),
                                        deadLetterQueueName));

    SetQueueAttributesResult response =
        amazonSQSClient.setQueueAttributes(request);
}
```

```java
private Map<String, String> createQueueAttributes(
                        String queueName, String deadLetterQueueName) {

    Map<String, String> attributes = new HashMap<String, String>();

    String queueNameTargetARN = "arn:aws:sqs:" + region.getName() + ":" +
                                awsUserAccountId + ":" + queueName;

    String queueNameDefaultPolicyId =
        queueNameTargetARN + "/SQSDefaultPolicy";

    String deadLetterTargetARN = "arn:aws:sqs:" + region.getName() + ":" +
                                awsUserAccountId + ":" + deadLetterQueueName;

    attributes.put("DelaySeconds", "0");

    attributes.put("MaximumMessageSize", "262144");

    attributes.put("MessageRetentionPeriod", "1209600");

    attributes.put("ReceiveMessageWaitTimeSeconds", "0");

    attributes.put("VisibilityTimeout", "30");

    attributes.put("Policy", "{" +
                        "\"Version\": \"2012-10-17\"," +
                        "\"Id\": \"" + queueNameDefaultPolicyId + "\"," +
                        "\"Statement\": [" +
                        " {" +
                        " \"Sid\": \"Sid1465389499769\"," +
                        " \"Effect\": \"Allow\"," +
                        " \"Principal\": \"*\"," +
                        " \"Action\": \"SQS:*\"," +
                        " \"Resource\": \"" + queueNameTargetARN + "\"" +
                        " }" +
                        "]}");

    attributes.put("RedrivePolicy",
            "{\"maxReceiveCount\":\"10\", \"deadLetterTargetArn\":\"" +
            deadLetterTargetARN + "\"}");

    return attributes;
}
```

```
{
  "sdkResponseMetadata": {
    "metadata": {
      "AWS_REQUEST_ID": "5813d728-2d8d-5ad6-b072-879239838ec2"
    }
  },
  "sdkHttpMetadata": {
    "httpHeaders": {
      "Server": "Server",
      "Connection": "keep-alive",
      "x-amzn-RequestId": "5813d728-2d8d-5ad6-b072-879239838ec2",
      "Content-Length": "225",
      "Date": "Thu, 01 Dec 2016 12:04:30 GMT",
      "Content-Type": "text/xml"
    },
    "httpStatusCode": 200
  }
}
```

There won't be any parameters in response specific to setting queue attributes apart from httpStatusCode, which will be used to identify whether the request was successful or not.

Get Queue Attributes

To get the queue attributes, you need to provide the attributes you need in return for the specific queueUrl using the getQueueAttributes method:

```
getQueueAttributes(queueUrl);

public void getQueueAttributes(String queueUrl) {
    GetQueueAttributesRequest request = new GetQueueAttributesRequest();

    request.setQueueUrl(queueUrl);

    request.setAttributeNames(getAttributeNames());

    GetQueueAttributesResult response =
        amazonSQSClient.getQueueAttributes(request);
}

private List<String> getAttributeNames() {
    List<String> attributeNames = new ArrayList<String>();

    attributeNames.add("DelaySeconds");

    attributeNames.add("MaximumMessageSize");

    attributeNames.add("MessageRetentionPeriod");

    attributeNames.add("ReceiveMessageWaitTimeSeconds");

    attributeNames.add("VisibilityTimeout");
```

```java
    attributeNames.add("Policy");

    return attributeNames;
}
```

```
{
  "attributes": {
    "Policy":
    "{\"Version\":\"2012-10-17\",\"Id\":\"arn:aws:sqs:us-west-2:298147259238:Chapter3SQSQueueName/SQSDefaultPolicy\",\"Statement\":[{\"Sid\":\"Sid1465389499769\",\
    "Effect\":\"Allow\",\"Principal\":\"*\",\"Action\":\"SQS:*\",\"Resource\":\"arn:aws:sqs:us-west-2:298147259238:Chapter3SQSQueueName\"}]}",
    "ReceiveMessageWaitTimeSeconds": "0",
    "DelaySeconds": "0",
    "MessageRetentionPeriod": "1209600",
    "MaximumMessageSize": "262144",
    "VisibilityTimeout": "30"
  },
  "sdkResponseMetadata": {
    "metadata": {
      "AWS_REQUEST_ID": "21b1bf95-914b-5659-802b-ef2f8545a24d"
    }
  },
  "sdkHttpMetadata": {
    "httpHeaders": {
      "Server": "Server",
      "Connection": "keep-alive",
      "x-amzn-RequestId": "21b1bf95-914b-5659-802b-ef2f8545a24d",
      "Content-Length": "1119",
      "Date": "Thu, 01 Dec 2016 12:04:30 GMT",
      "Content-Type": "text/xml"
    },
    "httpStatusCode": 200
  }
}
```

In response, you can see that under "attributes", all requested attributes values are returned.

List Queues

To list all queues, use the listQueues method:

```java
listQueues();

public void listQueues() {

    ListQueuesResult response = amazonSQSClient.listQueues();

}
```

```
{
  "queueUrls": [
    "https://sqs.us-west-2.amazonaws.com/298147259238/Chapter3SQSDeadLetterQueue",
    "https://sqs.us-west-2.amazonaws.com/298147259238/Chapter3SQSQueueName"
  ],
  "sdkResponseMetadata": {
    "metadata": {
      "AWS_REQUEST_ID": "d85c35d7-6771-543f-b718-656d737e002b"
    }
  },
  "sdkHttpMetadata": {
    "httpHeaders": {
      "Server": "Server",
      "Connection": "keep-alive",
      "x-amzn-RequestId": "d85c35d7-6771-543f-b718-656d737e002b",
      "Content-Length": "432",
      "Date": "Thu, 01 Dec 2016 12:04:31 GMT",
      "Content-Type": "text/xml"
    },
    "httpStatusCode": 200
  }
}
```

In response, you can see the `queueUrls` of all the queues available to the current user.

List Dead Letter Source Queues

To get a list of the dead letter's source queues that are assigned, use the `listDeadLetterSourceQueues` method:

```
listDeadLetterSourceQueues(deadLetterQueueUrl);

public void listDeadLetterSourceQueues(String queueUrl) {

    ListDeadLetterSourceQueuesRequest request =
        new ListDeadLetterSourceQueuesRequest();

    request.setQueueUrl(queueUrl);

    ListDeadLetterSourceQueuesResult response =
        amazonSQSClient.listDeadLetterSourceQueues(request);
}
```

```
{
  "queueUrls": [
    "https://sqs.us-west-2.amazonaws.com/298147259238/Chapter3SQSQueueName"
  ],
  "sdkResponseMetadata": {
    "metadata": {
      "AWS_REQUEST_ID": "188efeca-c1f9-5b1d-939c-ae1fbc6ee1c4"
    }
  },
  "sdkHttpMetadata": {
    "httpHeaders": {
      "Server": "Server",
      "Connection": "keep-alive",
      "x-amzn-RequestId": "188efeca-c1f9-5b1d-939c-ae1fbc6ee1c4",
      "Content-Length": "400",
      "Date": "Thu, 01 Dec 2016 12:04:31 GMT",
      "Content-Type": "text/xml"
    },
    "httpStatusCode": 200
  }
}
```

In response, you can see the `queueUrls` of source queues that have this requested dead letter queue.

Send Message

To send a message, use the `sendMessage` method:

```
private static final String MESSAGE_BODY = "Hello AWS SQS!!!";

sendMessage(queueUrl, MESSAGE_BODY);

public void sendMessage(String queueUrl, String body) {

    SendMessageRequest request = new SendMessageRequest(queueUrl, body);

    SendMessageResult response = amazonSQSClient.sendMessage(request);
}
```

```
{
  "mD5OfMessageBody": "2b28033cefe61c780b9e9245b13746e5",
  "messageId": "05e95564-365d-46db-80c4-869d29cd1704",
  "sdkResponseMetadata": {
    "metadata": {
      "AWS_REQUEST_ID": "92bb919c-cff2-5e02-835c-c126dbfdba16"
    }
  },
  "sdkHttpMetadata": {
    "httpHeaders": {
      "Server": "Server",
      "Connection": "keep-alive",
      "x-amzn-RequestId": "92bb919c-cff2-5e02-835c-c126dbfdba16",
      "Content-Length": "378",
      "Date": "Thu, 01 Dec 2016 12:04:31 GMT",
      "Content-Type": "text/xml"
    },
    "httpStatusCode": 200
  }
}
```

In response, the "mD5OfMessageBody" and "messageId" parameters are received.

Send Message with Add Message Attributes

To send a message with message attributes, you need to add message attributes along with key, value, and the value's datatype to the request and then call the sendMessage method:

```
sendMessageWithAddMessageAttributes(queueUrl, MESSAGE_BODY);

public void sendMessageWithAddMessageAttributes(String queueUrl, String body) {
    SendMessageRequest request = new SendMessageRequest(queueUrl, body);

    for(int i = 0 ; i < 5 ; i++) {
        request.addMessageAttributesEntry(
                        "Key-" + i,
                        createMessageAttributeValue("Value-" + i));
    }
```

```
    SendMessageResult response = amazonSQSClient.sendMessage(request);
}

private MessageAttributeValue createMessageAttributeValue(String value) {

    MessageAttributeValue messageAttributeValue =
        new MessageAttributeValue();

    messageAttributeValue.setStringValue(value);

    messageAttributeValue.setDataType("String");

    return messageAttributeValue;
}
```

For example we used a loop that will create 5 messsage attributes. This is just to demonstrate the adding of message attributes.

```
{
  "mD5OfMessageBody": "2b28033cefe61c780b9e9245b13746e5",
  "mD5OfMessageAttributes": "d9ba891ff0ff06dc24696ebd7b59eb1e",
  "messageId": "fb74ed74-2408-420a-99d9-7673d673307b",
  "sdkResponseMetadata": {
    "metadata": {
      "AWS_REQUEST_ID": "e2cac3c2-e81e-5b53-a40e-9378fc0ebf47"
    }
  },
  "sdkHttpMetadata": {
    "httpHeaders": {
      "Server": "Server",
      "Connection": "keep-alive",
      "x-amzn-RequestId": "e2cac3c2-e81e-5b53-a40e-9378fc0ebf47",
      "Content-Length": "459",
      "Date": "Thu, 01 Dec 2016 12:04:32 GMT",
      "Content-Type": "text/xml"
    },
    "httpStatusCode": 200
  }
}
```

In response, the "mD5OfMessageBody", "mD5OfMessageAttributes", and "messageId" parameters are received.

Send Message with Set Message Attributes

In addition to adding message attributes, you can also use the setMessageAttributes method of the SendMessageRequest object. To set message attributes, you need to create Map<String, MessageAttributeValue>:

```
sendMessageWithSetMessageAttributes(queueUrl, MESSAGE_BODY);

public void sendMessageWithSetMessageAttributes(String queueUrl, String body) {
    SendMessageRequest request = new SendMessageRequest(queueUrl, body);

    request.setMessageAttributes(createMessageAttributeValuesMap());

    SendMessageResult response = amazonSQSClient.sendMessage(request);
}

private Map<String, MessageAttributeValue> createMessageAttributeValuesMap() {
    Map<String, MessageAttributeValue> messageAttributeValuesMap =
        new HashMap<String, MessageAttributeValue>();

    for(int i = 0 ; i < 5 ; i++) {
        messageAttributeValuesMap.put(
                            "Key-" + i,
                            createMessageAttributeValue("Value-" + i));
    }

    return messageAttributeValuesMap;
}
```

```
{
  "mD5OfMessageBody": "2b28033cefe61c780b9e9245b13746e5",
  "mD5OfMessageAttributes": "d9ba891ff0ff06dc24696ebd7b59eb1e",
  "messageId": "0d6b98d1-24de-4236-a56e-5d6bfeac87e1",
  "sdkResponseMetadata": {
    "metadata": {
      "AWS_REQUEST_ID": "50c5df4f-3cad-550e-ba95-8ff528bd611a"
    }
  },
  "sdkHttpMetadata": {
    "httpHeaders": {
      "Server": "Server",
      "Connection": "keep-alive",
      "x-amzn-RequestId": "50c5df4f-3cad-550e-ba95-8ff528bd611a",
      "Content-Length": "459",
      "Date": "Thu, 01 Dec 2016 12:04:32 GMT",
      "Content-Type": "text/xml"
    },
    "httpStatusCode": 200
  }
}
```

In response, "mD5OfMessageBody", "mD5OfMessageAttributes", and "messageId" parameters are received.

Send Message with Timer

To send a message with a delay, use the setDelaySeconds method:

```
sendMessageWithTimer(queueUrl, MESSAGE_BODY);

public void sendMessageWithTimer(String queueUrl, String body) {

    SendMessageRequest request = new SendMessageRequest(queueUrl, body);

    request.setDelaySeconds(30);

    SendMessageResult response = amazonSQSClient.sendMessage(request);
}
```

```
{
  "mD5OfMessageBody": "2b28033cefe61c780b9e9245b13746e5",
  "messageId": "53bcfd42-12f9-485a-88f4-c17a3e526f25",
  "sdkResponseMetadata": {
    "metadata": {
      "AWS_REQUEST_ID": "605766ac-c0c2-5048-a61f-3616d4d2d45c"
    }
  },
  "sdkHttpMetadata": {
    "httpHeaders": {
      "Server": "Server",
      "Connection": "keep-alive",
      "x-amzn-RequestId": "605766ac-c0c2-5048-a61f-3616d4d2d45c",
      "Content-Length": "378",
      "Date": "Thu, 01 Dec 2016 12:04:32 GMT",
      "Content-Type": "text/xml"
    },
    "httpStatusCode": 200
  }
}
```

In response, "mD5OfMessageBody" and "messageId" parameters are received.

Send Message Batch

To send messages in batches, use the sendMessageBatch method:

```
sendMessageBatch(queueUrl, MESSAGE_BODY);

public void sendMessageBatch(String queueUrl, String body) {
    SendMessageBatchRequest request = new SendMessageBatchRequest(queueUrl);
```

```
    request.setEntries(createSendMessageBatchRequestEntry(body));

    SendMessageBatchResult response =
        amazonSQSClient.sendMessageBatch(request);
}

private List<SendMessageBatchRequestEntry>
    createSendMessageBatchRequestEntry(String body) {

    List<SendMessageBatchRequestEntry> entries =
        new ArrayList<SendMessageBatchRequestEntry>();

    SendMessageBatchRequestEntry sendMessageBatchRequestEntry;

    for(int i = 0; i < 5; i++) {
        sendMessageBatchRequestEntry = new SendMessageBatchRequestEntry();

        sendMessageBatchRequestEntry.setId(UUID.randomUUID().toString());

        sendMessageBatchRequestEntry.setMessageBody(body + "-" + i);

        //  sendMessageBatchRequestEntry.setDelaySeconds(30);

        entries.add(sendMessageBatchRequestEntry);
    }

    return entries;
}
```

By doing this, you will have created SendMessageBatchRequestEntry in a loop of 5 to demonstrate adding sample messages:

```
{
  "successful": [
    {
      "id": "0178f441-1abf-4e22-9502-6bfc5f5a5f55",
      "messageId": "f2aae8a1-d9cc-481f-8f3d-b7f764bd43d1",
      "mD5OfMessageBody": "ce67e1b50d724f5cebe918ead1adada6"
    },
    {
      "id": "8adfeb5a-70be-4d27-9c3a-f51cdeff3621",
      "messageId": "c3b6f91d-b98f-434a-a155-39b065197d2a",
      "mD5OfMessageBody": "db18e2bbc3094759354094f8fa161243"
    },
    {
      "id": "87c4f5a2-a3ba-4b74-a640-a3b11e19f0ca",
      "messageId": "a5ba06e7-62df-4a02-9752-af12eb6f8863",
      "mD5OfMessageBody": "507e11ab30f81e47c1b2c937cd6c31d3"
    },
    {
      "id": "31df5109-d5bd-46f4-9aaf-717fee89e73a",
      "messageId": "103c5215-24b5-4f80-a760-8a1fc7da80a7",
      "mD5OfMessageBody": "17066a6f6fa26444ae2359446af0dfee"
    },
    {
      "id": "dd4168e0-852b-4947-98dc-250ab2ef4de3",
      "messageId": "92e8b1d4-38bb-4758-ba33-560329f2dbfa",
      "mD5OfMessageBody": "94e51dd81cf7289705dcf1f0aaba4f2c"
    }
  ],
  "sdkResponseMetadata": {
    "metadata": {
      "AWS_REQUEST_ID": "91d53493-7e6b-5003-9775-64296a7a6417"
    }
  },
  "sdkHttpMetadata": {
    "httpHeaders": {
      "Server": "Server",
      "Connection": "keep-alive",
      "x-amzn-RequestId": "91d53493-7e6b-5003-9775-64296a7a6417",
      "Content-Length": "1430",
      "Date": "Thu, 01 Dec 2016 12:04:33 GMT",
      "Content-Type": "text/xml"
    },
    "httpStatusCode": 200
  }
}
```

In response, you have received an individual message's response parameters.

Receive Message with Acknowledgement

You need to acknowledge (delete) the messages to queue that the consumer has successfully received it. To do this, first receive the messages:

```
receiveMessageWithAck(queueUrl);

public void receiveMessageWithAck(String queueUrl) {
    List<Message> messages = receiveMessage(queueUrl, "receiveMessageWithAck");
```

```java
        for (Message message : messages) {
            acknowledgeMessageReceivedToQueue(message, queueUrl);
        }
    }

private List<Message> receiveMessage(String queueUrl, String operationType) {
    ReceiveMessageRequest request = new ReceiveMessageRequest(queueUrl);

    request.withMaxNumberOfMessages(10);

    ReceiveMessageResult response = amazonSQSClient.receiveMessage(request);

    return response.getMessages();
}

private void acknowledgeMessageReceivedToQueue(Message message,
                                               String queueUrl) {
    String receiptHandle = message.getReceiptHandle();

    DeleteMessageRequest deleteMessageRequest =
        new DeleteMessageRequest(queueUrl, receiptHandle);

    DeleteMessageResult response =
        amazonSQSClient.deleteMessage(deleteMessageRequest);
}
```

```
{
    "messages": {
        {
            "messageId": "5b46ed76-2488-436a-95d9-767dd0782075b",
            "receiptHandle": 
            "AQEBpbvrx03Hq3QQ2fNRLl3kDg7i fpBhC5ndOvIX/0QZnTrmnkba81db0jrdjrfV9L2mMyh0gZ6X7ury/6206E2eNOQEaaYp2SgpBfpkacc8lkedrr4pooo06RmZksVyTEgILqvot9vfbmfbk13lxYy7o0QaMKeqxPahf4icZREx0r+POlnlZeggBC7Pdn0r/ta36Z1VUNifG6C9EE/45lAlZt4lt90d40SMM0I/SrQ1K2nvXvQpryhbmnb9hDMyhfSrEQGksb0v0n0u0u6fo/sIk5g8e45/cDg4Q//IDd0m5H3HhhvovnnCBCv7+2nshn0NgyQDvdJ/vaPu2YCl+202LfH3b67L0nwyy0+hrohoZ0eMYvq09l/0hNEX/5BwSn6mehhagy90n0n0nSA9/w008l9/n008d/",
            "mD5Of8ody": "5k3£90ham6v41n749dc64249b17749c9",
            "messageAttributes": {}
        },
        {
            "messageId": "a5ba50c7-52d5-4c02-9780-af12ab465888",
            "receiptHandle": 
            "AQEBAL+Q1KvkbhpGpFwq44rvrQji49rsnfHJ1hfd04cfcs07ncheqoru9n3mi6qDsfYr0r8Encdw81v4wvygy0vp8Tn0c11DYLiT3h1khh8Cy/hwpw8PA/KZ1YdoV72b8llNmqLsndnd8R9rYlIqv6xcd0rcb6edEss9QvnntDTh/LS1ev/KyDvdaixhkdhyVr/Iog/HBcdlscpx4vJr05/dbVI37Y7+dfhhsn7wcZ8HFlll7YcpcfAM6qxN7YX2keEcr7nhmm27rTkoyrhk0LQQKcSn8Yzoot6Jn6inaKyheQCfR/S0Enjm0Ok8by3bu3dwnDh/brnC0JnncS+qpAd5jtyvkskwylgY0ppevy12PYnFqxc0ksSnExPSdMmMbgpypp75du4K00+h1SQ\u0008d\u008ml",
            "mD5Of8ody": "907a11ab0081d49c1kdc907cd5c8142",
            "messageAttributes": {}
        },
        {
            "messageId": "100c8219-2fb6-4780-8a18-Za18c7da80d7",
            "receiptHandle": 
            "AQEBPbpkpioy6m80fXMY0yfINnFdy5CvaQQv+1Bk9QEpZg+x4kxAqfIN5RCS261+x/nsh31hbm6dyvk/vdsxLpx5ncfXpovh28d/4z+9nn02gxHLKd9dz/cq/bBfAqdLgEhcb779+CqB0vri9QayYqYWxf7L00v0qQS2a0LYNMb1r028J76b1LPrQcdTBsSm8SpnS0L/IT3qcdvY/N9D0Cl6/OJ/HXKUGL4y7800x1ncded0f202bvdnb/nkfyfaCnpIQ117IuQ0ShnbayQu0cfQ2009maXdnNBapnY09xfK11Tbn0BLhX2qv/AFN8b9vBas87sn873cqRkhRo0p0aY1Lpd86m0Q\u0008d\u008ml",
            "mD5Of8ody": "176d4a4888s06444ac223944fn30dfoc",
            "messageAttributes": {}
        }
    },
    "sdkResponseMetadata": {
        "metadata": {
            "AWS_REQUEST_ID": "a5c7cafe-5b85-5ed5-aa19-9a444f343se1"
        }
    },
    "sdkHttpMetadata": {
        "httpHeaders": {
            "Server": "Server",
            "Connection": "keep-alive",
            "x-amzn-RequestId": "a5c7cafe-5b85-5ed5-aa19-9a444f343se1",
            "Content-Length": "2081",
            "Date": "Thu, 01 Dec 2016 12:04:32 GMT",
            "Content-Type": "text/xml"
        },
        "httpStatusCode": 200
    }
}
```

Once the messages are received, you will iterate over the messages and invoke the deleteMessage method that has the message's receiptHandle parameter:

```
{
  "sdkResponseMetadata": {
    "metadata": {
      "AWS_REQUEST_ID": "8c739006-0db4-5bc1-b5be-c0bc19a54fd5"
    }
  },
  "sdkHttpMetadata": {
    "httpHeaders": {
      "Server": "Server",
      "Connection": "keep-alive",
      "x-amzn-RequestId": "8c739006-0db4-5bc1-b5be-c0bc19a54fd5",
      "Content-Length": "215",
      "Date": "Thu, 01 Dec 2016 12:04:33 GMT",
      "Content-Type": "text/xml"
    },
    "httpStatusCode": 200
  }
}
```

There won't be any parameters in response specific to deleting message apart from "httpStatusCode", which will be used to identify whether the request was successful or not.

Receive Message with Change Visibility

To change the visibility of received messages, first retrieve the messages from the queue and then invoke the changeMessageVisibility method:

```
receiveMessageWithChangeVisibility(queueUrl);

public void receiveMessageWithChangeVisibility(String queueUrl) {
    List<Message> messages =
        receiveMessage(queueUrl, "receiveMessageWithChangeVisibility");

    for (Message message : messages) {
        changeMessageVisibility(queueUrl, message.getReceiptHandle(), 10);
    }
}

private void changeMessageVisibility(String queueUrl, String receiptHandle,
                                              Integer visibilityTimeout) {
    ChangeMessageVisibilityRequest request =
                                      new ChangeMessageVisibilityRequest(
                                      queueUrl,
                                      receiptHandle,
                                      visibilityTimeout);
```

```
ChangeMessageVisibilityResult response =
    amazonSQSClient.changeMessageVisibility(request);
}
```

```
{
    "messages": [
        {
            "messageId": "05e95564-365d-46db-80c4-869d29cd1704",
            "receiptHandle":
"AQEBaoBnaXMayQOQZaXUL2O4ZieCHC5o8i29mmsuLYGMIXPOHB6YhOQFnZrhNNeqjOQckBULy4FEX3f1HUXIx6/IfAGLa6VIP4yCNpOwaPMd0ge6vasm0j5Uxd8sds/vKaalP/dGET8xkNv4828XbIGJ9DE13tKluw83muOqTi11HCSayxc9M
HYNVyFj589cQYaKcecS8OuJNMUaiiH5JU4sUAIanaZ9VNBNa8zQYcaK77szICuBQOSpQz7K0Iv8Con6VMB98XMscTaHPvbgpUesmqRnjOA8vtNqp6z6LmhTP7GUuqujyvvvntImpzpXwZ42va8Vtc2EUETaPH6f4ZEXIOc/VnQsWiaN87c78Y
zdI063QMBwsm/pd6aQ6Ls+tz6gYzmuF87zh647I1iQeRO8NyA\u003d\u003d",
            "mD5OfBody": "7b28033cerfe61c780b5e9245b13746e5",
            "body": "Hello AWS SQS!!!",
            "messageAttributes": {}
        }
    ],
    "sdkResponseMetadata": {
        "metadata": {
            "AWS_REQUEST_ID": "fa720947-a0b2-5b7e-ad4c-58fdb4a0bf6a"
        }
    },
    "sdkHttpMetadata": {
        "httpHeaders": {
            "Server": "Server",
            "Connection": "keep-alive",
            "x-amzn-RequestId": "fa720947-a0b2-5b7e-ad4c-58fdb4a0bf6a",
            "Content-Length": "867",
            "Date": "Thu, 01 Dec 2016 12:04:34 GMT",
            "Content-Type": "text/xml"
        },
        "httpStatusCode": 200
    }
}
```

Once the messages are received, you will iterate over them and invoke the changeMessageVisibility method by passing the message's recieptHandle parameters.

```
{
    "sdkResponseMetadata": {
        "metadata": {
            "AWS_REQUEST_ID": "66871437-5fc1-5c85-b6df-448d4bd32891"
        }
    },
    "sdkHttpMetadata": {
        "httpHeaders": {
            "Server": "Server",
            "Connection": "keep-alive",
            "x-amzn-RequestId": "66871437-5fc1-5c85-b6df-448d4bd32891",
            "Content-Length": "235",
            "Date": "Thu, 01 Dec 2016 12:04:34 GMT",
            "Content-Type": "text/xml"
        },
        "httpStatusCode": 200
    }
}
```

There won't be any parameters in response specific to changing a message visibility apart from "httpStatusCode", which will be used to identify whether the request was successful or not.

Receive Message with Change Visibility Batch

To change the visibility in the batch of received messages, you will first retrieve the messages from the queue and then invoke the changeMessageVisibilityBatch method:

```
receiveMessageWithChangeVisibilityBatch(queueUrl);

public void receiveMessageWithChangeVisibilityBatch(String queueUrl) {
    List<Message> messages = receiveMessage(
                                queueUrl,
                                "receiveMessageWithChangeVisibilityBatch");

    changeMessageVisibilityBatch(queueUrl, messages);
}

private void changeMessageVisibilityBatch(String queueUrl,
                                            List<Message> messages) {
    ChangeMessageVisibilityBatchRequest request =
        new ChangeMessageVisibilityBatchRequest();

    request.setQueueUrl(queueUrl);

    List<ChangeMessageVisibilityBatchRequestEntry> entries =
        new ArrayList<ChangeMessageVisibilityBatchRequestEntry>();

    ChangeMessageVisibilityBatchRequestEntry entry;

    for(Message message: messages) {
        entry = new ChangeMessageVisibilityBatchRequestEntry(
                                        UUID.randomUUID().toString(),
                                        message.getReceiptHandle());

        entry.setVisibilityTimeout(10);

        entries.add(entry);
    }

    request.setEntries(entries);

    ChangeMessageVisibilityBatchResult response =
        amazonSQSClient.changeMessageVisibilityBatch(request);
}
```

```
{
  "messages": [
    {
      "messageId": "f2aae8a1-d9cc-481f-8f3d-b7f764bd49d1",
      "receiptHandle":
"AQEBBwJ92sbGISg9JiAUIoBXH27xqmU5AG35DKyvBnUqUpfSU/pbTRKYI5VS01eu3iUy6q63MVU0SF3BCKZuqqe6nnt6aC2hLi20hRv6p188mhK0pThNE3Tdq5v4Jq73AsCjDghKbY4GCg5UUJhnFriiXn22AYEbQteRiasdEYkGcYJxhT0s
vVNJSBn5647QExJpCwEupq6VaC2nsEaYjdvtZAV8nl44khnwWVZderfBCxMxi00ZC1v20RTKdqx/Cc/++pcvhXUXnPAVp5RGGUBM4c4iAx1tmBwdW4BIS/1Z9nROKAoejAou+BQ68Uyfvcvcpp1BhHy6NVAP6RQ5q4tMbBbxqOKwj7ZFbYIZQ9vKN
mUD46ULsgJz1qvcmmDm86YaMQEZvK8E0vaP1XPzrHr+s+tusg\u003d\u003d",
      "mD5OfBody": "ce67e1b60d724f5cebe518ead1adada6",
      "body": "Hello AWS SQS!!!-0",
      "messageAttributes": {}
    },
    {
      "messageId": "c8b6f91d-b98f-434a-a155-39b065197d2a",
      "receiptHandle":
"AQEBMaa6zF9RdOhvRc0PwZI4vP4uV7DUMnHmdBymizRjuruYPKPeBOA3mBQXK/6CPrui1rUy4HLCudVpTsmNTBZW21HXt96/eQYoys17cLnJVOH1Og4WcT6FBGRqy9UVEP9fsyC1I1SmUEbj+8c7HutfHHKTsPmbyyyRcfABOYf5aYDMAYgh5
EX6U1d1SU11Ai1C/JNn5qqVhKeeCrj2f11lOeaZD4zp6drviqGXe5epB0f4158560EfdCI220v8Nt3aqQ5r4qHFYi6Qnxj3kqGQK1/98Gc/TruN9+9xS/G7cs+JnUhJJzmmN+k0e1AsnB1LbY4fPiJj9HdUaRQSq4FcSc3squI+BZmd5Vk8nq
      "mD5OfBody": "db18a2bbc3094753854094f8fa161243",
      "body": "Hello AWS SQS!!!-1",
      "messageAttributes": {}
    }
  ],
  "sdkResponseMetadata": {
    "metadata": {
      "AWS_REQUEST_ID": "302fcd91-c2dc-520a-a6cc-9d2bd6cfc61e"
    }
  },
  "sdkHttpMetadata": {
    "httpHeaders": {
      "Server": "Server",
      "Connection": "keep-alive",
      "x-amzn-RequestId": "302fcd91-c2dc-520a-a6cc-9d2bd6cfc61e",
      "Content-Length": "1476",
      "Date": "Thu, 01 Dec 2016 12:04:35 GMT",
      "Content-Type": "text/xml"
    },
    "httpStatusCode": 200
  }
}
```

In response, you can see the messages are received with "messageId",
"receiptHandle", "mD5OfBody", "body", and "messageAttributes" parameters.

```
{
  "successful": [
    {
      "id": "49d2120b-453b-4215-918f-957461a89b9d"
    },
    {
      "id": "54343cb3-870c-43a0-9f0e-ad185c3fa8e0"
    }
  ],
  "sdkResponseMetadata": {
    "metadata": {
      "AWS_REQUEST_ID": "d8d7cba9-cd3d-5ff2-9e4c-9b13d92e7be6"
    }
  },
  "sdkHttpMetadata": {
    "httpHeaders": {
      "Server": "Server",
      "Connection": "keep-alive",
      "x-amzn-RequestId": "d8d7cba9-cd3d-5ff2-9e4c-9b13d92e7be6",
      "Content-Length": "574",
      "Date": "Thu, 01 Dec 2016 12:04:35 GMT",
      "Content-Type": "text/xml"
    },
    "httpStatusCode": 200
  }
}
```

In response, you can see that the change visibility status for each message is provided.

145

Purge Queue

To purge the queue, use the purgeQueue method:

```
purgeQueue(queueUrl);

public void purgeQueue(String queueUrl) {

    PurgeQueueRequest request = new PurgeQueueRequest(queueUrl);

    PurgeQueueResult response = amazonSQSClient.purgeQueue(request);
}
```

```
{
  "sdkResponseMetadata": {
    "metadata": {
      "AWS_REQUEST_ID": "29db084b-8140-5d65-9d1d-58f195530971"
    }
  },
  "sdkHttpMetadata": {
    "httpHeaders": {
      "Server": "Server",
      "Connection": "keep-alive",
      "x-amzn-RequestId": "29db084b-8140-5d65-9d1d-58f195530971",
      "Content-Length": "209",
      "Date": "Thu, 01 Dec 2016 12:04:35 GMT",
      "Content-Type": "text/xml"
    },
    "httpStatusCode": 200
  }
}
```

There won't be any parameters in response specific to purging the queue apart from "httpStatusCode", which will be used to identify whether the request was successful or not.

Delete Queue

To delete a queue, use the deleteQueue method:

```
deleteQueue(queueUrl);

public void deleteQueue(String queueUrl) {
    DeleteQueueRequest request = new DeleteQueueRequest(queueUrl);

    DeleteQueueResult response = amazonSQSClient.deleteQueue(request);

}
```

```
{
  "sdkResponseMetadata": {
    "metadata": {
      "AWS_REQUEST_ID": "0959b8cf-5285-5cce-94d5-e8754691f8da"
    }
  },
  "sdkHttpMetadata": {
    "httpHeaders": {
      "Server": "Server",
      "Connection": "keep-alive",
      "x-amzn-RequestId": "0959b8cf-5285-5cce-94d5-e8754691f8da",
      "Content-Length": "211",
      "Date": "Thu, 01 Dec 2016 12:04:36 GMT",
      "Content-Type": "text/xml"
    },
    "httpStatusCode": 200
  }
}
```

There won't be any parameters in response specific to deleting the queue apart from "httpStatusCode", which will be used to identify whether the request was successful or not.

Monitor Using CloudWatch

CloudWatch allows monitoring the SQS using different metrics. It will trigger an alarm when a threshold is exceeded on specific metrics. The following steps, shown in Figure 3-31, can be used to create an alarm:

1. Go to the CloudWatch Management Console and click the Alarms button.

Figure 3-31. *CloudWatch Alarm*

Click the Create Alarm button.

The Create Alarm screen, which is shown in Figure 3-32, will be displayed where you will do the next two steps:

- Select metric

- Define alarm

Figure 3-32. *Create Alarm screen*

2. First, select the metric for SQS. Click the Browse Metrics button and select SQS in the drop-down list, as shown in Figure 3-33.

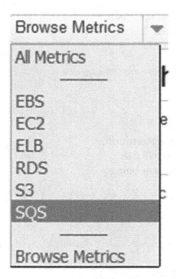

Figure 3-33. *Browse Metrics screen*

You can see all the metrics that can be configured on SQS in Figure 3-34.

Figure 3-34. *SQS Metric Listing screen*

3.   For our case, select ApproximateNumberOfMessagesVisible
     metrics. Then click the Next button. (See Figure 3-35.)

Figure 3-35. *SQS metric selected*

4.   Define the alarm settings by providing a name, description,
     and threshold values on the defined alarm. You will use
     "greater than" or "equal to" operations on messages being
     visible. (See Figure 3-36.)

Figure 3-36. *Define alarm*

5.   You will also define actions to trigger notification when the
     alarm state is "ALARM." To configure the action, select the value
     Send notification to: or create a new notification by clicking the
     New List button. Enter the topic name and the e-mail address
     where notifications need to be sent. (See Figure 3-37.)

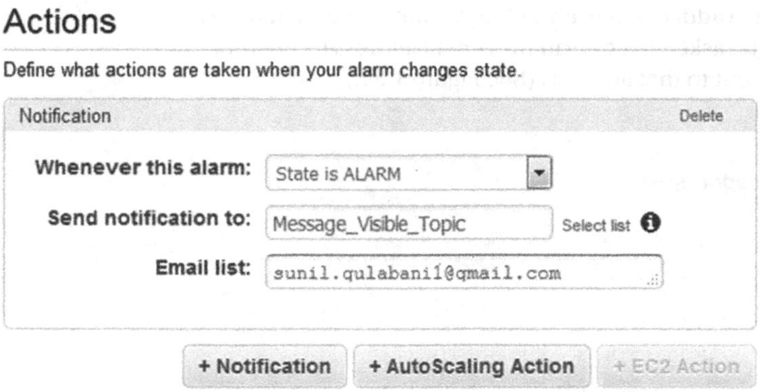

Actions

Define what actions are taken when your alarm changes state.

Notification	Delete

Whenever this alarm: State is ALARM ▾

Send notification to: Message_Visible_Topic   Select list ❶

Email list: sunil.qulabani1@qmail.com

+ Notification   **+ AutoScaling Action**   + EC2 Action

Figure 3-37. Define actions

6. Click the Create Alarm button, as shown in Figure 3-38.

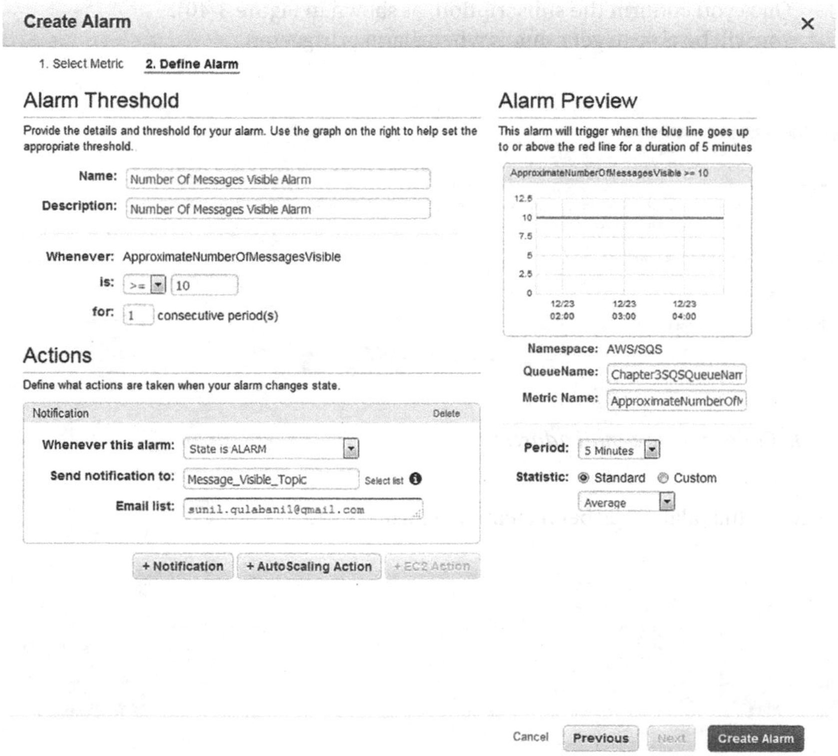

Create Alarm   ✕

1. Select Metric   **2. Define Alarm**

Alarm Threshold

Provide the details and threshold for your alarm. Use the graph on the right to help set the appropriate threshold.

Name: Number Of Messages Visible Alarm

Description: Number Of Messages Visible Alarm

Whenever: ApproximateNumberOfMessagesVisible

is: >= ▾ 10

for: 1 consecutive period(s)

Actions

Define what actions are taken when your alarm changes state.

Notification	Delete

Whenever this alarm: State is ALARM ▾

Send notification to: Message_Visible_Topic   Select list ❶

Email list: sunil.qulabani1@qmail.com

+ Notification   **+ AutoScaling Action**   + EC2 Action

Alarm Preview

This alarm will trigger when the blue line goes up to or above the red line for a duration of 5 minutes

ApproximateNumberOfMessagesVisible >= 10

12.5
10
7.5
5
2.5
0
12/23 12/23 12/23
02:00 03:00 04:00

Namespace: AWS/SQS
QueueName: Chapter3SQSQueueNam
Metric Name: ApproximateNumberOfN

Period: 5 Minutes ▾

Statistic: ◉ Standard ○ Custom
Average ▾

Cancel **Previous** Next **Create Alarm**

Figure 3-38. Create Alarm screen

7. If you have added a new e-mail that is not subscribed to SNS, you will be asked to confirm the e-mail address by opening the link sent to that address. (See Figure 3-39.)

Figure 3-39. *Confirm new e-mail address*

8. Once you confirm the subscription, as shown in Figure 3-40), you will be able to get e-mails when alarm is triggered.

Figure 3-40. *Confirm new e-mail address*

You can see that alarm has been created in Figure 3-41.

Figure 3-41. *Alarm listing*

9. To test that the alarm has been generated, add 20 messages to the queue. (See Figure 3-42.)

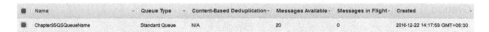

Name	Queue Type	Content-Based Deduplication	Messages Available	Messages in Flight	Created
Chapter3SQSQueueName	Standard Queue	N/A	20	0	2016-12-22 14:17:53 GMT+05:30

Figure 3-42. *Queue listing*

10. You can see that alarm state has changed to "ALARM" in Figure 3-43.

State	Name	Threshold	Config Status
☑ ALARM	Number Of Messages Visible Alarm	ApproximateNumberOfMessagesVisible >= 10 for 5 minutes	

1 Alarm selected

Alarm: Number Of Messages Visible Alarm

| Details | History |

State Details: State changed to ALARM at 2016/12/23. Reason: Threshold Crossed: 1 datapoint (20.0) was greater than or equal to the threshold (10.0).

Description: Number Of Messages Visible Alarm

Threshold: ApproximateNumberOfMessagesVisible >= 10 for 5 minutes

Actions: In ALARM: • Send message to topic "Message_Visible_Topic" (sunil.gulabani1@gmail.com)

Namespace: AWS/SQS

Metric Name: ApproximateNumberOfMessagesVisible

Dimensions: QueueName = Chapter3SQSQueueName

Statistic: Average

Period: 5 minutes

Figure 3-43. *Alarm generated*

11. The e-mail has also been triggered, as shown in Figure 3-44.

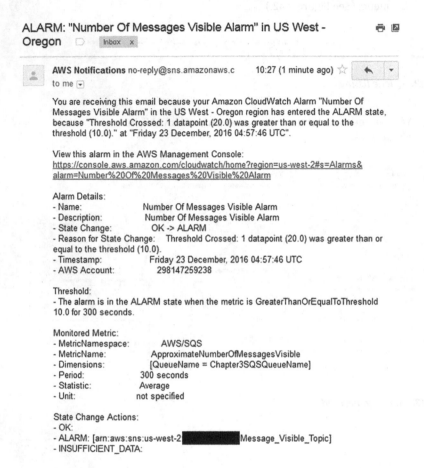

Figure 3-44. Alarm e-mail

12. After the messages are read and deleted from the queue, the alarm state will go back to "OK," as shown in Figure 3-45.

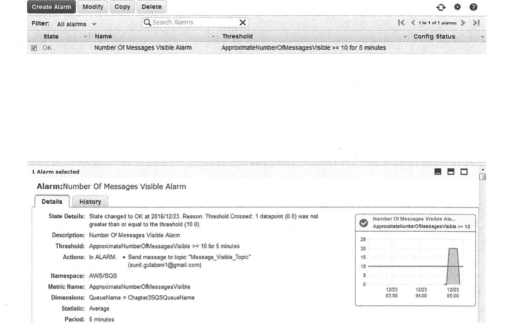

Figure 3-45. *Alarm state "OK"*

Summary

In this chapter, I have demonstrated how to create a queue and configure the queue attributes using AWS Management Console, AWS CLI, and AWS Java SDK. I have also explained how to authorize the queue to grant access to a specific AWS Account ID so that users can access the queue. Lastly, I discussed how to configure a CloudWatch alarm in your queue, which is invoked once the threshold value has been crossed.

In Chapter 4, I will explain how to create and configure Kinesis Streams and how to implement producer and consumer applications.

CHAPTER 4

■ ■ ■

Hands-on Kinesis

Amazon Kinesis is used for data streaming. It can handle heavy loads and provide performance in real-time processing. Kinesis data can be offloaded to Amazon S3 for future look-up on data. Amazon Kinesis captures data records using streams, delivers data records to other AWS services using Firehose, and can analyze captured data using Kinesis analytics.

In this chapter, I will cover the following topics:

- Introduction to AWS Kinesis Stream and Firehose

- Features

- Using AWS Management Console

- Using AWS CLI

- Using AWS SDK—Java

- Monitoring Using CloudWatch

Introduction to AWS Kinesis Stream and Firehose

AWS Kinesis Stream is a stream of data records used for real-time data transfer. AWS Kinesis Stream follows the pattern of producer and consumer to push and read data respectively from streams. Kinesis Stream can be used to process and aggregate data by integrating different AWS resources such as S3, Redshift, Elastic Search, and so on. For example, to analyze the call data records of telecommunication network, which are enormous records, the processing needs to be in real time. Whenever call data records are generated, applications will push data to Kinesis Stream, and the consumer application will read data from the stream and process it. This generates reports and billing for specific call data records. Simultaneously, Kinesis Stream also invokes events to store raw data to S3 as per configuration. This makes it possible for an application to serve high throughput, reliability, and durability.

AWS Kinesis Firehose is a delivery system for Kinesis stream. You don't need a separate application for AWS Kinesis Firehose; it is the configuration-based mechanism that triggers events to deliver data records when Kinesis receives data records. You can also transform this data before pushing it to other resources. With this, you can integrate several AWS resources such as Simple Storage Services (S3), Redshift, Elastic Search (ES), and so on. In this chapter, I will focus on the Amazon Kinesis Stream.

© Sunil Gulabani 2017
S. Gulabani, *Practical Amazon EC2, SQS, Kinesis, and S3*,
DOI 10.1007/978-1-4842-2841-8_4

Features

Following are the main features of Kinesis Stream:

Real-Time Data Streaming and Processing

Kinesis provides real-time data streaming. Producer applications can add data records to the stream and consumers can read the data after it is added. Data streaming between the producer, who is adding records, and the consumer, who is reading the record, is less than one second.

Durability and Elasticity

Kinesis Stream provides high availability and durability of the data stream. This ensures that data is not lost and real-time complex processing can be achieved. Kinesis Stream can scale based on the traffic flow of data records.

Managed Service

Kinesis is a fully AWS-managed service. You don't need to look after the Kinesis infrastructure to manage it; you just need to configure Kinesis Streams during its creation.

Concurrent Consumers

AWS Kinesis doesn't restrict the consumer applications to read data records. Multiple consumer applications can read the same record and process it. For example, you can achieve two tasks on data records—store raw data on S3 and process data records. You can have two consumer applications where one application will store raw data to S3 and the second application will process the data. In addition to this, you can also use Kinesis Client Library (KCL) to have multiple consumer workers to process data records.

Using AWS Management Console

AWS Management Console can be used to manage Kinesis Streams. It provides an easy way to configure Kinesis Streams. The following section shows how to configure Kinesis Streams.

Create Streams

Streams are an important part of Kinesis. Streams have the capability to capture data records. Streams follow the publisher and subscriber model. The following steps will lead to the creation of Kinesis Streams:

1. Sign in to the AWS console and click Kinesis under All Services ➤ Analytics category, as shown in Figure 4-1.

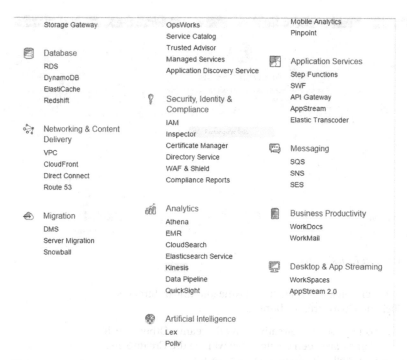

Figure 4-1. *AWS Management Console—Kinesis*

This will take you to the Kinesis screen, as shown in Figure 4-2, where you can see three different types of services:

- Amazon Kinesis Firehose

- Amazon Kinesis Analytics

- Amazon Kinesis Streams

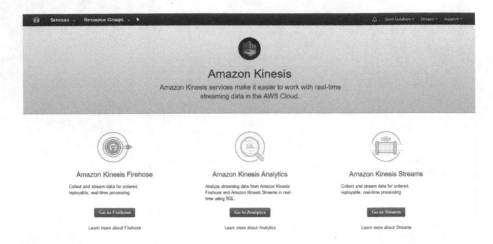

Figure 4-2. Amazon Kinesis screen

2. In this chapter, we will focus on Amazon Kinesis Streams. Click the Go to Streams button.

3. Here you can see the already-created streams. Otherwise, if no streams have been created, you will see the Create Stream button and click it, as shown in Figure 4-3.

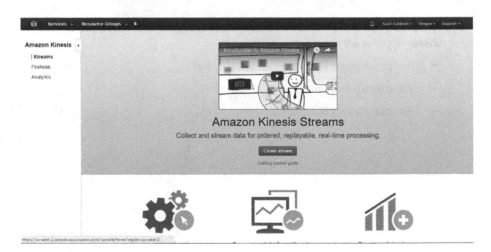

Figure 4-3. Amazon Kinesis Stream screen

4. Next, you will be filling up the stream name and shard count for creating a new stream, as shown in Figure 4-4.

■ **Note** Shards are created under a stream, which are uniquely identified as group of data records. You can have multiple shards under a stream, which will help to distribute load on shards.

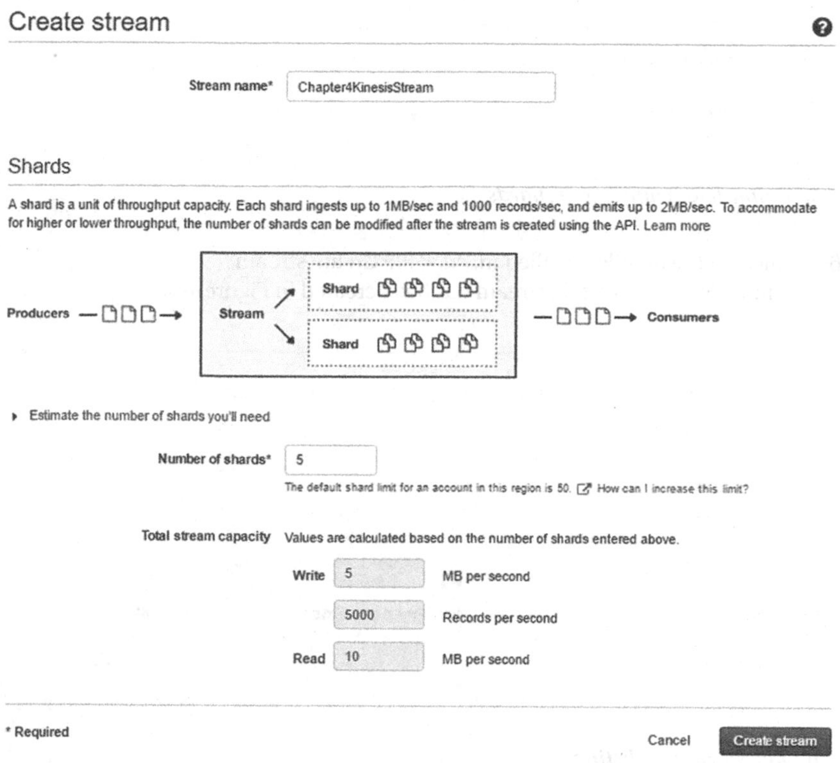

Create stream ❓

Stream name* Chapter4KinesisStream

Shards

A shard is a unit of throughput capacity. Each shard ingests up to 1MB/sec and 1000 records/sec, and emits up to 2MB/sec. To accommodate for higher or lower throughput, the number of shards can be modified after the stream is created using the API. Learn more

Producers — ☐☐☐→ Stream Shard 🦑🦑🦑🦑 / Shard 🦑🦑🦑🦑 — ☐☐☐→ Consumers

▸ Estimate the number of shards you'll need

Number of shards* 5

The default shard limit for an account in this region is 50. ☐ How can I increase this limit?

Total stream capacity Values are calculated based on the number of shards entered above.

Write 5 MB per second

5000 Records per second

Read 10 MB per second

---

* Required   Cancel **Create stream**

Figure 4-4. Create Kinesis Stream screen

5. Using the Estimate the number of shards you'll need link, you can predict how many shards you will need based on record size, records written per second, and number of consumer applications that will subscribe to stream. (See Figure 4-5.)

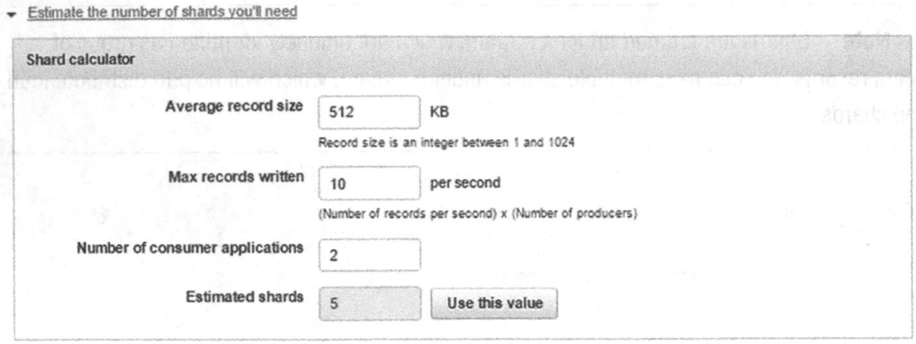

▼ Estimate the number of shards you'll need

Shard calculator		
Average record size	512	KB
	Record size is an integer between 1 and 1024	
Max records written	10	per second
	(Number of records per second) x (Number of producers)	
Number of consumer applications	2	
Estimated shards	5	Use this value

Figure 4-5. *Estimate the number of shards*

6. Once all the details are filled in, click the Create stream button. You can see that stream has been created in Figure 4-6.

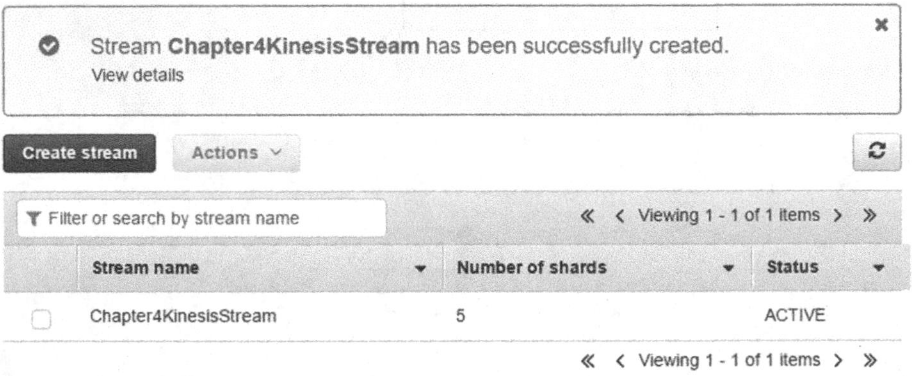

✓ Stream **Chapter4KinesisStream** has been successfully created.
View details   ✕

Create stream   Actions ⌄   ⟳

▼ Filter or search by stream name   ≪ ‹ Viewing 1 - 1 of 1 items › ≫

Stream name	▼	Number of shards	▼	Status	▼
☐ Chapter4KinesisStream		5		ACTIVE	

≪ ‹ Viewing 1 - 1 of 1 items › ≫

Figure 4-6. *Kinesis Stream listing*

Edit Shards

At times, you will want to scale up or scale down the Kinesis shards because of data traffic that is going on in the Kinesis Stream. If this is the case, you need to increase or decrease the shard count.

1. To edit the shard count, click the Kinesis Stream or select the Kinesis Stream and click the Actions ➤ Details menu, as shown in Figure 4-7.

Figure 4-7. Kinesis Stream action menu

2. You will land on the Kinesis Stream's details page, shown in Figure 4-8, where you can configure different parameters.

Figure 4-8. Kinesis Stream details

3. To edit the shard count, click the Edit button of Shards section. This will enable the "Open shards" input box to change count. (See Figure 4-9.)

Shards   Cancel   Save

In order to adapt to changes in the rate of data flow through the stream, Amazon Kinesis Streams supports scaling, which enables you to adjust the number of shards in your stream. Learn more

Open shards   4   ❶

Specify a number between half and double the current number of open shards for this stream (i.e between 2 and 10) up to a maximum of your shard limit. The default shard limit for accounts in this region is 50. ☑ How can I increase this limit?
Note: The operation takes several minutes and your application will remain in "Updating" state during that time.

Closed shards   0   ❶

Figure 4-9. Edit shards

4. Here you can define the number of shards between half and double the current number of open shards. Once you have finished the changes, click the Save button. Updating shard count takes time. (See Figure 4-10.)

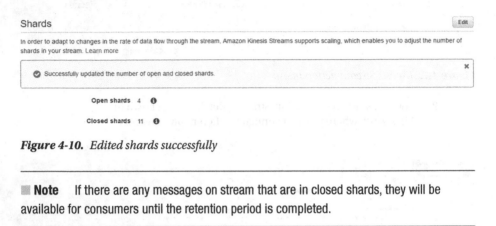

Shards   Edit

In order to adapt to changes in the rate of data flow through the stream, Amazon Kinesis Streams supports scaling, which enables you to adjust the number of shards in your stream. Learn more

✓ Successfully updated the number of open and closed shards.   ✕

Open shards   4   ❶

Closed shards   11   ❶

Figure 4-10. *Edited shards successfully*

■ **Note** If there are any messages on stream that are in closed shards, they will be available for consumers until the retention period is completed.

Configure Data Retention Period

The data retention period defines the time for a message to be retained on stream. For example, if we configured 24 hours as the data retention period, the stream will keep the message for 24 hours so that consumer applications can read the message within the specified duration.

1. To configure the data retention period for messages on stream, click the Edit button. (See Figure 4-11.)

Data retention period   Cancel   Save

The data retention period can be increased from 24 hours up to 168 hours for an additional cost. See ☑ Kinesis Streams pricing.

Data retention period   24   hours ❶

Specify a data retention period between 24 and 168 hours

Figure 4-11. *Configure data retention period*

2. Change the value and click the Save button. Changes may take up to 30 seconds to go into effect. (See Figure 4-12.)

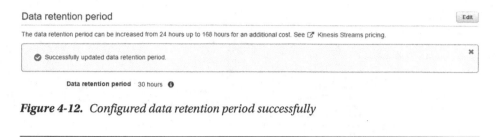

Figure 4-12. *Configured data retention period successfully*

■ **Note**   The minimum and maximum data retention periods can be 24 hours and 168 hours, respectively.

Configure Shard Level Metrics

Shard level metrics help to identify the performance of shards. Using these metrics, you can determine if you need resharding.

1. By default, no shard level metrics are enabled. To enable the shard level metrics, click the Edit button and select the metrics you want to enable. (See Figure 4-13.)

Shard level metrics   Cancel **Save**

Enabling shard level metrics will make data available in 1-minute periods at an additional cost. See "Custom Metrics" in ☑ CloudWatch pricing.

Shard level metrics ☑ *All shard level metrics*

        ☑ IncomingBytes
        ☑ IncomingRecords
        ☑ OutgoingBytes
        ☑ OutgoingRecords
        ☑ WriteProvisionedThroughputExceeded
        ☑ ReadProvisionedThroughputExceeded
        ☑ IteratorAgeMilliseconds

Figure 4-13. *Configure shard level metrics*

2. Once you select the metrics, click the Save button. Changes may take up to 70 seconds to go into effect. (See Figure 4-14.)

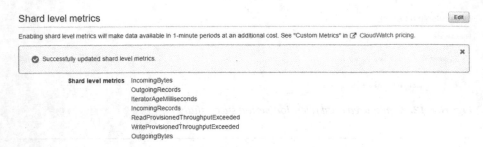

Figure 4-14. *Configured shard level metrics successfully*

Configure Tags

Tags are logical names and values that are assigned to AWS services. Tags are used to aggregate AWS resources and find out costs by grouping similar tags.

1. Click the Tags tab on the Kinesis Stream detail page, shown in Figure 4-15. Here you can see the tag listing, add new tags, edit existing tags, and remove tags.

2. To add tags, add key and value and click the Save button.

Figure 4-15. *Add tags*

3. You can also edit the existing created tags by clicking the edit icon of each tag. (See Figure 4-16.)

Figure 4-16. *Added tags successfully and edited tags*

4. To delete tags, click the delete (cross) icon shown for each tag.
    Clicking the delete icon will prompt users to confirm deletion.
    (See Figure 4-17.)

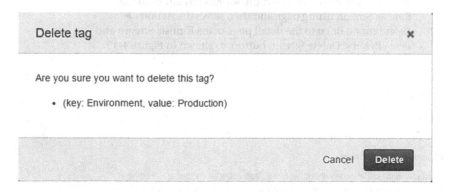

Figure 4-17. *Delete tag confirmation*

5. Changes will be saved by clicking the Delete button, as shown
    in Figure 4-18.

Figure 4-18. *Deleted tag successfully*

Delete Stream

The delete stream command deletes the stream permanently. Data records that are present on Kinesis Stream are removed and can't be recovered once deleted.

1. To delete a stream, first select the Kinesis Stream from the Kinesis Stream listing page and then select the Actions ➤ Delete menu or go to the detail page of the Kinesis Stream and then click the Delete Stream button, as shown in Figure 4-19.

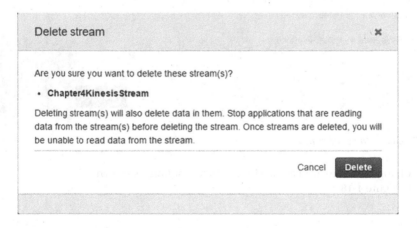

Figure 4-19. *Delete stream confirmation*

2. Click the Delete button to delete the stream. The deleting process may take time.

Using AWS CLI

In Chapter 1, I explained how to install AWS CLI. In this section, I will show how to use AWS CLI to manage AWS Kinesis.

create-stream

To create stream using AWS CLI, you need to provide the stream name and shard count in a command:

```
>aws kinesis create-stream --stream-name "Chapter4KinesisStream"
--shard-count 5
```

```
C:\Users\Dell>aws kinesis create-stream --stream-name "Chapter4KinesisStream" --shard-count 5

C:\Users\Dell>
```

There won't be any output for this request. create-stream has a limitation where it only supports 5 transactions per second per account.

■ **Note**   For more parameters in detail, refer to `http://docs.amazonaws.cn/cli/latest/reference/kinesis/create-stream.html`.

---

describe-stream

The describe-stream command will provide details of the stream. You need to pass the stream name to get the details:

```
>aws kinesis describe-stream --stream-name "Chapter4KinesisStream"
```

```
C:\Users\Dell>aws kinesis describe-stream --stream-name "Chapter4KinesisStream"
{
    "StreamDescription": {
        "RetentionPeriodHours": 24,
        "StreamName": "Chapter4KinesisStream",
        "Shards": [
            {
                "ShardId": "shardId-000000000000",
                "HashKeyRange": {
                    "EndingHashKey": "68056473384187692692674921486353642290",
                    "StartingHashKey": "0"
                },
                "SequenceNumberRange": {
                    "StartingSequenceNumber": "49569174031364017882077503751619586115517200604164259842"
                }
            },
            {
                "ShardId": "shardId-000000000001",
                "HashKeyRange": {
                    "EndingHashKey": "136112946768375385385349842972707284581",
                    "StartingHashKey": "68056473384187692692674921486353642291"
                },
                "SequenceNumberRange": {
                    "StartingSequenceNumber": "49569174031386318627276034374761121833789848965670240274"
                }
            },
            {
                "ShardId": "shardId-000000000002",
                "HashKeyRange": {
                    "EndingHashKey": "204169420152563078078024764459060926872",
                    "StartingHashKey": "136112946768375385385349842972707284582"
                },
                "SequenceNumberRange": {
                    "StartingSequenceNumber": "49569174031408619372474564997902657552062497327176220706"
                }
            },
            {
                "ShardId": "shardId-000000000003",
                "HashKeyRange": {
                    "EndingHashKey": "272225893536750770770699685945414569163",
                    "StartingHashKey": "204169420152563078078024764459060926873"
                },
                "SequenceNumberRange": {
                    "StartingSequenceNumber": "49569174031430920117673095621044193270335145688682201138"
                }
            },
            {
                "ShardId": "shardId-000000000004",
                "HashKeyRange": {
                    "EndingHashKey": "340282366920938463463374607431768211455",
                    "StartingHashKey": "272225893536750770770699685945414569164"
                },
                "SequenceNumberRange": {
                    "StartingSequenceNumber": "49569174031453220862871626244185728988607794050188181570"
                }
            }
        ],
        "StreamARN": "arn:aws:kinesis:us-west-2:              :stream/Chapter4KinesisStream",
        "EnhancedMonitoring": [
            {
                "ShardLevelMetrics": []
            }
        ],
        "StreamStatus": "ACTIVE"
    }
}
```

By default, all shards details will be provided. To get a paginated response, you need to pass the `"max-items"` parameter in a request:

```
>aws kinesis describe-stream --stream-name "Chapter4KinesisStream"
--max-items 1
```

```
C:\Users\Dell>aws kinesis describe-stream --stream-name "Chapter4KinesisStream" --max-items 1
{
    "NextToken": "eyJib3RvX3RydW5jYXRlX2Ftb3VudCI6IDEsICJFeGNsdXNpdmVTdGFydFNoYXJkSWQiOiBudWxsfQ==",
    "StreamDescription": {
        "RetentionPeriodHours": 24,
        "StreamName": "Chapter4KinesisStream",
        "Shards": [
            {
                "ShardId": "shardId-000000000000",
                "HashKeyRange": {
                    "EndingHashKey": "68056473384187692692674921486353642290",
                    "StartingHashKey": "0"
                },
                "SequenceNumberRange": {
                    "StartingSequenceNumber": "49569174031364017882077503751619586115517200604164259842"
                }
            }
        ],
        "StreamARN": "arn:aws:kinesis:us-west-2:███████████:stream/Chapter4KinesisStream",
        "EnhancedMonitoring": [
            {
                "ShardLevelMetrics": []
            }
        ],
        "StreamStatus": "ACTIVE"
    }
}
```

In the output, you can see the `"NextToken"` parameter is returned. This means that you still have records to be fetched. To fetch the next set of records, pass the `"NextToken"` parameter value as `"starting-token"`:

```
>aws kinesis describe-stream --stream-name "Chapter4KinesisStream"
--starting-token "eyJib3RvX3RydW5jYXRlX2Ftb3VudCI6IDEsICJFeGNsdXNpdm
VTdGFydFNoYXJkSWQiOiBudWxsfQ==" --max-items 2
```

```
C:\Users\Dell>aws kinesis describe-stream --stream-name "Chapter4KinesisStream" --starting-token "eyJib3RvX3RydW5jYXRlX2Ftb3VudCI6IDEsICJFeGNsdXNpdmVTdGFydFNoYXJkSWQiOi
BudWxsfQ==" --max-items 2
{
    "NextToken": "eyJib3RvX3RydW5jYXRlX2Ftb3VudCI6IDIsICJFeGNsdXNpdmVTdGFydFNoYXJkSWQiOiBudWxsfQ==",
    "StreamDescription": {
        "RetentionPeriodHours": 24,
        "StreamName": "Chapter4KinesisStream",
        "Shards": [
            {
                "ShardId": "shardId-000000000001",
                "HashKeyRange": {
                    "EndingHashKey": "136112046768375385385349842972707284581",
                    "StartingHashKey": "68056473384187692692674921486353642291"
                },
                "SequenceNumberRange": {
                    "StartingSequenceNumber": "49569174031386318622726034374761121833789848965670240274"
                }
            },
            {
                "ShardId": "shardId-000000000002",
                "HashKeyRange": {
                    "EndingHashKey": "204169420152563070070824764459060926872",
                    "StartingHashKey": "136112046768375385385349842972707284582"
                },
                "SequenceNumberRange": {
                    "StartingSequenceNumber": "49569174031408619372474564997902657552062497327176220706"
                }
            }
        ],
        "StreamARN": "arn:aws:kinesis:us-west-2:███████████:stream/Chapter4KinesisStream",
        "EnhancedMonitoring": [
            {
                "ShardLevelMetrics": []
            }
        ],
        "StreamStatus": "ACTIVE"
    }
}
```

The describe-stream command has a limitation in that it only supports 10 transactions per second per account.

■ **Note** For more parameters in detail, refer to `http://docs.amazonaws.cn/cli/latest/reference/kinesis/describe-stream.html`.

---

list-streams

To list your Kinesis Streams, execute the following command:

```
>aws kinesis list-streams
```

```
C:\Users\Dell>aws kinesis list-streams
{
    "StreamNames": [
        "Chapter4KinesisStream",
        "Chapter4KinesisStream1",
        "Chapter4KinesisStream2",
        "Chapter4KinesisStream3"
    ]
}
```

By default, the total number of streams returned is 10. To pass the limit, you can use "max-items" in the request:

```
>aws kinesis list-streams --max-items 2
```

```
C:\Users\Dell>aws kinesis list-streams --max-items 2
{
    "StreamNames": [
        "Chapter4KinesisStream",
        "Chapter4KinesisStream1"
    ],
    "NextToken": "eyJFeGNsdXNpdmVTdGFydFN0cmVhbU5hbWUiOiBudWxsLCAiYm90b190cnVuY2F0ZV9hbW91bnQiOiAyfQ=="
}
```

Using the "NextToken" parameter value, you can get the next set of records by passing a value for "starting-token" in the request:

```
>aws kinesis list-streams --starting-token "eyJFeGNsdXNpdmVTdGFydFN0cmVhbU5hbWUiOiBudWxsLCAiYm90b190cnVuY2F0ZV9hbW91bnQiOiAyfQ==" --max-items 2
```

```
C:\Users\Dell>aws kinesis list-streams --starting-token "eyJFeGNsdXNpdmVTdGFydFN0cmVhbU5hbWUiOiBudWxsLCAiYm90b190cnVuY2F0ZV9hbW91bnQiOiAyfQ==" --max-items 2
{
    "StreamNames": [
        "Chapter4KinesisStream2",
        "Chapter4KinesisStream3"
    ]
}
```

The list-stream command has the limitation of only supporting 5 transactions per second per account.

■ **Note** For more parameters in detail, refer to http://docs.amazonaws.cn/cli/latest/reference/kinesis/list-streams.html.

---

increase-stream-retention-period

The increase-stream-retention period refers to the time period that data will be retained in a Kinesis Stream after adding messages to stream. You need to provide "retention-period-hours" parameter in hours:

```
>aws kinesis increase-stream-retention-period --stream-name
"Chapter4KinesisStream" --retention-period-hours 72
```

```
C:\Users\Dell>aws kinesis increase-stream-retention-period --stream-name "Chapter4KinesisStream" --retention-period-hours 72
C:\Users\Dell>
```

By default, the retention period is 24 hours. You can provide any value between 24 hours (1 day) and 168 hours (7 days). To check if the retention period is set properly, you can use the describe-stream command:

```
>aws kinesis describe-stream --stream-name "Chapter4KinesisStream"
--max-items 1
```

```
C:\Users\Dell>aws kinesis describe-stream --stream-name "Chapter4KinesisStream" --max-items 1
{
    "NextToken": "eyJib3RvX3RydW5jYXRlX2Ftb3VudCI6IDEsICJFeGNsdXNpdmVTdGFydFNoYXJkSWQiOiBudWxsfQ==",
    "StreamDescription": {
        "RetentionPeriodHours": 72,
        "StreamName": "Chapter4KinesisStream",
        "Shards": [
            {
                "ShardId": "shardId-000000000000",
                "HashKeyRange": {
                    "EndingHashKey": "680564733841876926926749214863536422290",
                    "StartingHashKey": "0"
                },
                "SequenceNumberRange": {
                    "StartingSequenceNumber": "49569174031364017882077503751619586115517200604164259842"
                }
            }
        ],
        "StreamARN": "arn:aws:kinesis:us-west-2:            :stream/Chapter4KinesisStream",
        "EnhancedMonitoring": [
            {
                "ShardLevelMetrics": []
            }
        ],
        "StreamStatus": "ACTIVE"
    }
}
```

■ **Note** For more parameters in detail, refer to http://docs.amazonaws.cn/cli/ latest/reference/kinesis/increase-stream-retention-period.html.

---

decrease-stream-retention-period

This command decreases the stream-retention period for data after they are added to the stream:

```
>aws kinesis decrease-stream-retention-period --stream-name
"Chapter4KinesisStream" --retention-period-hours 24
```

```
C:\Users\Dell>aws kinesis decrease-stream-retention-period --stream-name "Chapter4KinesisStream" --retention-period-hours 24
C:\Users\Dell>
```

To check if the retention period is set properly, use the describe-stream command:

```
>aws kinesis describe-stream --stream-name "Chapter4KinesisStream"
--max-items 1
```

```
C:\Users\Dell>aws kinesis describe-stream --stream-name "Chapter4KinesisStream" --max-items 1
{
    "NextToken": "eyJib3RvX3RydW5jYXRlX2Ftb3VudCI6IDEsICJFeGNsdXNpdmVTdGFydFNoYXJkSWQiOiBudWxsfQ==",
    "StreamDescription": {
        "RetentionPeriodHours": 24,
        "StreamName": "Chapter4KinesisStream",
        "Shards": [
            {
                "ShardId": "shardId-000000000000",
                "HashKeyRange": {
                    "EndingHashKey": "680564733841876926926749214863536422900",
                    "StartingHashKey": "0"
                },
                "SequenceNumberRange": {
                    "StartingSequenceNumber": "49569174031364017882077503751619586115517200604164259842"
                }
            }
        ],
        "StreamARN": "arn:aws:kinesis:us-west-2:          :stream/Chapter4KinesisStream",
        "EnhancedMonitoring": [
            {
                "ShardLevelMetrics": []
            }
        ],
        "StreamStatus": "ACTIVE"
    }
}
```

The minimum retention period you can set is 24 hours (1 day).

■ **Note**   For more parameters in detail, refer to `http://docs.amazonaws.cn/cli/`
`latest/reference/kinesis/decrease-stream-retention-period.html`.

---

enable-enhanced-monitoring

The enable-enhanced-monitoring command enables shard level metrics:

```
>aws kinesis enable-enhanced-monitoring --stream-name
"Chapter4KinesisStream" --shard-level-metrics "IncomingBytes"
"OutgoingBytes"
```

```
>aws kinesis enable-enhanced-monitoring --stream-name
"Chapter4KinesisStream" --shard-level-metrics "IncomingRecords"
"OutgoingRecords"
```

```
C:\Users\Dell>aws kinesis enable-enhanced-monitoring --stream-name "Chapter4KinesisStream" --shard-level-metrics "IncomingBytes" "OutgoingBytes"
{
    "StreamName": "Chapter4KinesisStream",
    "CurrentShardLevelMetrics": [],
    "DesiredShardLevelMetrics": [
        "IncomingBytes",
        "OutgoingBytes"
    ]
}
C:\Users\Dell>aws kinesis enable-enhanced-monitoring --stream-name "Chapter4KinesisStream" --shard-level-metrics "IncomingRecords" "OutgoingRecords"
{
    "StreamName": "Chapter4KinesisStream",
    "CurrentShardLevelMetrics": [
        "IncomingBytes",
        "OutgoingBytes"
    ],
    "DesiredShardLevelMetrics": [
        "IncomingBytes",
        "OutgoingRecords",
        "IncomingRecords",
        "OutgoingBytes"
    ]
}
```

The following shard level metric values are valid:

- IncomingBytes: Number of bytes put on the shard

- IncomingRecords: Number of records put on the shard

- OutgoingBytes: Number of bytes fetched from the shard

- OutgoingRecords: Number of records fetched from the shard

- WriteProvisionedThroughputExceeded: Number of PutRecord and PutRecords failed due to throttling for the shard

- ReadProvisionedThroughputExceeded: Number of GetRecords failed due to throttling for the shard

- IteratorAgeMilliseconds: Age of last record in all GetRecords calls made on the shard

- ALL

■ **Note**   For more parameters in detail, refer to http://docs.amazonaws.cn/cli/
latest/reference/kinesis/enable-enhanced-monitoring.html.

disable-enhanced-monitoring

The disable-enhanced-monitoring command disables shard level metrics:

```
>aws kinesis disable-enhanced-monitoring --stream-name
"Chapter4KinesisStream" --shard-level-metrics "IncomingBytes"
"OutgoingBytes"

>aws kinesis disable-enhanced-monitoring --stream-name
"Chapter4KinesisStream" --shard-level-metrics "IncomingRecords"
"OutgoingRecords"
```

```
C:\Users\Dell>aws kinesis disable-enhanced-monitoring --stream-name "Chapter4KinesisStream" --shard-level-metrics "IncomingBytes" "OutgoingBytes"
{
    "StreamName": "Chapter4KinesisStream",
    "CurrentShardLevelMetrics": [
        "IncomingBytes",
        "OutgoingRecords",
        "IncomingRecords",
        "OutgoingBytes"
    ],
    "DesiredShardLevelMetrics": [
        "OutgoingRecords",
        "IncomingRecords"
    ]
}

C:\Users\Dell>aws kinesis disable-enhanced-monitoring --stream-name "Chapter4KinesisStream" --shard-level-metrics "IncomingRecords" "OutgoingRecords"
{
    "StreamName": "Chapter4KinesisStream",
    "CurrentShardLevelMetrics": [
        "OutgoingRecords",
        "IncomingRecords"
    ],
    "DesiredShardLevelMetrics": []
}
```

The following shard level metric values are valid:

- IncomingBytes

- IncomingRecords

- OutgoingBytes

- OutgoingRecords

- WriteProvisionedThroughputExceeded

- ReadProvisionedThroughputExceeded

- IteratorAgeMilliseconds

- ALL

■ **Note**   For more parameters in detail, refer to http://docs.amazonaws.cn/cli/
latest/reference/kinesis/disable-enhanced-monitoring.html.

put-record

To send a single data record to a Kinesis Stream, use the put-record command. You need to provide the stream name, partition key, and data blob. Based on the partition key, the shard is chosen and then data will be transported to that shard:

```
>aws kinesis put-record --stream-name "Chapter4KinesisStream" --data "DUMMY
DATA" --partition-key "123"
```

```
C:\Users\Dell>aws kinesis put-record --stream-name "Chapter4KinesisStream" --data "DUMMY DATA" --partition-key "123"
{
    "ShardId": "shardId-000000000000",
    "SequenceNumber": "49569181828774975057915174435979388609624180136595161090"
}
```

In response, you get the shard ID, where data is stored, and the sequence number of the data for that shard.

If you need to store the data on a specific shard, you can also pass the hash key, which will override the partition key hash. To demonstrate the explicit-hash-key command, you will get the starting hash key and ending hash key for the shard ID "shardId-000000000004" using the describe-stream command. Then select any value between the starting hash key and ending hash key:

```
>aws kinesis put-record --stream-name "Chapter4KinesisStream" --data "DUMMY
DATA" --partition-key "123" --explicit-hash-key "27222589353675077077069968
5945414569165"
```

```
C:\Users\Dell>aws kinesis put-record --stream-name "Chapter4KinesisStream" --data "DUMMY DATA" --partition-key "123" --explicit-hash-key "27222589353675077077069968595
414569165"
{
    "ShardId": "shardId-000000000004",
    "SequenceNumber": "49569181828864178038709297761129116673851112958860460098"
}
```

In response, you can see that data is stored on the shard ID "shardId-000000000004". The data blob size should be equal to or less than 1MB. The partition key can have a maximum length of 256 characters.

■ **Note** For more parameters in detail, refer to http://docs.amazonaws.cn/cli/latest/reference/kinesis/put-record.html.

---

put-records

To send multiple data records to a Kinesis Stream, use the put-records command. You need to provide the stream name, an array of records that have the partition key, and the data blob for each record:

```
>aws kinesis put-records --stream-name "Chapter4KinesisStream"
--records Data="DUMMY DATA 1",PartitionKey="456" Data="DUMMY DATA
2",PartitionKey="789" Data="DUMMY DATA 3",PartitionKey="123",ExplicitHashK
ey="272225893536750770770699685945414569165"
```

In response, you can see successful and unsuccessful records. Any data record failure won't affect the processing of other data records.

You can also add your data records in a JSON file:

```
>aws kinesis put-records --stream-name "Chapter4KinesisStream" --records
file://put-records-data.json
```

```
put-records-data.json
[
  {
    "Data": "DUMMY DATA 1",
    "PartitionKey": "456"
  },
  {
    "Data": "DUMMY DATA 2",
    "PartitionKey": "789"
  },
  {
    "Data": "DUMMY DATA 3",
    "PartitionKey": "123",
"ExplicitHashKey": "272225893536750770770699685945414569165"
  }
]
```

```
C:\Users\Dell>aws kinesis put-records --stream-name "Chapter4KinesisStream" --records file://put-records-data.json
{
    "FailedRecordCount": 0,
    "Records": [
        {
            "ShardId": "shardId-000000000000",
            "SequenceNumber": "49569181828774975057915176137757668513106296924778004482"
        },
        {
            "ShardId": "shardId-000000000002",
            "SequenceNumber": "49569181828819576548312237384039531023831979018615259170"
        },
        {
            "ShardId": "shardId-000000000004",
            "SequenceNumber": "49569181828864178038709298630325020312016504999976632386"
        }
    ]
}
```

The put-records command can contain a maximum of 500 data records. The maximum data record size can be 1MB. For an entire batch of records, the size should not exceed 5MB, including partition keys.

■ **Note**   For more parameters in detail, refer to `http://docs.amazonaws.cn/cli/latest/reference/kinesis/put-records.html`.

---

get-shard-iterator

This command provides the Kinesis shard iterator. The shard iterator identifies from which position you need to start reading data records. The shard iterator provided from this command expires in five minutes. You need to provide the shard-iterator-type to determine how data will be read from the shard:

```
>aws kinesis get-shard-iterator --stream-name "Chapter4KinesisStream"
--shard-id "shardId-000000000000" --shard-iterator-type "TRIM_HORIZON"
```

```
C:\Users\Dell>aws kinesis get-shard-iterator --stream-name "Chapter4KinesisStream" --shard-id "shardId-000000000000" --shard-iterator-type "TRIM_HORIZON"
{
    "ShardIterator": "AAAAAAAAAAGJz6AeV+wzd7GaNxL+LJ547JiS+NnzTwMGS+OhTbpUUOnYguZQHOtFbkdVNZ5CpcFV37h8aFXVY1I1diyYk7P7d9ooPkxjLDU+xn2o9dnfhYWZv/9l7OwHxAKz/kdQ8zgNfROgtD
vP9d0kcV4hdN8V6b4/s6nFxz4xv49POtzPOqN5+EdzEf8zfK638JY7L87pzs2DzjTVm93b6SyRJ+fLgKzyb4GBySKuO2586ux8fA==".
}
C:\Users\Dell>
```

The following are valid values for shard-iterator-type:

- AT_SEQUENCE_NUMBER: You need to pass the starting-sequence-number parameter, which says to read the record from the mentioned sequence number.

- AFTER_SEQUENCE_NUMBER: You need to pass the starting-sequence-number parameter, which says to read the record after the mentioned sequence number.

- TRIM_HORIZON: This value is used to read from the oldest data record available in the shard.

- LATEST: This value allows you to read from the latest record available in the shard.

- AT_TIMESTAMP: You need to pass the timestamp parameter, which says to read the data records after the specified timestamp.

The get-shard-iterator command only supports 5 transactions per second per account per open shard.

■ **Note**   For more parameters in detail, refer to `http://docs.amazonaws.cn/cli/latest/reference/kinesis/get-shard-iterator.html`.

---

get-records

The get-records command helps to read data records from the stream's shard. You need to provide the shard iterator to specify from which location the data records need to be read. For the first time, the shard iterator can be fetched using the get-shard-iterator command. For the next request, use the "NextShardIterator" response parameter of the get-records request. For our case, we will use the shard ID "shardId-000000000004" to read data records:

```
>aws kinesis get-shard-iterator --stream-name "Chapter4KinesisStream"
--shard-id "shardId-000000000004" --shard-iterator-type "LATEST"
```

```
>aws kinesis get-records --shard-iterator "AAAAAAAAAAEwbn15NNj8HZYnLK3mzJ
WdveOH/UNE9IjGzh3ckBOWTb8OkqJA2/pqPBbC2VooaaChnt/8dj4BT9r8xahKZRZlGHIt+
5Fo5Cs1xvCfgsDsOgYuXadcpJ1sLWF1vECDGSF/QqFpDOx96wDAs3HvmRDagN5PIGYq6MKs
KrBVHLPz4UwlkmC4/TywYDMezKjdtg9Fr/rXxKOOhpboqLfDDYaV+NF6KfGaxBD5HOVk
SjQcag=="
```

```
>aws kinesis put-records --stream-name "Chapter4KinesisStream"
--records file://put-records-data.json
```

You can use the "NextShardInterator" value in the get-records call:

```
>aws kinesis get-records --shard-iterator "AAAAAAAAAAEz7IL+mZqHRqPAE39P5
TO1WD3gvsK4O/+uWUyRJa4ziaW+elBs3AsBDIX8uOyJLTpxmNQOhbFZ4DHk/jGisT9R4dO
fOclh1Gk1ggNccyxHIGFKuhXO+6m7C2qxFm+AvK+nToUpZKFct2bKcwThfVlIqChGF4d3n
FwpjHFPyU4EPtzLcSWTyB8Ng+YFLNJLCml+iaipyXCxW/+O45Ho6Q4y7eZsWl/
sdZqxl01wO7OfAA=="
```

You can see that the "Data" parameter has Base64, so you need to decode it to see what the actual readable data is. You can use any online Base64 decoder. To limit the records to be fetched, provide the "limit" parameter in request. The maximum number of records returned is 10,000.

■ **Note**   For more parameters in detail, refer to http://docs.amazonaws.cn/cli/latest/reference/kinesis/get-records.html.

---

merge-shards

Based on the historic data, we have shards that are not used frequently or shards that are not used to their full capacity. So we came to a decision to merge two adjacent shards to make use of shards' capacity at their fullest. The merge shard operation can only be processed on ACTIVE streams:

```
>aws kinesis merge-shards --stream-name "Chapter4KinesisStream"
--shard-to-merge "shardId-000000000003" --adjacent-shard-to-merge
"shardId-000000000004"
```

There won't be any output for this request. To check if the merge-shards operation executed successfully or not, invoke the describe-stream command:

```
>aws kinesis describe-stream --stream-name "Chapter4KinesisStream"
--max-items 3 --starting-token "eyJib3RvX3RydW5jYXRlX2Ftb3VudCI6ID
MsICJFeGNsdXNpdmVTdGFydFNoYXJkSWQiOiBudWxsfQ=="
```

The merge-shards command only supports 5 transactions per second per account.

■ **Note**   For more parameters in detail, refer to http://docs.amazonaws.cn/cli/
latest/reference/kinesis/merge-shards.html.

---

split-shard

To increase the shard capacity, you can use the split-shard operation. This will split a single shard into two new shards. To split a shard, you need to provide the shard ID and a new starting hash key. A new hash key can be calculated by averaging the starting and ending hash keys of the current shard, or you can choose any hash key that is between the starting and ending hash keys.

First, choose a shard to split and then get the starting and ending hash keys using the describe-stream command:

```
>aws kinesis describe-stream --stream-name "Chapter4KinesisStream"
--max-items 1
```

```
C:\Users\Dell>aws kinesis describe-stream --stream-name "Chapter4KinesisStream" --max-items 1
{
    "NextToken": "eyJib3RvX3RydW5jYXRlX2Ftb3VudCI6IDEsICJFeGNsdXNpdmVTdGFydFNoYXJkSWQiOiBudWxsfQ==",
    "StreamDescription": {
        "RetentionPeriodHours": 24,
        "StreamName": "Chapter4KinesisStream",
        "Shards": [
            {
                "ShardId": "shardId-000000000000",
                "HashKeyRange": {
                    "EndingHashKey": "680564733841876926926749214863 53642290",
                    "StartingHashKey": "0"
                },
                "SequenceNumberRange": {
                    "StartingSequenceNumber": "49569315168677042265861731873137961544857055494859128834"
                }
            }
        ],
        "StreamARN": "arn:aws:kinesis:us-west-2:███████████:stream/Chapter4KinesisStream",
        "EnhancedMonitoring": [
            {
                "ShardLevelMetrics": []
            }
        ],
        "StreamStatus": "ACTIVE"
    }
}
```

Calculate the new hash key by averaging the starting and ending hash keys:

NewHashKey = (StartingHashKey + EndingHashKey) / 2

NewHashKey = (0 + 680564733841876926926749214863 53642290) / 2

NewHashKey = 340282366920938463374607 43176821145

>aws kinesis split-shard --stream-name "Chapter4KinesisStream" --shard-to-split "shardId-000000000000" --new-starting-hash-key "340282366920938463374 60743176821145"

```
C:\Users\Dell>aws kinesis split-shard --stream-name "Chapter4KinesisStream" --shard-to-split "shardId-000000000000" --new-starting-hash-key "340282366920938463 374607 43176821145"
C:\Users\Dell>
```

To check that the shard has been split properly, invoke the describe-stream command:

>aws kinesis describe-stream --stream-name "Chapter4KinesisStream"

```
C:\Users\Dell>aws kinesis describe-stream --stream-name "Chapter4KinesisStream"
{
    "StreamDescription": {
        "RetentionPeriodHours": 24,
        "StreamName": "Chapter4KinesisStream",
        "Shards": [
            {
                "ShardId": "shardId-000000000000",
                "HashKeyRange": {
                    "EndingHashKey": "68056473384187692692674921486353642290",
                    "StartingHashKey": "0"
                },
                "SequenceNumberRange": {
                    "EndingSequenceNumber": "49569315168688192638460997184707520478173942686284775426",
                    "StartingSequenceNumber": "49569315168677042265861731873137961544857055494859128834"
                }
            },

        . . . . . . . . . . . .

            {
                "ShardId": "shardId-000000000006",
                "HashKeyRange": {
                    "EndingHashKey": "34028236692093846337460743176821144",
                    "StartingHashKey": "0"
                },
                "ParentShardId": "shardId-000000000000",
                "SequenceNumberRange": {
                    "StartingSequenceNumber": "49569316091526480071455978716169055103591729043907543138"
                }
            },
            {
                "ShardId": "shardId-000000000007",
                "HashKeyRange": {
                    "EndingHashKey": "68056473384187692692674921486353642290",
                    "StartingHashKey": "34028236692093846337460743176821145"
                },
                "ParentShardId": "shardId-000000000000",
                "SequenceNumberRange": {
                    "StartingSequenceNumber": "49569316091548780816654509339310590821864377405413523570"
                }
            }
        ],
        "StreamARN": "arn:aws:kinesis:us-west-2:███████████:stream/Chapter4KinesisStream",
        "EnhancedMonitoring": [
            {
                "ShardLevelMetrics": []
            }
        ],
        "StreamStatus": "ACTIVE"
    }
}
```

The split-shard operation only supports 5 transactions per second per account.

■ **Note**   For more parameters in detail, refer to http://docs.amazonaws.cn/cli/ latest/reference/kinesis/split-shard.html.

---

add-tags-to-stream

This command will add or update tags to the Kinesis Stream. Each stream can have up to 10 tags. If an existing tag is requested to add, it will overwrite the existing one:

```
>aws kinesis add-tags-to-stream --stream-name "Chapter4KinesisStream" --tags
Chapter=4,Environment=Production
```

```
C:\Users\Dell>aws kinesis add-tags-to-stream --stream-name "Chapter4KinesisStream" --tags Chapter=4,Environment=Production
C:\Users\Dell>
```

■ **Note**   For more parameters in detail, refer to http://docs.amazonaws.cn/cli/
latest/reference/kinesis/add-tags-to-stream.html.

---

list-tags-for-stream

This command lists the tags of the Kinesis Stream:

>aws kinesis list-tags-for-stream --stream-name "Chapter4KinesisStream"

```
C:\Users\Dell>aws kinesis list-tags-for-stream --stream-name "Chapter4KinesisStream"
{
    "HasMoreTags": false,
    "Tags": [
        {
            "Value": "4",
            "Key": "Chapter"
        },
        {
            "Value": "Production",
            "Key": "Environment"
        }
    ]
}
```

To get the tags after a specific key, use "exclusive-start-tag-key":

>aws kinesis list-tags-for-stream --stream-name "Chapter4KinesisStream"
--exclusive-start-tag-key "Chapter"

```
C:\Users\Dell>aws kinesis list-tags-for-stream --stream-name "Chapter4KinesisStream" --exclusive-start-tag-key "Chapter"
{
    "HasMoreTags": false,
    "Tags": [
        {
            "Value": "Production",
            "Key": "Environment"
        }
    ]
}
```

You can also set the limit of tags returned using the "limit" tag:

>aws kinesis list-tags-for-stream --stream-name "Chapter4KinesisStream"
--limit 1

```
C:\Users\Dell>aws kinesis list-tags-for-stream --stream-name "Chapter4KinesisStream" --limit 1
{
    "HasMoreTags": true,
    "Tags": [
        {
            "Value": "4",
            "Key": "Chapter"
        }
    ]
}
```

■ **Note**   For more parameters in detail, refer to http://docs.amazonaws.cn/cli/ latest/reference/kinesis/list-tags-for-stream.html.

remove-tags-from-stream

This command deletes the tag from the Kinesis Stream:

```
>aws kinesis remove-tags-from-stream --stream-name "Chapter4KinesisStream"
--tag-keys "Environment" "Chapter"
```

```
C:\Users\Dell>aws kinesis remove-tags-from-stream --stream-name "Chapter4KinesisStream" --tag-keys "Environment" "Chapter"
C:\Users\Dell>
```

To check whether the tags are removed or not, use the list-tags-for-stream command:

```
>aws kinesis list-tags-for-stream --stream-name "Chapter4KinesisStream"
```

```
C:\Users\Dell>aws kinesis list-tags-for-stream --stream-name "Chapter4KinesisStream"
{
    "HasMoreTags": false,
    "Tags": []
}
```

■ **Note**   For more parameters in detail, refer to http://docs.amazonaws.cn/cli/ latest/reference/kinesis/remove-tags-from-stream.html.

delete-stream

The delete-stream command deletes the stream along with all its shard and data records. Once the stream has been deleted, you cannot recover it. Only ACTIVE streams can be deleted:

```
>aws kinesis delete-stream --stream-name "Chapter4KinesisStream"
```

```
C:\Users\Dell>aws kinesis delete-stream --stream-name "Chapter4KinesisStream"

C:\Users\Dell>
```

To verify that the stream has been deleted, use the list-streams command:

```
>aws kinesis list-streams
```

```
C:\Users\Dell>aws kinesis list-streams
{
    "StreamNames": []
}
```

The delete-stream operation only supports 5 transactions per second per account.

■ **Note**   For more parameters in detail, refer to `http://docs.amazonaws.cn/cli/latest/reference/kinesis/delete-stream.html`.

Using AWS SDK—Java

In this section, I will explain how to use AWS Java SDK to manage AWS Kinesis.

Create AmazonKinesisClient

To create AmazonKinesisClient, first create the AWSCredentials using any of the credential provider mechanisms. In our case, we will use ProfileCredentialsProvider:

```
AWSCredentials credentials =
    new ProfileCredentialsProvider("sunilgulabani").getCredentials();

AmazonKinesisClient amazonKinesisClient = new AmazonKinesisClient(credentials);
```

This process will load the sunilgulabani profile's access key and secret key via the credentials file.

Create Stream

To create a stream using SDK, invoke the createStream method:

```
private static final String STREAM_NAME = "Chapter4KinesisStream";
private static final Integer SHARD_COUNT = 5;

createStream(STREAM_NAME, SHARD_COUNT);

public void createStream(String streamName, Integer shardCount) {
    // CreateStreamResult response =
    //     amazonKinesisClient.createStream(streamName, shardCount);

    CreateStreamRequest request = new CreateStreamRequest();

    request.setStreamName(streamName);

    request.setShardCount(shardCount);

    CreateStreamResult response = amazonKinesisClient.createStream(request);
}
```

```
{
  "sdkResponseMetadata": {
    "metadata": {
      "AWS_REQUEST_ID": "deb8e257-0d44-2624-8e55-8f86ed5ccf6e"
    }
  },
  "sdkHttpMetadata": {
    "httpHeaders": {
      "Server": "Apache-Coyote/1.1",
      "x-amzn-RequestId": "deb8e257-0d44-2624-8e55-8f86ed5ccf6e",
      "x-amz-id-2": "weZDGaHG53KTLjPkwdRgJEGKAGJK199NPEinTc+oC+r0JSvR5coEmkG0sz7hLT+0ihd12bapuWXs097iqblvbtRfqPCRVxPa",
      "Content-Length": "0",
      "Date": "Mon, 09 Jan 2017 10:53:05 GMT",
      "Content-Type": "application/x-amz-cbor-1.1"
    },
    "httpStatusCode": 200
  }
}
```

Describe Stream

To get details of the stream, invoke the describeStream method:

```
Integer shardListingLimit = null;
String exclusiveStartShardId = null;

describeStream(STREAM_NAME, shardListingLimit, exclusiveStartShardId);

publicDescribeStreamResultdescribeStream(
    String streamName, Integer limit, String exclusiveStartShardId) {
```

```java
// DescribeStreamResult response =
//     amazonKinesisClient.describeStream(streamName);

DescribeStreamRequest request = new DescribeStreamRequest();

request.setStreamName(streamName);

if(limit != null) {
    request.setLimit(limit);
}

if(!StringUtils.isNullOrEmpty(exclusiveStartShardId)) {
    request.setExclusiveStartShardId(exclusiveStartShardId);
}

DescribeStreamResult response =
    amazonKinesisClient.describeStream(request);

return response;
}
```

You can see that we are passing null in shardListingLimit and exclusiveStartShardId parameters to get all shards listed:

```
{
  "streamDescription": {
    "streamName": "Chapter4KinesisStream",
    "streamARN": "arn:aws:kinesis:us-west-2:          :stream/Chapter4KinesisStream",
    "streamStatus": "ACTIVE",
    "shards": [{
        "shardId": "shardId-000000000000",
        "hashKeyRange": {"startingHashKey": "0","endingHashKey": "68056473384187692692674921486353642290"},
        "sequenceNumberRange": {"startingSequenceNumber": "49569351636996464244219563273393190993363905632144877158 6"}
      },{
        "shardId": "shardId-000000000001",
        "hashKeyRange": {"startingHashKey": "68056473384187692692674921486353642291","endingHashKey": "136112946768375385385349842972707284581"},
        "sequenceNumberRange": {"startingSequenceNumber": "495693516370187631873941633570734456191170468295475201 8"}
      },{
        "shardId": "shardId-000000000002",
        "hashKeyRange": {"startingHashKey": "136112946768375385385349842972707284582","endingHashKey": "204169420152563078078024764459060926872"},
        "sequenceNumberRange": {"startingSequenceNumber": "495693516370410639325926939802149813701843530444607324 50"}
      },{
        "shardId": "shardId-000000000003",
        "hashKeyRange": {"startingHashKey": "204169420152563078078024764459060926873","endingHashKey": "272225893536750770770699685945414569163"},
        "sequenceNumberRange": {"startingSequenceNumber": "495693516370633646777912246033565170884570014059667128 82"}
      },{
        "shardId": "shardId-000000000004",
        "hashKeyRange": {"startingHashKey": "272225893536750770770699685945414569164","endingHashKey": "340282366920938463463374607431768211455"},
        "sequenceNumberRange": {"startingSequenceNumber": "495693516370856654229897552264980528067296497674726933 14"}
      }
    ],
    "hasMoreShards": false,
    "retentionPeriodHours": 24,
    "enhancedMonitoring": [{"shardLevelMetrics": []}]
  },
  "sdkResponseMetadata": {
    "metadata": {
      "AWS_REQUEST_ID": "c73b9e8a-8960-c5cc-97d6-f01189785f5c"
    }
  },
  "sdkHttpMetadata": {
    "httpHeaders": {
      "Server": "Apache-Coyote/1.1",
      "x-amzn-RequestId": "c73b9e8a-8960-c5cc-97d6-f01189785f5c",
      "x-amz-id-2": "SNKyIxCLT8aNS+1ZMzCdROlVSOI3MJ5xd7GLraWeEBNICZg+rvhzCjSReQwDhj3LjMePDtoehzGWmDameXUNEYegU6gvR110",
      "Content-Length": "1542",
      "Date": "Mon, 09 Jan 2017 10:56:30 GMT",
      "Content-Type": "application/x-amz-cbor-1.1"
    },
    "httpStatusCode": 200
  }
}
```

To get a paginated shard listing, pass values for limit and exlusiveStartShardId as null for first request:

```
Integer shardListingLimit = 1;
String exclusiveStartShardId = null;

DescribeStreamResultdescribeStreamResult =
    describeStream(STREAM_NAME,
                                shardListingLimit,
                                exclusiveStartShardId);

StreamDescriptionstreamDescription =
    describeStreamResult.getStreamDescription();

List<Shard> shards = streamDescription.getShards();

booleanhasMoreShards = streamDescription.getHasMoreShards();

while(hasMoreShards) {
    exclusiveStartShardId = shards.get(shards.size()-1).getShardId();
    describeStreamResult = describeStream(
                                STREAM_NAME,
                                shardListingLimit,
                                exclusiveStartShardId);

    streamDescription = describeStreamResult.getStreamDescription();

    shards = streamDescription.getShards();

    hasMoreShards = streamDescription.getHasMoreShards();
}
```

```
{
  "streamDescription": {
    "streamName": "Chapter4KinesisStream",
    "streamARN": "arn:aws:kinesis:us-west-2:          :stream/Chapter4KinesisStream",
    "streamStatus": "ACTIVE",
    "shards": [
      {
        "shardId": "shardId-000000000000",
        "hashKeyRange": {
          "startingHashKey": "0",
          "endingHashKey": "680564733841876926926749214863536422290"
        },
        "sequenceNumberRange": {
          "startingSequenceNumber": "49569351636996462442195632733931909933639056321448771586"
        }
      }
    ],
    "hasMoreShards": true,
    "retentionPeriodHours": 24,
    "enhancedMonitoring": [
      {
        "shardLevelMetrics": []
      }
    ]
  },
  "sdkResponseMetadata": {
    "metadata": {
      "AWS_REQUEST_ID": "c2c704cd-a07a-9ab8-922a-6a6da0620028"
    }
  },
  "sdkHttpMetadata": {
    "httpHeaders": {
      "Server": "Apache-Coyote/1.1",
      "x-amzn-RequestId": "c2c704cd-a07a-9ab8-922a-6a6da0620028",
      "x-amz-id-2": "pvxsTUHae11MGRuh7TRDYTpu0fV1vu17P1pGWEvHGKr5Jmqdv9j01GbDpKiXs/Zn4mNB8esutkrHlckZYKFXFinXCwFAoyiY",
      "Content-Length": "499",
      "Date": "Mon, 09 Jan 2017 10:56:31 GMT",
      "Content-Type": "application/x-amz-cbor-1.1"
    },
    "httpStatusCode": 200
  }
}
```

To get to the next page, pass the last shard ID obtained from the previous request:

```
{
  "streamDescription": {
    "streamName": "Chapter4KinesisStream",
    "streamARN": "arn:aws:kinesis:us-west-2:          :stream/Chapter4KinesisStream",
    "streamStatus": "ACTIVE",
    "shards": [
      {
        "shardId": "shardId-000000000001",
        "hashKeyRange": {
          "startingHashKey": "68056473384187692692674921486353642291",
          "endingHashKey": "136112946768375385385349842972707284581"
        },
        "sequenceNumberRange": {
          "startingSequenceNumber": "49569351637018763187394163357073445651911704682954752018"
        }
      }
    ],
    "hasMoreShards": true,
    "retentionPeriodHours": 24,
    "enhancedMonitoring": [
      {
        "shardLevelMetrics": []
      }
    ]
  },
  "sdkResponseMetadata": {
    "metadata": {
      "AWS_REQUEST_ID": "fe95ac3a-4f0f-f340-ae78-c29a4f1769d0"
    }
  },
  "sdkHttpMetadata": {
    "httpHeaders": {
      "Server": "Apache-Coyote/1.1",
      "x-amzn-RequestId": "fe95ac3a-4f0f-f340-ae78-c29a4f1769d0",
      "x-amz-id-2": "nPgiv+BJsfOWzH/7bN9vSvpAI+g7uEsEOBYIM0OBmZ6yGzy+sxU0ORJxFMN0gUC6omYxGQM7gCnn5RtQALuneQUHAlinZ1qF",
      "Content-Length": "538",
      "Date": "Mon, 09 Jan 2017 10:56:31 GMT",
      "Content-Type": "application/x-amz-cbor-1.1"
    },
    "httpStatusCode": 200
  }
}
```

Similarly you can get the result for the next page.

List Stream

To get all streams available under the AWS account, invoke the listStreams method:

```
Integer streamListingLimit = null;

String exclusiveStartStreamName = null;

listStreams(exclusiveStartStreamName, streamListingLimit);

public void listStreams(String exclusiveStartStreamName,
                                         Integer streamListingLimit) {

    // ListStreamsResult response = amazonKinesisClient.listStreams();

    ListStreamsRequest request = new ListStreamsRequest();

    if(!StringUtils.isNullOrEmpty(exclusiveStartStreamName)) {
        request.setExclusiveStartStreamName(exclusiveStartStreamName);
    }
```

```
    if(streamListingLimit != null) {
        request.setLimit(streamListingLimit);
    }

    ListStreamsResult response = amazonKinesisClient.listStreams(request);
}
```

Here we are passing a null value for exclusiveStartStreamName and streamListingLimit to get all streams:

```
{
  "streamNames": [
    "Chapter4KinesisStream",
    "Chapter4KinesisStream1",
    "Chapter4KinesisStream2",
    "Chapter4KinesisStream3",
    "Chapter4KinesisStream4",
    "Chapter4KinesisStream5"
  ],
  "hasMoreStreams": false,
  "sdkResponseMetadata": {
    "metadata": {
      "AWS_REQUEST_ID": "d7475086-6849-30ac-87aa-3e246851aa3c"
    }
  },
  "sdkHttpMetadata": {
    "httpHeaders": {
      "Server": "Apache-Coyote/1.1",
      "x-amzn-RequestId": "d7475086-6849-30ac-87aa-3e246851aa3c",
      "x-amz-id-2": "w4vW51ZhDZUoTVztObLmLLkvg5doG3ByUQ01Vcmy3vUkL96X636x+rr88KSY09cpF873h4onNr21NkkoYNVuL2sf2akOpPzk",
      "Content-Length": "169",
      "Date": "Mon, 09 Jan 2017 10:56:33 GMT",
      "Content-Type": "application/x-amz-cbor-1.1"
    },
    "httpStatusCode": 200
  }
}
```

To get a paginated stream listing, pass the streamListingLimit parameter to get the number of streams in a single request and exclusiveStartStreamName as null for the first request. For subsequent requests, pass the last stream name returned by the previous request:

```
{
  "streamNames": [
    "Chapter4KinesisStream1"
  ],
  "hasMoreStreams": true,
  "sdkResponseMetadata": {
    "metadata": {
      "AWS_REQUEST_ID": "f42d1493-89da-0ac3-a4c0-7a3189c29053"
    }
  },
  "sdkHttpMetadata": {
    "httpHeaders": {
      "Server": "Apache-Coyote/1.1",
      "x-amzn-RequestId": "f42d1493-89da-0ac3-a4c0-7a3189c29053",
      "x-amz-id-2": "8gf2DpykWYGf0IZ1jwhKzpIAL5gt8Bx+zc9tK77ROEV9HAVtZ1F0Q5wxnzfUCmTAi+RXFXqmdHf3Uw1t8wgmFmI9wyh8gma1",
      "Content-Length": "55",
      "Date": "Mon, 09 Jan 2017 10:56:33 GMT",
      "Content-Type": "application/x-amz-cbor-1.1"
    },
    "httpStatusCode": 200
  }
}
```

Similarly, you can get the result for the next page.

Increase Stream Retention Period

The stream retention period will retain the message to read in Kinesis. This period can be increased using the increaseStreamRetentionPeriod method:

```
increaseStreamRetentionPeriod(STREAM_NAME, 72);

public void increaseStreamRetentionPeriod(String streamName,
                                          Integer retentionPeriodHours) {

    IncreaseStreamRetentionPeriodRequest request =
        new IncreaseStreamRetentionPeriodRequest();

    request.setStreamName(streamName);

    request.setRetentionPeriodHours(retentionPeriodHours);

    IncreaseStreamRetentionPeriodResult response =
        amazonKinesisClient.increaseStreamRetentionPeriod(request);
}
```

```
{
  "sdkResponseMetadata": {
    "metadata": {
      "AWS_REQUEST_ID": "f390877f-8ea5-24d8-a37d-e9dd8ebdbe48"
    },
  },
  "sdkHttpMetadata": {
    "httpHeaders": {
      "Server": "Apache-Coyote/1.1",
      "x-amzn-RequestId": "f390877f-8ea5-24d8-a37d-e9dd8ebdbe48",
      "x-amz-id-2": "3L9W17161vG1Un2iJXxFe120SNe9/1/9dtaRJMuRICXRo7aamt6XGg29pVvxdcRKYUuqI78QHi5/RWY8yb9jjJCEFCbOqF/d",
      "Content-Length": "0",
      "Date": "Mon, 09 Jan 2017 10:56:34 GMT",
      "Content-Type": "application/x-amz-cbor-1.1"
    },
    "httpStatusCode": 200
  }
}
```

To verify that the stream retention period is being updated, use the describe stream operation:

```
describeStream(STREAM_NAME, 1, null);
```

```
{
  "streamDescription": {
    "streamName": "Chapter4KinesisStream",
    "streamARN": "arn:aws:kinesis:us-west-2:             :stream/Chapter4KinesisStream",
    "streamStatus": "ACTIVE",
    "shards": [
      {
        "shardId": "shardId-000000000000",
        "hashKeyRange": {
          "startingHashKey": "0",
          "endingHashKey": "680564733841876926926749214863536422290"
        },
        "sequenceNumberRange": {
          "startingSequenceNumber": "49569351636996462442195632733931909933639056321448771586"
        }
      }
    ],
    "hasMoreShards": true,
    "retentionPeriodHours": 72,
    "enhancedMonitoring": [
      {
        "shardLevelMetrics": []
      }
    ]
  },
  "sdkResponseMetadata": {
    "metadata": {
      "AWS_REQUEST_ID": "cf1afe3a-5c63-08d5-9ff7-90fcc17cbe80"
    }
  },
  "sdkHttpMetadata": {
    "httpHeaders": {
      "Server": "Apache-Coyote/1.1",
      "x-amzn-RequestId": "cf1afe3a-5c63-08d5-9ff7-90fcc17cbe80",
      "x-amz-id-2": "1OUHMQ51mEv8ydUytNIsScAk+pQn58ZajMpyOM1Fz81Tulyp49gWQuxMI1PyMLDvOykDQfoXObqod2TiJCSq7sf0tiYpZwlt",
      "Content-Length": "499",
      "Date": "Mon, 09 Jan 2017 10:57:10 GMT",
      "Content-Type": "application/x-amz-cbor-1.1"
    },
    "httpStatusCode": 200
  }
}
```

Decrease Stream Retention Period

The stream retention period will retain the message to read in Kinesis. This period can be decreased using the decreaseStreamRetentionPeriod method:

```
decreaseStreamRetentionPeriod(STREAM_NAME, 24);

public void decreaseStreamRetentionPeriod(String streamName,
                                          Integer retentionPeriodHours) {

    DecreaseStreamRetentionPeriodRequest request =
        new DecreaseStreamRetentionPeriodRequest();

    request.setStreamName(streamName);

    request.setRetentionPeriodHours(retentionPeriodHours);

    DecreaseStreamRetentionPeriodResult response =
        amazonKinesisClient.decreaseStreamRetentionPeriod(request);
}
```

```
{
  "sdkResponseMetadata": {
    "metadata": {
      "AWS_REQUEST_ID": "fd6187da-ac29-f2a8-ad8c-e91d313644fd"
    }
  },
  "sdkHttpMetadata": {
    "httpHeaders": {
      "Server": "Apache-Coyote/1.1",
      "x-amzn-RequestId": "fd6187da-ac29-f2a8-ad8c-e91d313644fd",
      "x-amz-id-2": "UXxszXomzYoH12VtAIlSqc50LlWztefKSIE2s2h3Nz2y6pmB/obR+q5EF49OETZDqCfQlc6n/P3kHY8kZyJWWq4uRuI/Rh4+",
      "Content-Length": "0",
      "Date": "Mon, 09 Jan 2017 10:57:11 GMT",
      "Content-Type": "application/x-amz-cbor-1.1"
    },
    "httpStatusCode": 200
  }
}
```

To verify that the stream retention period is being updated, use the describe stream operation:

```
describeStream(STREAM_NAME, 1, null);
```

```
{
  "streamDescription": {
    "streamName": "Chapter4KinesisStream",
    "streamARN": "arn:aws:kinesis:us-west-2:          :stream/Chapter4KinesisStream",
    "streamStatus": "ACTIVE",
    "shards": [
      {
        "shardId": "shardId-000000000000",
        "hashKeyRange": {
          "startingHashKey": "0",
          "endingHashKey": "68056473384187692692674921486353642290"
        },
        "sequenceNumberRange": {
          "startingSequenceNumber": "49569351636996462442195632733931909933639056321448771586"
        }
      }
    ],
    "hasMoreShards": true,
    "retentionPeriodHours": 24,
    "enhancedMonitoring": [
      {
        "shardLevelMetrics": []
      }
    ]
  },
  "sdkResponseMetadata": {
    "metadata": {
      "AWS_REQUEST_ID": "ca3bb1f1-53fb-0806-9ad6-df198c3c265f"
    }
  },
  "sdkHttpMetadata": {
    "httpHeaders": {
      "Server": "Apache-Coyote/1.1",
      "x-amzn-RequestId": "ca3bb1f1-53fb-0806-9ad6-df198c3c265f",
      "x-amz-id-2": "yAFwFjpwlOVGIiFRISlH0EGhbpugRBHNCkE9s2WK3Bvj2ncjeSFkOki2kxV35DuuloEBZ+A+tQBh+u0C3J7nS7K2Z/Ggqqyr",
      "Content-Length": "499",
      "Date": "Mon, 09 Jan 2017 10:57:44 GMT",
      "Content-Type": "application/x-amz-cbor-1.1"
    },
    "httpStatusCode": 200
  }
}
```

Enable Enhanced Monitoring

Enable enhanced monitoring will enable shard level metrics. To enable enhanced monitoring, invoke the enableEnhancedMonitoring method:

```
enableEnhancedMonitoring(STREAM_NAME);
```

```java
public void enableEnhancedMonitoring(String streamName) {
    EnableEnhancedMonitoringRequest request =
        new EnableEnhancedMonitoringRequest();

    request.setStreamName(streamName);

    request.setShardLevelMetrics(getShardLevelMetrics());

    EnableEnhancedMonitoringResult response =
        amazonKinesisClient.enableEnhancedMonitoring(request);
}
```

```json
{
    "streamName": "Chapter4KinesisStream",
    "currentShardLevelMetrics": [],
    "desiredShardLevelMetrics": [
      "IncomingBytes",
      "OutgoingRecords",
      "IteratorAgeMilliseconds",
      "IncomingRecords",
      "ReadProvisionedThroughputExceeded",
      "WriteProvisionedThroughputExceeded",
      "OutgoingBytes"
    ],
    "sdkResponseMetadata": {
      "metadata": {
        "AWS_REQUEST_ID": "c4fb93e5-1756-09f3-9416-fd0cc89127aa"
      }
    },
    "sdkHttpMetadata": {
      "httpHeaders": {
        "Server": "Apache-Coyote/1.1",
        "x-amzn-RequestId": "c4fb93e5-1756-09f3-9416-fd0cc89127aa",
        "x-amz-id-2": "ip+h/UQnIJb+xaSEvUbBX0f1gX0PB1X2QNofpFByUM6ES2R3AuXADgRPY0iPVDuHY3kW9D+G6Ig9QvNHwW3qpxjDwPZSYmic",
        "Content-Length": "246",
        "Date": "Mon, 09 Jan 2017 10:57:44 GMT",
        "Content-Type": "application/x-amz-cbor-1.1"
      },
      "httpStatusCode": 200
    }
}
```

Disable Enhanced Monitoring

Disable enhanced monitoring will disable shard level metrics. To disable enhanced monitoring, invoke disableEnhancedMonitoring method:

```
disableEnhancedMonitoring(STREAM_NAME);
```

```java
public void disableEnhancedMonitoring(String streamName) {
    DisableEnhancedMonitoringRequest request =
        new DisableEnhancedMonitoringRequest();
```

```
        request.setStreamName(streamName);

        request.setShardLevelMetrics(getShardLevelMetrics());

        DisableEnhancedMonitoringResult response =
            amazonKinesisClient.disableEnhancedMonitoring(request);
}
```

```
{
  "streamName": "Chapter4KinesisStream",
  "currentShardLevelMetrics": [
    "IncomingBytes",
    "OutgoingRecords",
    "IteratorAgeMilliseconds",
    "IncomingRecords",
    "ReadProvisionedThroughputExceeded",
    "WriteProvisionedThroughputExceeded",
    "OutgoingBytes"
  ],
  "desiredShardLevelMetrics": [],
  "sdkResponseMetadata": {
    "metadata": {
      "AWS_REQUEST_ID": "f1ca902f-1288-aa44-a127-ff20272e4052"
    }
  },
  "sdkHttpMetadata": {
    "httpHeaders": {
      "Server": "Apache-Coyote/1.1",
      "x-amzn-RequestId": "f1ca902f-1288-aa44-a127-ff20272e4052",
      "x-amz-id-2": "3zSvQ83D+oW3vU1GfunNAp3U8+9WAMYOaxPw7WmSs6KIhKQV4i6TBbYDUeQNDTIef4wHdUkJgbaXAHm2+3QYLaavgcqRZrhQ",
      "Content-Length": "246",
      "Date": "Mon, 09 Jan 2017 10:58:23 GMT",
      "Content-Type": "application/x-amz-cbor-1.1"
    },
    "httpStatusCode": 200
  }
}
```

Put Record

To add data records to the stream, invoke the putRecord method:

```
String explicitHashKey = null;
String partitionKey = "123";
String data = "Hello World Kinesis!!!";

putRecord(STREAM_NAME, partitionKey, data.getBytes(), explicitHashKey);

public void putRecord(String streamName, String partitionKey,
                                byte[] data, String explicitHashKey) {
    // PutRecordResult response = amazonKinesisClient.putRecord(streamName,
    //                                          ByteBuffer.wrap(data),
    //                                          partitionKey);

    PutRecordRequest request = new PutRecordRequest();

    request.setStreamName(streamName);
```

```
request.setPartitionKey(partitionKey);
request.setData(ByteBuffer.wrap(data));

if(!StringUtils.isNullOrEmpty(explicitHashKey)) {
    request.setExplicitHashKey(explicitHashKey);
}

PutRecordResult response = amazonKinesisClient.putRecord(request);
}
```

Here we are passing values for partitionKey and data, but, for now, the exclusiveHashKey parameter value is null. The partition key is used to identify to which shard data record needs to be added and the exclusiveHashKey parameter signifies to which shard we want to explicitly send data records:

```
{
    "shardId": "shardId-000000000000",
    "sequenceNumber": "49569351636996464244219563278893199009700663488268153651 4",
    "sdkResponseMetadata": {
        "metadata": {
            "AWS_REQUEST_ID": "cb2da314-1f51-c8d4-9bc0-cc3ba8c09ce5"
        }
    },
    "sdkHttpMetadata": {
        "httpHeaders": {
            "Server": "Apache-Coyote/1.1",
            "x-amzn-RequestId": "cb2da314-1f51-c8d4-9bc0-cc3ba8c09ce5",
            "x-amz-id-2": "DV/H/0669r3uxXzTaZncs7aQeD4Vad69DtmpYkZyDyoNaGNjeV1U0iVU3fDMflBEjpITdzLVru/v1oMhDWS1BxHcr1r1wwqT",
            "Content-Length": "104",
            "Date": "Mon, 09 Jan 2017 10:58:55 GMT",
            "Content-Type": "application/x-amz-cbor-1.1"
        },
        "httpStatusCode": 200
    }
}
```

To send data records to an explicit shard, pass the exclusiveHashKey parameter:

```
explicitHashKey = "272225893536750770770699685945414569165";

putRecord(STREAM_NAME, partitionKey, data.getBytes(), explicitHashKey);
```

```
{
    "shardId": "shardId-000000000004",
    "sequenceNumber": "49569351637085665422989755281499341895916843026599641154",
    "sdkResponseMetadata": {
        "metadata": {
            "AWS_REQUEST_ID": "c16c17b5-6955-17f1-9181-7885dec443c0"
        }
    },
    "sdkHttpMetadata": {
        "httpHeaders": {
            "Server": "Apache-Coyote/1.1",
            "x-amzn-RequestId": "c16c17b5-6955-17f1-9181-7885dec443c0",
            "x-amz-id-2": "Jpya3G7J9RXFJQWr19kzwJtk+9P/R7I+eHQWLivMuuyfX7axwbzgOYZJkuSfZJA7E3RmDnDxTx+5MvdZwAvP+sVbzK4p1Zho",
            "Content-Length": "104",
            "Date": "Mon, 09 Jan 2017 10:58:55 GMT",
            "Content-Type": "application/x-amz-cbor-1.1"
        },
        "httpStatusCode": 200
    }
}
```

Put Records

To send multiple data records to a stream in a single request, invoke the putRecords method:

```
List<PutRecordsRequestEntry> records = new ArrayList<>();
PutRecordsRequestEntry record = null;
explicitHashKey = null;

for(inti=0;i<5;i++) {
    record = createPutRecordsRequestEntry(
                                String.valueOf(i),
                                data + "-" + i,
                                explicitHashKey);

    records.add(record);
}

explicitHashKey = "272225893536750770770699685945414569165";

record = createPutRecordsRequestEntry(
                                String.valueOf(5),
                                data + "-" + 5,
                                explicitHashKey);

records.add(record);

putRecords(STREAM_NAME, records);

public void putRecords(String streamName,
                            List<PutRecordsRequestEntry> records) {
    PutRecordsRequest request = new PutRecordsRequest();

    request.setStreamName(streamName);

    request.setRecords(records);

    PutRecordsResult response = amazonKinesisClient.putRecords(request);
}
```

Here you can see that first we created multiple PutRecordsRequestEntry instances that have partition key, data, and exclusive hash key (optional). We then passed the list of PutRecordsRequestEntry to the putRecords method;

```
{
  "failedRecordCount": 0,
  "records": [
    {
      "sequenceNumber": "49569351637085665422989755281500550821736457655774347330",
      "shardId": "shardId-000000000004"
    },
    {
      "sequenceNumber": "49569351637063364677791224684070449435027742581919318066",
      "shardId": "shardId-000000000003"
    },
    {
      "sequenceNumber": "49569351637063364677791224684071658360847357211094024242",
      "shardId": "shardId-000000000003"
    },
    {
      "sequenceNumber": "49569351637085665422989755281501759747556072284949053506",
      "shardId": "shardId-000000000004"
    },
    {
      "sequenceNumber": "49569351637063364677791224684072867286666971840268730418",
      "shardId": "shardId-000000000003"
    },
    {
      "sequenceNumber": "49569351637085665422989755281502968673375686914123759682",
      "shardId": "shardId-000000000004"
    }
  ],
  "sdkResponseMetadata": {
    "metadata": {
      "AWS_REQUEST_ID": "e62cdc4d-533a-2dc6-b6c1-b37de4ab79f7"
    }
  },
  "sdkHttpMetadata": {
    "httpHeaders": {
      "Server": "Apache-Coyote/1.1",
      "x-amzn-RequestId": "e62cdc4d-533a-2dc6-b6c1-b37de4ab79f7",
      "x-amz-id-2": "FjZyOO+uiFA/zIRR4pmBxekb3BQ0Ev1Dx1tQuWezoJekweXAbF/14cHYN/h08Xo871qebPuwRhAOiPrLHpW4vVNyZZ+UT+QE",
      "Content-Length": "655",
      "Date": "Mon, 09 Jan 2017 10:58:55 GMT",
      "Content-Type": "application/x-amz-cbor-1.1"
    },
    "httpStatusCode": 200
  }
}
```

In response, we get failed and successful added data records individually.

Get Records

To read data records from Kinesis Streams, invoke the getRecords method. You need the shard iterator to read a data record from individual shards:

```
getRecords(STREAM_NAME);

public void getRecords(String streamName)
    throws UnsupportedEncodingException {

    GetRecordsRequest request = new GetRecordsRequest();

    request.setLimit(100);

    List<String>shardIterators = getShardIterators(
                                        streamName,
                                        ShardIteratorType.TRIM_HORIZON);
```

```java
    List<GetRecordsResult> response = new ArrayList<GetRecordsResult>();

    shardIterators.forEach(shardIterator -> {
        request.setShardIterator(shardIterator);

        GetRecordsResultgetRecordsResult =
            amazonKinesisClient.getRecords(request);

        response.add(getRecordsResult);
    });

    System.out.println("-------------");

    for(GetRecordsResult result: response) {
        for(Record record: result.getRecords()) {
            String data = new String(record.getData().array(), "UTF-8");

            System.out.println(data);
        }
    }
}

private List<String> getShardIterators(String streamName,
                                ShardIteratorTypeshardIteratorType) {
    List<String> shardIteratorList = new ArrayList<>();

    List<Shard>shardList = getShards(streamName);

    shardList.forEach(shard -> {
        GetShardIteratorResultshardIteratorResult =
            getShardIteratorResult(streamName, shardIteratorType, shard);

        shardIteratorList.add(shardIteratorResult.getShardIterator());
    });

    return shardIteratorList;
}

private GetShardIteratorResultgetShardIteratorResult(
                                String streamName,
                                ShardIteratorTypeshardIteratorType,
                                Shard shard) {

    // return amazonKinesisClient.getShardIterator(streamName,
    //              shard.getShardId(), shardIteratorType.toString());
```

```java
GetShardIteratorRequestshardIteratorRequest =
    new GetShardIteratorRequest();

shardIteratorRequest.setShardId(shard.getShardId());

shardIteratorRequest.setShardIteratorType(shardIteratorType);

shardIteratorRequest.setStreamName(streamName);

return amazonKinesisClient.getShardIterator(shardIteratorRequest);
}

public List<Shard> getShards(String streamName) {
    DescribeStreamResultdescribeStreamResult =
        describeStream(streamName, null, null);

    return describeStreamResult.getStreamDescription().getShards();
}
```

```
{
  "streamDescription": {
    "streamName": "Chapter4KinesisStream",
    "streamARN": "arn:aws:kinesis:us-west-2:          :stream/Chapter4KinesisStream",
    "streamStatus": "ACTIVE",
    "shards": [{
        "shardId": "shardId-000000000000",
        "hashKeyRange": {"startingHashKey": "0","endingHashKey": "68056473384187692692674921486353642290"},
        "sequenceNumberRange": {"startingSequenceNumber": "49569351636996464244219563273393190993363905632144877 1586"}
      },{
        "shardId": "shardId-000000000001",
        "hashKeyRange": {"startingHashKey": "68056473384187692692674921486353642291","endingHashKey": "136112946768375385385349842972707284581"},
        "sequenceNumberRange": {"startingSequenceNumber": "49569351637018763187394163557073445619117046829547 82018"}
      },{
        "shardId": "shardId-000000000002",
        "hashKeyRange": {"startingHashKey": "136112946768375385385349842972707284582","endingHashKey": "204169420182563078078024764459060926872"},
        "sequenceNumberRange": {"startingSequenceNumber": "49569351637041063932592693980214981370184353044460 732450"}
      },{
        "shardId": "shardId-000000000003",
        "hashKeyRange": {"startingHashKey": "204169420182563078078024764459060926873","endingHashKey": "272225893536750770770699685945414569163"},
        "sequenceNumberRange": {"startingSequenceNumber": "49569351637063364677791224603356517088457001405966 712882"}
      },{
        "shardId": "shardId-000000000004",
        "hashKeyRange": {"startingHashKey": "272225893536750770770699685945414569164","endingHashKey": "340282366920938463463374607431768211455"},
        "sequenceNumberRange": {"startingSequenceNumber": "49569351637085665422989755226498052806729649767472 693314"}
      }
    ],
    "hasMoreShards": false,
    "retentionPeriodHours": 24,
    "enhancedMonitoring": [{"shardLevelMetrics": []}]
  },
  "sdkResponseMetadata": {
    "metadata": {
      "AWS_REQUEST_ID": "fd3dc731-6853-364a-add0-a801dfc2627b"
    }
  },
  "sdkHttpMetadata": {
    "httpHeaders": {
      "Server": "Apache-Coyote/1.1",
      "x-amzn-RequestId": "fd3dc731-6853-364a-add0-a801dfc2627b",
      "x-amz-id-2": "eKJMTBYNM2gvbdqQn2GdvR7PMRmU5ugN42kJAEPVNi+fIRrekazdoNHWwm58H8WcrHt4erNBi6310uXbJY1sVPOLZuKOQcq",
      "Content-Length": "1542",
      "Date": "Mon, 09 Jan 2017 10:58:56 GMT",
      "Content-Type": "application/x-amz-cbor-1.1"
    },
    "httpStatusCode": 200
  }
}
```

Once shard IDs have been collected, get the shard iterator for each shard ID.

```
{
  "shardIterator":
"AAAAAAAAAAFaPwcyv5k3rxrFln3Irn2YrLuCZamtPllkELeyEWz5GqJiGJ1Lv0f5Xmdg8KtQLWwAhD1kGf8v9YoYPWrUbrfyn/JX4/1XVDHUAb7R9BNVtmlpsst3fFip26YIKA+R+v1EVQTaB38KM
85h0E+Bud7h2w/GU7EJyk6+vrz889BpEjhU5u3qNo8kWnSH1F72Op05aQpvHQyitLVUH1fOduIEu9R4QG68wDhdx7pAiUoNiQ\u003d\u003d",
  "sdkResponseMetadata": {
    "metadata": {
      "AWS_REQUEST_ID": "e34a2938-0d54-611d-b3a7-5744e5858156"
    }
  },
  "sdkHttpMetadata": {
    "httpHeaders": {
      "Server": "Apache-Coyote/1.1",
      "x-amzn-RequestId": "e34a2938-0d54-611d-b3a7-5744e5858156",
      "x-amz-id-2": "s+Ld3DaphDILziWyQcjMpUGUxpGp3E7seTw4H9Hnztd/L0e2FM49e57HscVufFyfdSFoAqL7DmccCt6+JJV0iBQlqnuTXv3H",
      "Content-Length": "266",
      "Date": "Mon, 09 Jan 2017 12:04:11 GMT",
      "Content-Type": "application/x-amz-cbor-1.1"
    },
    "httpStatusCode": 200
  }
}
```

Using the shard iterator, invoke the getRecords method. For subsequent get records request from the same shard, use the "nextShardIterator" parameter value received in response:

```
{
  "records": [
    {
      "sequenceNumber": "49569351636996462442195632788931990097006634882681536514",
      "approximateArrivalTimestamp": "Jan 9, 2017 4:28:55 PM",
      "data": {
        "hb": [72,101,108,108,111,32,87,111,114,108,100,32,75,105,110,101,115,105,115,33,33,33],
        "offset": 0,
        "isReadOnly": false,
        "bigEndian": true,
        "nativeByteOrder": false,
        "mark": -1,
        "position": 0,
        "limit": 22,
        "capacity": 22,
        "address": 0
      },
      "partitionKey": "123"
    }
  ],
  "nextShardIterator":
"AAAAAAAAAAFSRBC11q/L5WPn2B1y2/p+zHuv5iCNorNFgBMxldg+VlsI1p6/odZoycBAO2drFFSZc4+KnVM/TS+xL7yUd1mM17HucatW4HGWDKdvUXtpn/wrp72OqYUbXKyO9LZyMvAImBWss
Q5U2nBykHXRSLU13qX00/sdWvRjLtnzDOmpvVotXfDncfxIe4u8DJyxAfhwiylW0JmThc41e0WOxry/dFpbh9HYcqoUmW+pOwMbtw\u003d\u003d",
  "millisBehindLatest": 0,
  "sdkResponseMetadata": {
    "metadata": {
      "AWS_REQUEST_ID": "eb575343-897f-4294-bbba-3c703eee16a5"
    }
  },
  "sdkHttpMetadata": {
    "httpHeaders": {
      "Server": "Apache-Coyote/1.1",
      "x-amzn-RequestId": "eb575343-897f-4294-bbba-3c703eee16a5",
      "x-amz-id-2": "5o3SKerpcx3J3MQJKvukNJcQlhQgW7wXPnMUQGoAA1XH17VILRZRxtmTPR4UhdA8891iAYIuDCKVKleoCwNCpdTyER4hIH87",
      "Content-Length": "459",
      "Date": "Mon, 09 Jan 2017 10:58:58 GMT",
      "Content-Type": "application/x-amz-cbor-1.1"
    },
    "httpStatusCode": 200
  }
}
```

Merge Shards

When a Kinesis Stream's shard is not effectively being used and you can merge two adjacent shards into a single shard, invoke the mergeShards method:

```
List<Shard>shardList = getShards(STREAM_NAME);
mergeShards(
    STREAM_NAME,
    shardList.get(3).getShardId(),
    shardList.get(4).getShardId());
```

```java
public void mergeShards(String streamName,
                                String shardIdToMerger,
                                String adjacentShardIdToMerge) {

    // MergeShardsResult response = amazonKinesisClient.mergeShards(
    //                                 streamName,
    //                                 shardIdToMerger,
    //                                 adjacentShardIdToMerge);

    MergeShardsRequest request = new MergeShardsRequest();

    request.setStreamName(streamName);

    request.setShardToMerge(shardIdToMerger);

    request.setAdjacentShardToMerge(adjacentShardIdToMerge);

    MergeShardsResult response = amazonKinesisClient.mergeShards(request);
}
```

Here we are merging "shardId-000000000003" and "shardId-000000000004" into a single shard. To merge the shards first, you need the shard ID that can be obtained using describe stream:

```
{
  "streamDescription": {
    "streamName": "Chapter4KinesisStream",
    "streamARN": "arn:aws:kinesis:us-west-2:          :stream/Chapter4KinesisStream",
    "streamStatus": "ACTIVE",
    "shards": [{
        "shardId": "shardId-000000000000",
        "hashKeyRange": {"startingHashKey": "0","endingHashKey": "68056473384187692692674921486353642290"},
        "sequenceNumberRange": {"startingSequenceNumber": "49569351636996464244219563273393190993639056321448771586"}
      }, {
        "shardId": "shardId-000000000001",
        "hashKeyRange": {"startingHashKey": "68056473384187692692674921486353642291","endingHashKey": "136112946768375385385349842972707284581"},
        "sequenceNumberRange": {"startingSequenceNumber": "49569351637018763187394163357073445651911704682954752018"}
      }, {
        "shardId": "shardId-000000000002",
        "hashKeyRange": {"startingHashKey": "136112946768375385385349842972707284582","endingHashKey": "204169420152563078078024764459060926872"},
        "sequenceNumberRange": {"startingSequenceNumber": "49569351637041063932592693980214981370184353044460732450"}
      }, {
        "shardId": "shardId-000000000003",
        "hashKeyRange": {"startingHashKey": "204169420152563078078024764459060926873","endingHashKey": "272225893536750770770699685945414569163"},
        "sequenceNumberRange": {"startingSequenceNumber": "49569351637063366677791224603356517088457001405966712882"}
      }, {
        "shardId": "shardId-000000000004",
        "hashKeyRange": {"startingHashKey": "272225893536750770770699685945414569164","endingHashKey": "340282366920938463463374607431768211455"},
        "sequenceNumberRange": {"startingSequenceNumber": "49569351637085665422987552264980528067296497674472693314"}
      }
    ],
    "hasMoreShards": false,
    "retentionPeriodHours": 24,
    "enhancedMonitoring": [{"shardLevelMetrics": []}]
  },
  "sdkResponseMetadata": {
    "metadata": {
      "AWS_REQUEST_ID": "ea1f2c18-f4ac-7139-baf2-432c433d2508"
    }
  },
  "sdkHttpMetadata": {
    "httpHeaders": {
      "Server": "Apache-Coyote/1.1",
      "x-amzn-RequestId": "ea1f2c18-f4ac-7139-baf2-432c433d2508",
      "x-amz-id-2": "U/GG6Nm2kedxoENze8zrxfCs4zxIhcjEKn3QZ8oekBtDE37AveEuTWwCEm1SmVVD7VmdIQ+a3Iq/JNeC13i5pMJzHXX3N7Cq",
      "Content-Length": "1542",
      "Date": "Mon, 09 Jan 2017 10:59:00 GMT",
      "Content-Type": "application/x-amz-cbor-1.1"
    },
    "httpStatusCode": 200
  }
}
```

Once shard IDs are obtained, invoke the mergeShards operation by setting the shard to merge and the adjacent shard to merge:

```
{
  "sdkResponseMetadata": {
    "metadata": {
      "AWS_REQUEST_ID": "cd121a8a-2572-82c6-9dff-75bf92e3d6f7"
    }
  },
  "sdkHttpMetadata": {
    "httpHeaders": {
      "Server": "Apache-Coyote/1.1",
      "x-amzn-RequestId": "cd121a8a-2572-82c6-9dff-75bf92e3d6f7",
      "x-amz-id-2": "h5DlnHLguP3WTiHQjy17GAqQL6xSYm9B3zfwz1J0S01WvGOnjfcifkXR6jb75YVhwLnH9nRYMfP/R7OKNZ+KzvwvGYXvkp71",
      "Content-Length": "0",
      "Date": "Mon, 09 Jan 2017 10:59:00 GMT",
      "Content-Type": "application/x-amz-cbor-1.1"
    },
    "httpStatusCode": 200
  }
}
```

To verify that the mergeShards operation is being carried out, invoke describe stream:

```
describeStream(STREAM_NAME, null, null);
```

```
{
  "streamDescription": {
    "streamName": "Chapter4KinesisStream",
    "streamARN": "arn:aws:kinesis:us-west-2:          :stream/Chapter4KinesisStream",
    "streamStatus": "ACTIVE",
    "shards": [{
        "shardId": "shardId-000000000000",
        "hashKeyRange": {"startingHashKey": "0","endingHashKey": "68056473384187692692674921486383642290"},
        "sequenceNumberRange": {"startingSequenceNumber": "49569351636996462442195632733931909933639056321448771586"}
      },{
        "shardId": "shardId-000000000001",
        "hashKeyRange": {"startingHashKey": "68056473384187692692674921486353642291","endingHashKey": "136112946768375385385349842972707284581"},
        "sequenceNumberRange": {"startingSequenceNumber": "49569351637018763187394163857073445651911704682954752018"}
      },{
        "shardId": "shardId-000000000002",
        "hashKeyRange": {"startingHashKey": "136112946768375385385349842972707284582","endingHashKey": "204169420162563078078024764459060926872"},
        "sequenceNumberRange": {"startingSequenceNumber": "49569351637041063932592693980214981370184353044460732450"}
      },{
        "shardId": "shardId-000000000003",
        "hashKeyRange": {"startingHashKey": "204169420162563078078024764459060926873","endingHashKey": "272225893536750770770699685945414569163"},
        "sequenceNumberRange": {"startingSequenceNumber": "49569351637063364677791224603385651708845700140596671282","endingSequenceNumber":
        "49569351637074515050390489914926076021773737277104596802"}
      },{
        "shardId": "shardId-000000000004",
        "hashKeyRange": {"startingHashKey": "272225893536750770770699685945414569164","endingHashKey": "340282366920938463463374607431768211455"},
        "sequenceNumberRange": {"startingSequenceNumber": "49569351637085665422985755226498052806729649767472693314","endingSequenceNumber":
        "49569351637096815795589020538067611740046386538610567234"}
      },{
        "shardId": "shardId-000000000005",
        "parentShardId": "shardId-000000000003",
        "adjacentParentShardId": "shardId-000000000004",
        "hashKeyRange": {"startingHashKey": "204169420162563078078024764459060926873","endingHashKey": "340282366920938463463374607431768211455"},
        "sequenceNumberRange": {"startingSequenceNumber": "49569351774123744667960434431285041592153857610001416274"}
      }
    ],
    "hasMoreShards": false,
    "retentionPeriodHours": 24,
    "enhancedMonitoring": [{"shardLevelMetrics": []}]
  },
  "sdkResponseMetadata": {"metadata": {"AWS_REQUEST_ID": "e76abd9c-9fbf-98f7-b787-d2f837df8087"}
  },
  "sdkHttpMetadata": {
    "httpHeaders": {
      "Server": "Apache-Coyote/1.1",
      "x-amzn-RequestId": "e76abd9c-9fbf-98f7-b787-d2f837df8087",
      "x-amz-id-2": "rxHNG6xIyGf91kpgZG+qiTiX2f+0bNWGLB2HhgjguScHhSD6w3GVnTkI6ZD0C/158rKLiOdP5zdXRPE1svq305dUQRPqSNj3",
      "Content-Length": "2039",
      "Date": "Mon, 09 Jan 2017 10:59:47 GMT",
      "Content-Type": "application/x-amz-cbor-1.1"
    },
    "httpStatusCode": 200
  }
}
```

In response to describe stream, you can see that the new shard ID "shardId-000000000005" has been created.

Split Shard

A split shard will split a single shard into two shards. The decision to split a shard should be made when there is heavy traffic on a single shard and it can be divided into different shards. This will make it faster for consumer applications to read data records:

```
List<Shard>shardList = getShards(STREAM_NAME);

splitShard(STREAM_NAME, shardList.get(0));

public void splitShard(String streamName, Shard shard) {
    SplitShardRequest request = new SplitShardRequest();

    request.setStreamName(streamName);

    request.setShardToSplit(shard.getShardId());

    String startHashKey = shard.getHashKeyRange().getStartingHashKey();

    String endHashKey = shard.getHashKeyRange().getEndingHashKey();

    BigIntegertempHashKey =
        new BigInteger(startHashKey).add(new BigInteger(endHashKey));

    String childHashKey =
        tempHashKey.divide(new BigInteger("2")).toString();

    request.setNewStartingHashKey(childHashKey);

    SplitShardResult response = amazonKinesisClient.splitShard(request);
}
```

Here we have calculated the average of the starting and ending hash keys of the shard to be split to get the child's new starting hash key. You can have any algorithm to choose a child's new starting hash key. To invoke splitShard, first you need the shard ID to be split, which can be obtained by using describe stream and choosing the shard ID.

```
{
  "streamDescription": {
    "streamName": "Chapter4KinesisStream",
    "streamARN": "arn:aws:kinesis:us-west-2:          :stream/Chapter4KinesisStream",
    "streamStatus": "ACTIVE",
    "shards": [{
        "shardId": "shardId-000000000000",
        "hashKeyRange": {"startingHashKey": "0","endingHashKey": "68056473384187692692674921486353642290"},
        "sequenceNumberRange": {"startingSequenceNumber": "49569351636396462442195632733931909933639056321448771586"}
      },{
        "shardId": "shardId-000000000001",
        "hashKeyRange": {"startingHashKey": "68056473384187692692674921486353642291","endingHashKey": "136112946768375385385349842972707284581"},
        "sequenceNumberRange": {"startingSequenceNumber": "49569351637018763187394163357073445651911704682954752018"}
      },{
        "shardId": "shardId-000000000002",
        "hashKeyRange": {"startingHashKey": "136112946768375385385349842972707284582","endingHashKey": "204169420152563078078024764459060926872"},
        "sequenceNumberRange": {"startingSequenceNumber": "49569351637041063932592693980214981370184353044460732450"}
      },
      {
        "shardId": "shardId-000000000003",
        "hashKeyRange": {"startingHashKey": "204169420152563078078024764459060926873","endingHashKey": "272225893536750770770699685945414569163"},
        "sequenceNumberRange": {"startingSequenceNumber": "49569351637045150503904899145260760217373737271045586802","endingSequenceNumber":
        "49569351637074515050390489914526076021773737271045586802"}
      },{
        "shardId": "shardId-000000000004",
        "hashKeyRange": {"startingHashKey": "272225893536750770770699685945414569164","endingHashKey": "340282366920938463463374607431768211455"},
        "sequenceNumberRange": {"startingSequenceNumber": "49569351637085665422989755226498052806729643767472693314","endingSequenceNumber":
        "49569351637096815795589020538067611740046385638610567234"}
      },{
        "shardId": "shardId-000000000005",
        "parentShardId": "shardId-000000000003",
        "adjacentParentShardId": "shardId-000000000004",
        "hashKeyRange": {"startingHashKey": "204169420152563078078024764459060926873","endingHashKey": "340282366920938463463374607431768211455"},
        "sequenceNumberRange": {"startingSequenceNumber": "49569351774128744667960434431235041592153885761000141627 4"}
      }
    ],
    "hasMoreShards": false,
    "retentionPeriodHours": 24,
    "enhancedMonitoring": [{"shardLevelMetrics": []}]
  },
  "sdkResponseMetadata": {"metadata": {"AWS_REQUEST_ID": "d8514015-dad7-af6e-88bc-2f7172b7b71e"}},
  "sdkHttpMetadata": {
    "httpHeaders": {
      "Server": "Apache-Coyote/1.1",
      "x-amzn-RequestId": "d8514015-dad7-af6e-88bc-2f7172b7b71e",
      "x-amz-id-2": "qRP9xwUk2EhVOJgvJQKMf87JX71+HpICLJy2fDzwz3ub/XAnS0YJegHKjrxyvGl1Kg46iZhbQ9y++r99EQRsPL3/v12A6OKH",
      "Content-Length": "2039",
      "Date": "Mon, 09 Jan 2017 10:59:48 GMT",
      "Content-Type": "application/x-amz-cbor-1.1"
    },
    "httpStatusCode": 200
  }
}
```

Once the shard ID is obtained, invoke the `splitShard` method:

```
{
  "sdkResponseMetadata": {
    "metadata": {
      "AWS_REQUEST_ID": "fb895f9c-34e0-e72b-ab64-30f99c80ff5b"
    }
  },
  "sdkHttpMetadata": {
    "httpHeaders": {
      "Server": "Apache-Coyote/1.1",
      "x-amzn-RequestId": "fb895f9c-34e0-e72b-ab64-30f99c80ff5b",
      "x-amz-id-2": "HUqqqbu9dItBQsXsZiBeLmN3fqAZsM5g9PBEnz9Qa1QqaPUgL+qICe+B1/Vf6P0zVngbK3uqKg8n8s2ByWcbLhnjR+hNnjAD",
      "Content-Length": "0",
      "Date": "Mon, 09 Jan 2017 10:59:48 GMT",
      "Content-Type": "application/x-amz-cbor-1.1"
    },
    "httpStatusCode": 200
  }
}
```

To verify that the shard is being split, invoke describe stream:

```
describeStream(STREAM_NAME, null, null);
```

```
{
    "streamDescription": {
        "streamName": "Chapter4KinesisStream","streamARN": "arn:aws:kinesis:us-west-2:████████:stream/Chapter4KinesisStream","streamStatus": "ACTIVE",
        "shards": [{
            "shardId": "shardId-000000000000",
            "hashKeyRange": {"startingHashKey": "0","endingHashKey": "6805647338418769269267492148635364229"},
            "sequenceNumberRange": {"startingSequenceNumber": "49569351686996462442195632733931909933689056321448771586","endingSequenceNumber":
            "49569351637007612814794898046501468966955795284963098626"}
        }, {
            "shardId": "shardId-000000000001",
            "hashKeyRange": {"startingHashKey": "6805647338418769269267492148635364229","endingHashKey": "13611294768375385385349842972707284581"},
            "sequenceNumberRange": {"startingSequenceNumber": "49569351637018763187394163357034466519117046829547620187"}
        }, {
            "shardId": "shardId-000000000002",
            "hashKeyRange": {"startingHashKey": "13611294768375385385349842972707284582","endingHashKey": "20416942015256307807802476445906092687"},
            "sequenceNumberRange": {"startingSequenceNumber": "49569351637041063932592693980214981370184353044460732450"}
        }, {
            "shardId": "shardId-000000000003",
            "hashKeyRange": {"startingHashKey": "20416942015256307807802476445906092687","endingHashKey": "27222589353675077077069968594541456916"},
            "sequenceNumberRange": {"startingSequenceNumber": "49569351637045150503904899149260760217373737277104586802"}
        }, {
            "shardId": "shardId-000000000004",
            "hashKeyRange": {"startingHashKey": "27222589353675077077069968594541456916","endingHashKey": "34028236692093846346337460743176821145"},
            "sequenceNumberRange": {"startingSequenceNumber": "49569351637085665452298975522649805280672964976747269331","endingSequenceNumber":
            "49569351637096815785589020538067611740046385658961056723"}
        }, {
            "shardId": "shardId-000000000005",
            "parentShardId": "shardId-000000000003",
            "adjacentParentShardId": "shardId-000000000004",
            "hashKeyRange": {"startingHashKey": "20416942015256307807802476445906092687","endingHashKey": "34028236692093846346337460743176821145"},
            "sequenceNumberRange": {"startingSequenceNumber": "49569351774123744667960434431236041592153857610001416274"}
        }, {
            "shardId": "shardId-000000000006",
            "parentShardId": "shardId-000000000000",
            "hashKeyRange": {"startingHashKey": "0","endingHashKey": "34028236692093846346337460743176821144"},
            "sequenceNumberRange": {"startingSequenceNumber": "49569351790202581956010101371628229446678332934818974934"}
        }, {
            "shardId": "shardId-000000000007",
            "parentShardId": "shardId-000000000000",
            "hashKeyRange": {"startingHashKey": "34028236692093846346337460743176821145","endingHashKey": "6805647338418769269267492148635364229"},
            "sequenceNumberRange": {"startingSequenceNumber": "49569351790224882701299544339423883018600597770905729778"}
        }
        ], "hasMoreShards": false, "retentionPeriodHours": 24, "enhancedMonitoring": [{"shardLevelMetrics": []}]
    },
    "sdkResponseMetadata": {"metadata": {"AWS_REQUEST_ID": "f8f44966-4926-b508-a819-26e3b2ed4f5b"}},
    "sdkHttpMetadata": {
        "httpHeaders": {"Server": "Apache-Coyote/1.1","x-amzn-RequestId": "f8f44966-4926-b508-a819-26e3b2ed4f5b","x-amz-id-2":
        "QYnibgTGRf51JwZ98GwLuZzmy9ZRrDpy6mPUfL/C2K5J7G9LmSNWs4s3F/3/hpuxtu49OubXVhfDgNHZGuNqz3IiXAVjcybe","Content-Length": "2668","Date": "Mon, 09 Jan 2017 11:00:21
        GMT","Content-Type": "application/x-amz-cbor-1.1"},
        "httpStatusCode": 200
    }
}
```

Add Tags to Stream

This process adds or updates tags to the Kinesis Stream. You can add up to 10 tags for each stream. To add or update tags, invoke the addTagsToStream method:

```java
Map<String, String> tags = new HashMap<>();

tags.put("Environment", "Production");

tags.put("Chapter", "4");

addTagsToStream(STREAM_NAME, tags);

public void addTagsToStream(String streamName, Map<String, String> tags) {
    AddTagsToStreamRequest request = new AddTagsToStreamRequest();

    request.setStreamName(streamName);

    request.setTags(tags);

    AddTagsToStreamResult response =
        amazonKinesisClient.addTagsToStream(request);
}
```

```
{
  "sdkResponseMetadata": {
    "metadata": {
      "AWS_REQUEST_ID": "edef21ef-cc62-ec7a-bd02-4e6a37a91629"
    }
  },
  "sdkHttpMetadata": {
    "httpHeaders": {
      "Server": "Apache-Coyote/1.1",
      "x-amzn-RequestId": "edef21ef-cc62-ec7a-bd02-4e6a37a91629",
      "x-amz-id-2": "v1Yj3hvEDXYP+U1Z1sg8+XLCTNATs7kgJvvs11ROZaSxLwp0eaeutZQfhTQTrBwPnY8/tmeVNE9LEJsgViSwfqSB6P3Gw6gj",
      "Content-Length": "0",
      "Date": "Mon, 09 Jan 2017 11:00:21 GMT",
      "Content-Type": "application/x-amz-cbor-1.1"
    },
    "httpStatusCode": 200
  }
}
```

List Tags for Stream

To get the list of tags attached to a stream, invoke the listTagsForStream method:

```
listTagsForStream(STREAM_NAME);
```

```
public void listTagsForStream(String streamName) {
    ListTagsForStreamRequest request = new ListTagsForStreamRequest();

    request.setStreamName(streamName);

    ListTagsForStreamResult response =
        amazonKinesisClient.listTagsForStream(request);
}
```

```
{
  "tags": [
    {
      "key": "Chapter",
      "value": "4"
    },
    {
      "key": "Environment",
      "value": "Production"
    }
  ],
  "hasMoreTags": false,
  "sdkResponseMetadata": {
    "metadata": {
      "AWS_REQUEST_ID": "e58a5031-3561-def1-b567-3f949b778d07"
    }
  },
  "sdkHttpMetadata": {
    "httpHeaders": {
      "Server": "Apache-Coyote/1.1",
      "x-amzn-RequestId": "e58a5031-3561-def1-b567-3f949b778d07",
      "x-amz-id-2": "a1zT/A0x6VnBBDs2N2JnMaQK1ZxfrmWED/nTuEA+udcXtgLIxTvL6OqsA1Nw2mUY70t1XB52y23k53ZTbposPpeozu9z+5nZ",
      "Content-Length": "79",
      "Date": "Mon, 09 Jan 2017 11:00:53 GMT",
      "Content-Type": "application/x-amz-cbor-1.1"
    },
    "httpStatusCode": 200
  }
}
```

Remove Tags from Stream

To remove tags from a stream, invoke the removeTagsFromStream method:

```
List<String>tagKeys = new ArrayList<>();

tagKeys.add("Environment");

removeTagsFromStream(STREAM_NAME, tagKeys);

public void removeTagsFromStream(String streamName, List<String>tagKeys) {
    RemoveTagsFromStreamRequest request = new RemoveTagsFromStreamRequest();

    request.setStreamName(streamName);

    request.setTagKeys(tagKeys);

    RemoveTagsFromStreamResult response =
        amazonKinesisClient.removeTagsFromStream(request);
}
```

```
{
  "sdkResponseMetadata": {
    "metadata": {
      "AWS_REQUEST_ID": "d6d92740-b0c8-6a00-8634-48a61eda39f6"
    }
  },
  "sdkHttpMetadata": {
    "httpHeaders": {
      "Server": "Apache-Coyote/1.1",
      "x-amzn-RequestId": "d6d92740-b0c8-6a00-8634-48a61eda39f6",
      "x-amz-id-2": "otLit1NnvPV1KMnvvc8z1qcc6BkxsA0SeAQG2zzrYkOm0Yx07y4J0tG8H/wYdWYxJcwzwFTsQLVO1XsNIuydO/ANYmcHr/em",
      "Content-Length": "0",
      "Date": "Mon, 09 Jan 2017 11:00:53 GMT",
      "Content-Type": "application/x-amz-cbor-1.1"
    },
    "httpStatusCode": 200
  }
}
```

To verify that the tag is being removed, invoke the list stream operation:

```
listTagsForStream(STREAM_NAME);
```

```
{
  "tags": [
    {
      "key": "Chapter",
      "value": "4"
    }
  ],
  "hasMoreTags": false,
  "sdkResponseMetadata": {
    "metadata": {
      "AWS_REQUEST_ID": "eeb32d05-2bc8-dcaf-be5e-42c3be2e809d"
    }
  },
  "sdkHttpMetadata": {
    "httpHeaders": {
      "Server": "Apache-Coyote/1.1",
      "x-amzn-RequestId": "eeb32d05-2bc8-dcaf-be5e-42c3be2e809d",
      "x-amz-id-2": "14if7GeBYWcc56KxdKrufgtvQ/yitnYUOy/PzaNjuAJAF6uAUB2+pIRXs/freUyaJzExl9o2UhEeSnx1m5uipT7rPVmcHExK",
      "Content-Length": "44",
      "Date": "Mon, 09 Jan 2017 11:01:26 GMT",
      "Content-Type": "application/x-amz-cbor-1.1"
    },
    "httpStatusCode": 200
  }
}
```

Delete Stream

To delete a stream permanently, invoke the deleteStream method:

```
deleteStream(STREAM_NAME);

public void deleteStream(String streamName) {
    // DeleteStreamResult response =
    // amazonKinesisClient.deleteStream(streamName);

    DeleteStreamRequest request = new DeleteStreamRequest();

    request.setStreamName(streamName);

    DeleteStreamResult response =
        amazonKinesisClient.deleteStream(request);
}
```

```
{
  "sdkResponseMetadata": {
    "metadata": {
      "AWS_REQUEST_ID": "c4cfb9cf-0f25-7a62-9422-d6089ac32650"
    }
  },
  "sdkHttpMetadata": {
    "httpHeaders": {
      "Server": "Apache-Coyote/1.1",
      "x-amzn-RequestId": "c4cfb9cf-0f25-7a62-9422-d6089ac32650",
      "x-amz-id-2": "JpHLk5nMOZk4AhyfDnQnw9kBI5Qbj6HeKUebIxpVDlDnn7cWUSGak1QeH4wJCJN1+LXkATcfVMv7M8q2LQM6SxgXm+LdQtlI",
      "Content-Length": "0",
      "Date": "Mon, 09 Jan 2017 11:01:27 GMT",
      "Content-Type": "application/x-amz-cbor-1.1"
    },
    "httpStatusCode": 200
  }
}
```

To verify that the stream has been deleted, invoke list stream operation:

```
listStreams(null, null);
```

```
{
  "streamNames": [
    "Chapter4KinesisStream1",
    "Chapter4KinesisStream2",
    "Chapter4KinesisStream3",
    "Chapter4KinesisStream4",
    "Chapter4KinesisStream5"
  ],
  "hasMoreStreams": false,
  "sdkResponseMetadata": {
    "metadata": {
      "AWS_REQUEST_ID": "edca6b15-4ab7-b9b3-bd27-1bb4ad459947"
    }
  },
  "sdkHttpMetadata": {
    "httpHeaders": {
      "Server": "Apache-Coyote/1.1",
      "x-amzn-RequestId": "edca6b15-4ab7-b9b3-bd27-1bb4ad459947",
      "x-amz-id-2": "rVKIEH1w+WE1LwGhnfB1ph7DfXRmDSV49JnAQN724o/OXb1Xw+5KTw/nNKRiI2IpFY1UWXV54CJDABHZjPnRfwca39x/HSKR",
      "Content-Length": "147",
      "Date": "Mon, 09 Jan 2017 11:05:05 GMT",
      "Content-Type": "application/x-amz-cbor-1.1"
    },
    "httpStatusCode": 200
  }
}
```

Monitor Using CloudWatch

CloudWatch allows monitoring the Kinesis having different metrics. It will trigger an alarm when a threshold is exceeded on specific metrics. The following steps will guide you to create an alarm:

1. Go to the CloudWatch Management Console and click Alarms from left navigation, as shown in Figure 4-20.

Figure 4-20. CloudWatch alarm

2. Click Create Alarm.

3. The Create Alarm screen will be displayed, which has two steps, as shown in Figure 4-21:

   • Select Metric

   • Define Alarm

Create Alarm ✕

1. **Select Metric**   2. Define Alarm

Browse Metrics ▾ 🔍 Search Metrics ✕

CloudWatch Metrics by Category

Your CloudWatch metric summary has loaded. Total metrics: **59**

Kinesis Metrics : 17

  Stream Metrics : 17

Lambda Metrics : 28

  Across All Functions : 4
  By Function Name : 12
  By Resource : 12

Logs Metrics : 4

  Account Metrics : 2
  Log Group Metrics : 2

S3 Metrics : 10

  Storage Metrics : 10

Update Graph   ▪ ▪ ▫ ▫

Cancel   Previous   **Next**   Create Alarm

Figure 4-21. *Create Alarm screen*

4.   First of all, select the metric for Kinesis. Click Browse Metrics and select Kinesis, as shown in Figure 4-22.

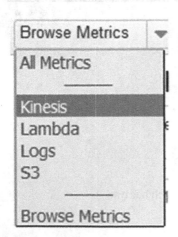

Figure 4-22. *Browse Metrics screen*

5. You can see all the metrics that can be configured on Kinesis in Figure 4-23.

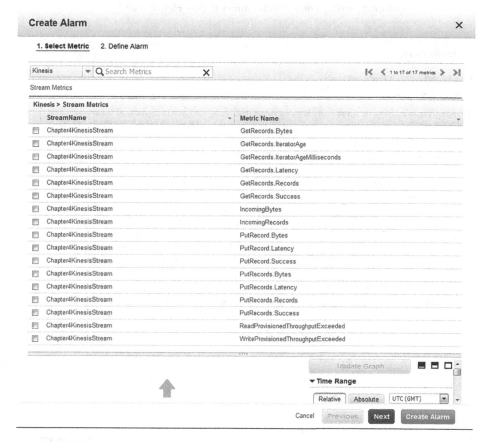

Figure 4-23. Kinesis metric listing

6. For our case, select the PutRecord.Bytes metric. Click the Next button. (See Figure 4-24.)

Figure 4-24. Kinesis metric selected

7. Define the alarm settings by providing the name, a description, and threshold values on the alarm to be generated. Use the sum of data records that should be greater than or equal to operation during a one-minute interval. (See Figure 4-25.)

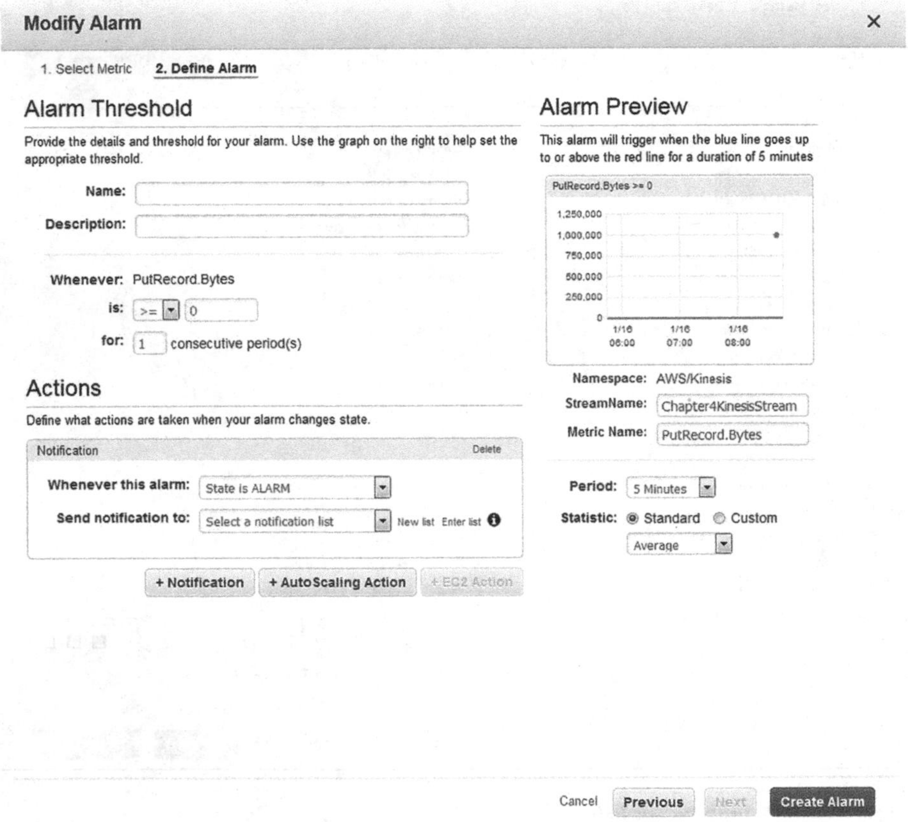

Figure 4-25. *Define alarm*

8. You can also configure Actions to trigger notification when the alarm state is "ALARM." To configure it, select from the drop-down list "Send notification to" or create a new notification by clicking New List. Enter the topic name and the e-mail address where notifications need to be sent. (See Figure 4-26.)

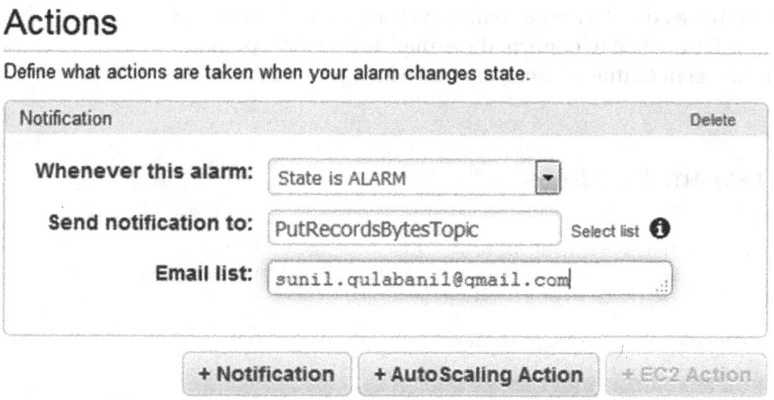

Actions

Define what actions are taken when your alarm changes state.

Notification	Delete

Whenever this alarm: State is ALARM ▾

Send notification to: PutRecordsBytesTopic   Select list ⓘ

Email list: sunil.qulabanil@qmail.com

+ Notification   **+ AutoScaling Action**   + EC2 Action

Figure 4-26. Define actions

> 9. Click the Create Alarm button, as shown in Figure 4-27.

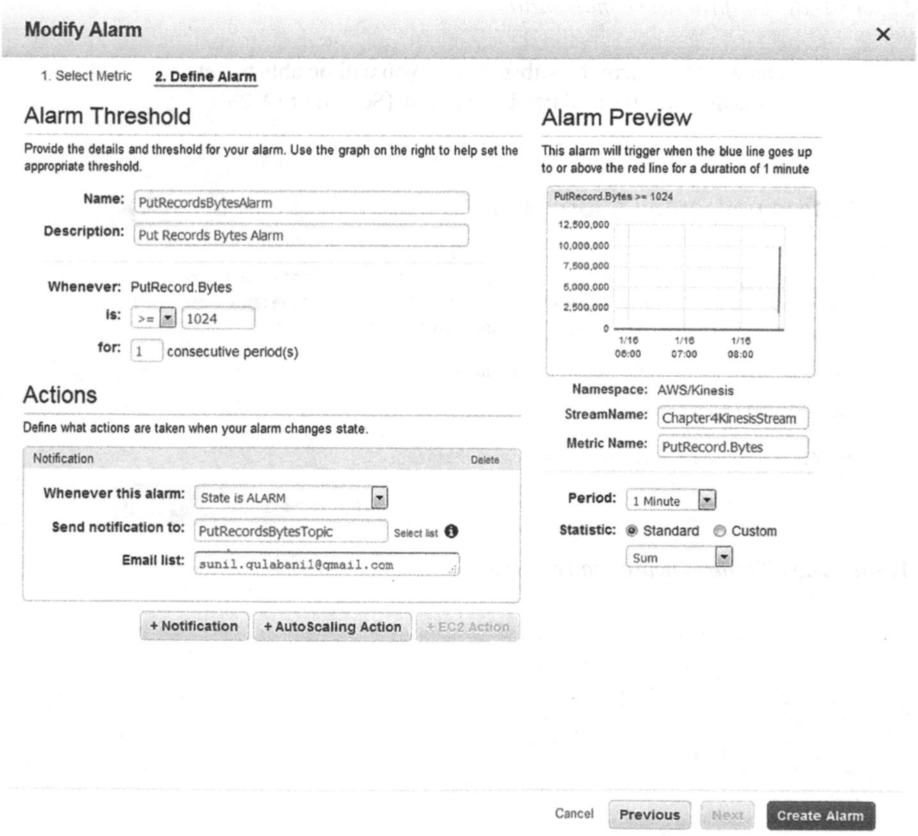

Modify Alarm   ✕

1. Select Metric   **2. Define Alarm**

Alarm Threshold

Provide the details and threshold for your alarm. Use the graph on the right to help set the appropriate threshold.

Name: PutRecordsBytesAlarm

Description: Put Records Bytes Alarm

Whenever: PutRecord.Bytes

is: >= ▾ 1024

for: 1 consecutive period(s)

Actions

Define what actions are taken when your alarm changes state.

Notification	Delete

Whenever this alarm: State is ALARM ▾

Send notification to: PutRecordsBytesTopic   Select list ⓘ

Email list: sunil.qulabanil@qmail.com

+ Notification   **+ AutoScaling Action**   + EC2 Action

Alarm Preview

This alarm will trigger when the blue line goes up to or above the red line for a duration of 1 minute

PutRecord.Bytes >= 1024

```
12,500,000
10,000,000
 7,500,000
 5,000,000
 2,500,000
         0
          1/16      1/16      1/16
          06:00     07:00     08:00
```

Namespace: AWS/Kinesis

StreamName: Chapter4KinesisStream

Metric Name: PutRecord.Bytes

Period: 1 Minute ▾

Statistic: ● Standard ○ Custom

Sum ▾

Cancel   **Previous**   Next   **Create Alarm**

Figure 4-27. Create alarm

10. If you have added a new e-mail that is not subscribed to SNS, you will be asked to confirm the e-mail address by opening the link sent to that address, as shown in Figure 4-28.

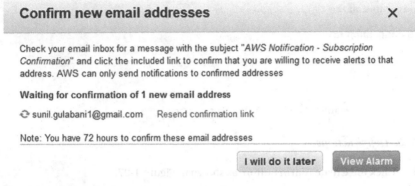

Figure 4-28. Confirm new e-mail address

11. Once you confirm the subscription, you will be able to get messages when the alarm is triggered. (See Figure 4-29.)

Figure 4-29. Confirm new e-mail address

You can see that alarm has been created in Figure 4-30.

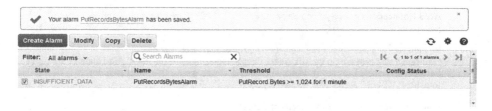

Figure 4-30. Alarm listing

12. To test that the alarm has been generated, we added multiple data records to the stream with 1MB of data for each record.

13. You can see that alarm state is changed to "ALARM" in Figure 4-31.

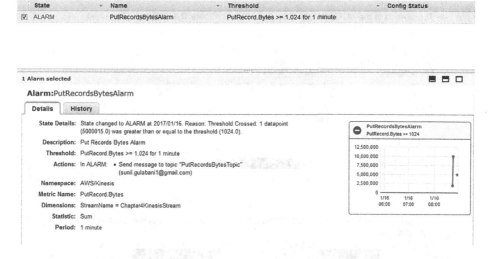

Figure 4-31. Alarm status changed

14. An e-mail has also been triggered, as shown in Figure 4-32.

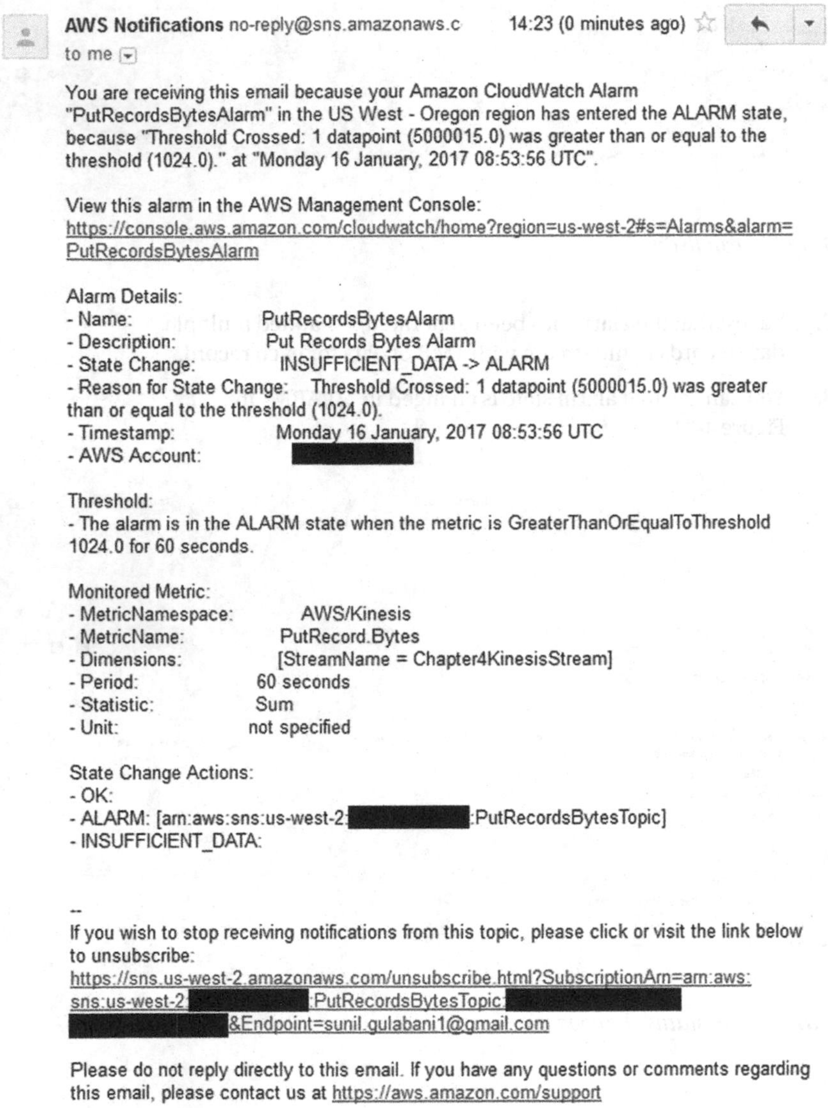

AWS Notifications no-reply@sns.amazonaws.c   14:23 (0 minutes ago) ☆   ↰   ▾
to me ▾

You are receiving this email because your Amazon CloudWatch Alarm
"PutRecordsBytesAlarm" in the US West - Oregon region has entered the ALARM state,
because "Threshold Crossed: 1 datapoint (5000015.0) was greater than or equal to the
threshold (1024.0)." at "Monday 16 January, 2017 08:53:56 UTC".

View this alarm in the AWS Management Console:
https://console.aws.amazon.com/cloudwatch/home?region=us-west-2#s=Alarms&alarm=
PutRecordsBytesAlarm

Alarm Details:
- Name: PutRecordsBytesAlarm
- Description: Put Records Bytes Alarm
- State Change: INSUFFICIENT_DATA -> ALARM
- Reason for State Change: Threshold Crossed: 1 datapoint (5000015.0) was greater
than or equal to the threshold (1024.0).
- Timestamp: Monday 16 January, 2017 08:53:56 UTC
- AWS Account: ███████████

Threshold:
- The alarm is in the ALARM state when the metric is GreaterThanOrEqualToThreshold
1024.0 for 60 seconds.

Monitored Metric:
- MetricNamespace: AWS/Kinesis
- MetricName: PutRecord.Bytes
- Dimensions: [StreamName = Chapter4KinesisStream]
- Period: 60 seconds
- Statistic: Sum
- Unit: not specified

State Change Actions:
- OK:
- ALARM: [arn:aws:sns:us-west-2:███████████:PutRecordsBytesTopic]
- INSUFFICIENT_DATA:

--
If you wish to stop receiving notifications from this topic, please click or visit the link below
to unsubscribe:
https://sns.us-west-2.amazonaws.com/unsubscribe.html?SubscriptionArn=arn:aws:
sns:us-west-2:███████████:PutRecordsBytesTopic:███████████
███████████&Endpoint=sunil.gulabani1@gmail.com

Please do not reply directly to this email. If you have any questions or comments regarding
this email, please contact us at https://aws.amazon.com/support

Figure 4-32. *Alarm e-mail*

15. After messages are read from the stream, the alarm state will
go back to "OK" if the data record sizes that are continuously
sent are less than 1024 bytes. The alarm state will be
"INSUFFICIENT_DATA" when there are no put record activity
on the stream. (See Figure 4-33.)

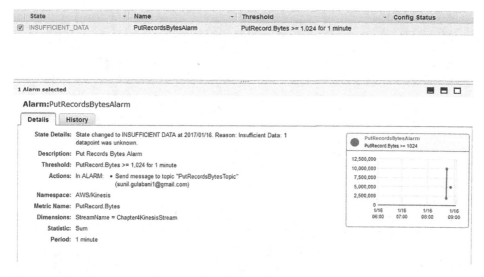

Figure 4-33. Alarm status changed—Insufficient Data

Summary

In this chapter, I discussed how to create a Kinesis Stream and configure the shards to efficiently meet your requirements. I also explained how to use AWS Management Console, AWS CLI, and AWS Java SDK to manage Kinesis Streams. Furthermore, I covered how to create a CloudWatch alarm on Kinesis Streams, which is invoked once the threshold value is crossed.

In Chapter 5, I will guide you in creating and configuring S3 buckets and uploading objects.

CHAPTER 5

■ ■ ■

Hands-on Simple Storage Service (S3)

Amazon S3 provides a storage service where you can store files. You can also use S3 for serving static data to web sites or applications, host a static web site on S3, and stream photos and videos to different web sites along with AWS CloudFront.

In this chapter, I will cover the following topics:

- Introduction to S3

- Features of S3

- Using AWS Management Console

- Using AWS CLI

- Using AWS SDK—Java

- Monitoring using CloudWatch

Introduction to AWS S3

AWS Simple Storage Service (S3) is a web service exposed over the Internet to store and retrieve data. It provides infrastructure that is reliable, scalable, and cost-efficient. Amazon uses AWS S3 to serve its global network of web sites. You can even host static web sites over AWS S3.

AWS S3 stores data objects in buckets. A bucket is simply a logical container that is used to identify the namespace of data objects. Each AWS user account can create up to 100 buckets. You can also create folders under the bucket, and inside folders you can store data objects. Consequently, it becomes easier to separate the logical storage of data objects. Each data object has a unique key within a bucket. You can access the data objects using the following URL: http://BUCKET_NAME.s3.amazonaws.com/DATA_OBJECT_KEY.

Here BUCKET_NAME will be the actual bucket name in which DATA_OBJECT_KEY resides. (See Figure 5-1.)

© Sunil Gulabani 2017
S. Gulabani, *Practical Amazon EC2, SQS, Kinesis, and S3*,
DOI 10.1007/978-1-4842-2841-8_5

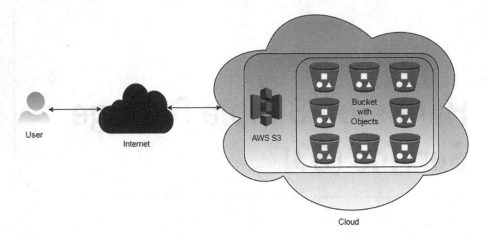

Figure 5-1. *AWS S3*

AWS S3 allows users to store an unlimited number of data objects, and the data objects' size can be up to 5GB. Each data object has metadata associated with it. You can assign permissions for those who can access the data objects. Permissions will enforce security for unauthorized access to our data objects. Data objects can also be made public that can be accessible over HTTP or BitTorrent.

Features

The main features of S3 are discussed in the sections that follow.

Scalability

AWS S3 provides infrastructure to store and retrieve data objects based on configuration. It scales automatically when we store a large number of data objects. There won't be any configuration changes from the user's end.

Availability

AWS S3 ensures that data objects are available at all times. You don't need to manage anything if you have heavy traffic overnight.

■ **Note**   For more details on AWS S3 SLA, please visit `https://aws.amazon.com/s3/sla/`.

Cost Efficiency

AWS S3 follows the pay-as-you-go strategy, meaning you only have to pay for the data objects you have stored and retrieved on AWS S3. For startups and small-scale companies, it becomes inexpensive to use data storage infrastructure.

Static Web Hosting

AWS S3 provides static web site hosting that can be mapped. When you have static HTML web sites, you can opt for hosting on S3 rather than purchasing the hosting space.

■ **Note**   Amazon's global network of web sites is hosted on AWS S3.

Using AWS Management Console

AWS Management Console can be used to manage S3. It provides an easy way to configure the S3. The following explanation shows how to configure S3.

Create Bucket

Buckets are a core part of S3. Buckets are used to stores objects that have content and metadata describing for the object. The following steps show how to create a bucket:

1. Sign in to AWS Management Console and click S3 under the All Services ➤ Storage category. (See Figure 5-2.)

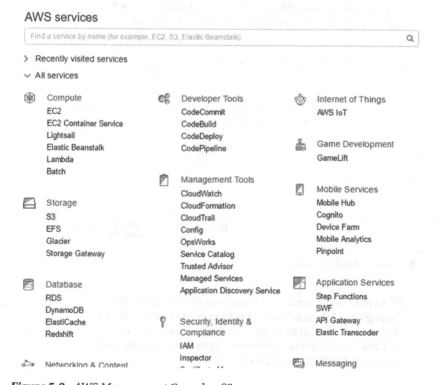

Figure 5-2. *AWS Management Console—S3*

2. This will take you to the S3 screen shown in Figure 5-3.

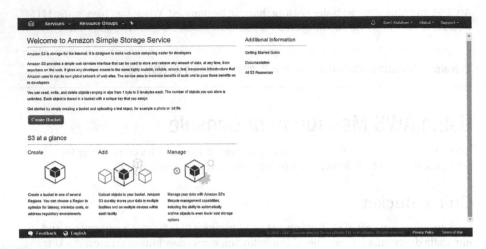

Figure 5-3. *S3 landing screen*

3. Click the Create Bucket button to create a bucket. This will open the Create a Bucket window shown in Figure 5-4.

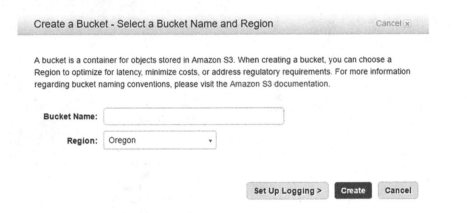

Figure 5-4. *Create a Bucket screen*

4. Fill in the bucket name as "chapter5-s3-bucket" and select the region as "Oregon" where the bucket will be located. The bucket name should be unique across all buckets in Amazon S3. Choose a bucket name carefully as this bucket name will be reflected in the URL of the data object.

■ **Note**   Bucket naming conventions can be found at http://docs.aws.amazon.com/
AmazonS3/latest/UG/CreatingaBucket.html.

5.   You can also set up logging for the activities carried on in
the newly created bucket. To enable logging, click the Set Up
Logging button and enable the logging check box. Select the
target bucket and target prefix in which logs will be dumped.
(See Figure 5-5.)

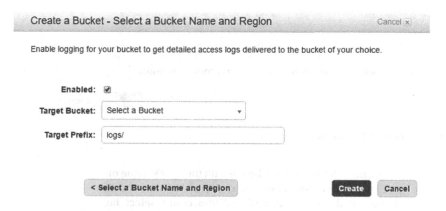

Figure 5-5. *Create bucket; set up logging*

6.   Once the bucket name and region has been determined and
the logging has been set up (optional), click the Create button.

7.   Figure 5-6 shows the bucket listing.

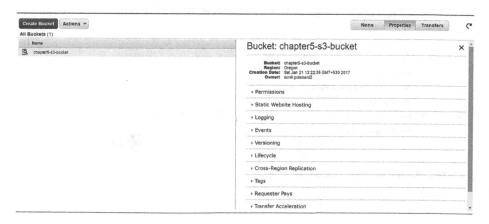

Figure 5-6. *Bucket listing*

Bucket Permissions

Bucket permissions authorize users to access the data objects stored under the bucket. You can grant permissions on bucket.

1. By default, the owner of the bucket has all rights. To add permissions, click Add more permissions. (See Figure 5-7.)

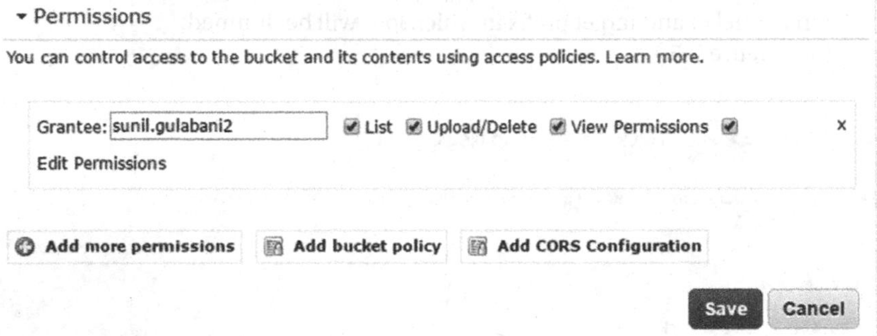

Figure 5-7. *Bucket permissions*

2. The grantee slot should be filled in with the user's name or group to which permissions will be given. The name should be associated with an e-mail of an AWS account. Select the permissions check boxes that need to be granted, as shown in Figure 5-8.

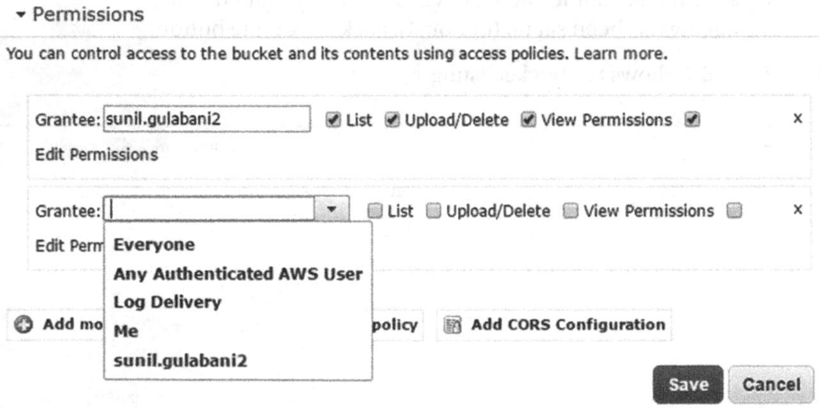

Figure 5-8. *Add more permissions*

3. Once the grantee's name has been given and the permissions have been selected, click the Save button.

■ **Note**   For more details on grantees, see `http://docs.aws.amazon.com/AmazonS3/`
`latest/dev/acl-overview.html#SpecifyingGrantee`.

---

4. To remove any permissions, click the "x" icon displayed in each permission box.

5. To add a bucket policy, click the Add bucket policy link. This will open the window shown in Figure 5-9.

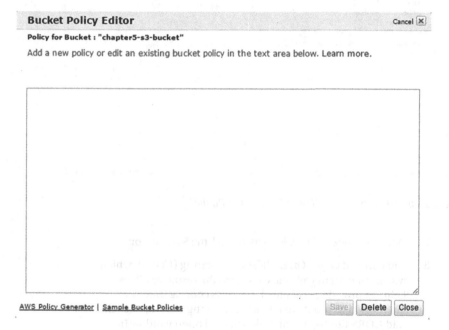

Figure 5-9. *Add Bucket Policy screen*

6. You can use the AWS policy generator or sample bucket policies to create a bucket policy. I created a bucket policy for reading bucket data objects to public, as shown in Figure 5-10.

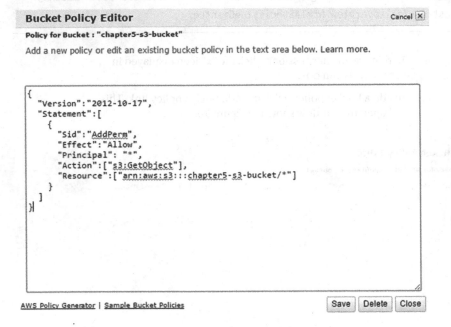

Figure 5-10. Add a bucket policy—GetObject to Public

7. Once the bucket policy is created, click the Save button.

8. You can add Cross-Origin Resource Sharing (CORS), which will grant certain web sites to access the resources. This helps to provide access to all requests coming from the mentioned web site. To add a CORS configuration, click the Add CORS Configuration link. This will open window in Figure 5-11.

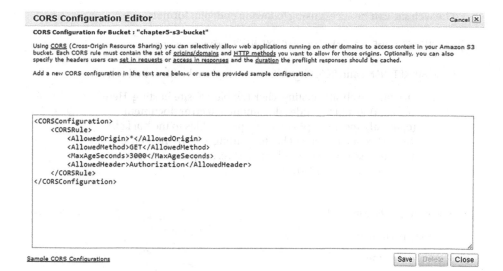

Figure 5-11. Add CORS configuration

Static Web Site Hosting

You can host a web site having static content on AWS S3.

1. To enable the static web site hosting, click Static Website Hosting. (See Figure 5-12.)

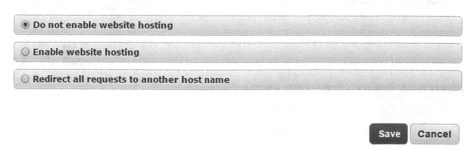

Figure 5-12. Static web site hosting

The web site can be access using following endpoint format:

`http://BUCKET_NAME.s3-website-REGION_NAME.amazonaws.com.`

Here `BUCKET_NAME` and `REGION_NAME` will be replaced with actual values.

2. To enable web site hosting, click Enable website hosting. Here you need to add the index document and error document (optional) and also upload the respective files to the bucket. The index document will be the landing page of the web site. You can also set custom rules to redirect requests on specific content. (See Figure 5-13.)

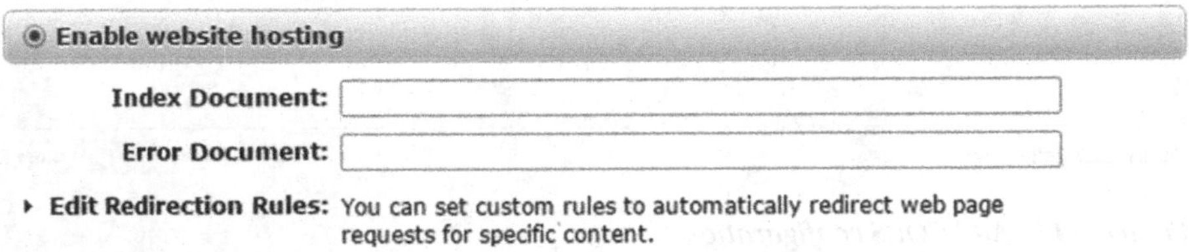

Figure 5-13. Enable web site hosting

3. If you need to redirect the request to a specific URL, you can click Redirect all requests to another host name. Add your URL in the Redirect all requests to input box where redirection needs to happen. You can specify the URL with HTTP or HTTPS protocol. If you don't provide a URL with protocol, it will consider the original request's protocol. (See Figure 5-14.)

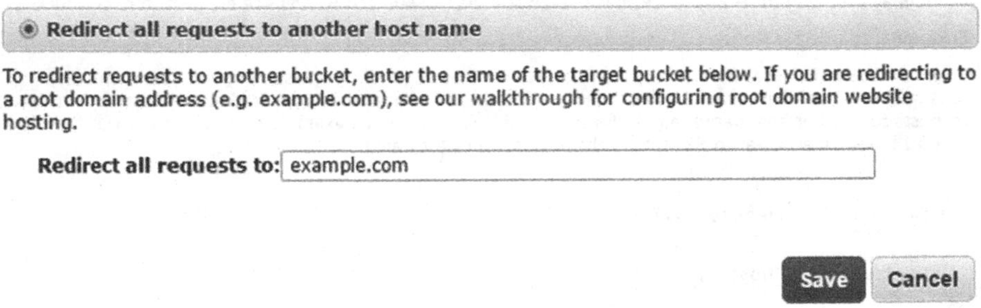

Figure 5-14. Redirect all requests to another hostname

4. Once the configuration is complete, click the Save button. In addition to this configuration, you also need to provide public read permission on buckets or objects so that it is accessible to the public.

■ **Note** To map an AWS S3 web site to custom domain, please see `http://docs.aws.` `amazon.com/AmazonS3/latest/dev/website-hosting-custom-domain-walkthrough.html`.

Logging

You can enable the logging on your bucket activity. To enable logging, click the Enabled check box and provide the target bucket and prefix where you need to store the logs, as shown in Figure 5-15.

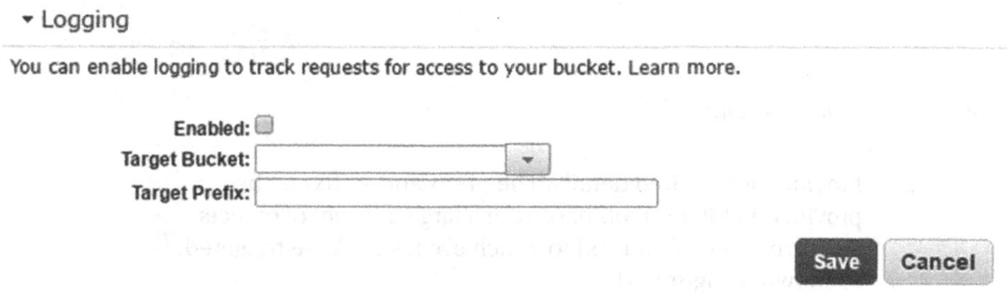

▼ Logging

You can enable logging to track requests for access to your bucket. Learn more.

Enabled: ☐
Target Bucket: [▼]
Target Prefix: [   ]

[Save] [Cancel]

Figure 5-15. *Bucket logging*

Events

You can configure the events on the bucket activities. When a new object is added to the bucket, notification should be sent to SNS or SQS or trigger the lambda function to carry out some processing. For example, logs are being added to the bucket. You want to filter out logs so you can configure an event that will trigger whenever a log file is added to the bucket.

1. To create an event, click Events, as shown in Figure 5-16.

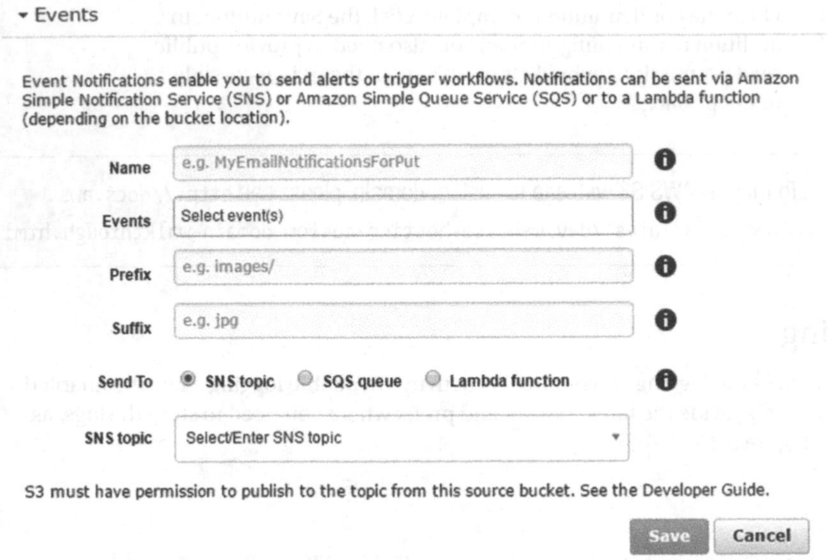

▾ Events

Event Notifications enable you to send alerts or trigger workflows. Notifications can be sent via Amazon Simple Notification Service (SNS) or Amazon Simple Queue Service (SQS) or to a Lambda function (depending on the bucket location).

Name	e.g. MyEmailNotificationsForPut	❶
Events	Select event(s)	❶
Prefix	e.g. images/	❶
Suffix	e.g. jpg	❶
Send To	● SNS topic ○ SQS queue ○ Lambda function	❶
SNS topic	Select/Enter SNS topic ▾	

S3 must have permission to publish to the topic from this source bucket. See the Developer Guide.

Save   Cancel

Figure 5-16. *Bucket events*

2. Provide the required details. The prefix and suffix can be provided to filter out objects from a large number of objects. Select the type of event(s) to which event should be triggered, as shown in Figure 5-17.

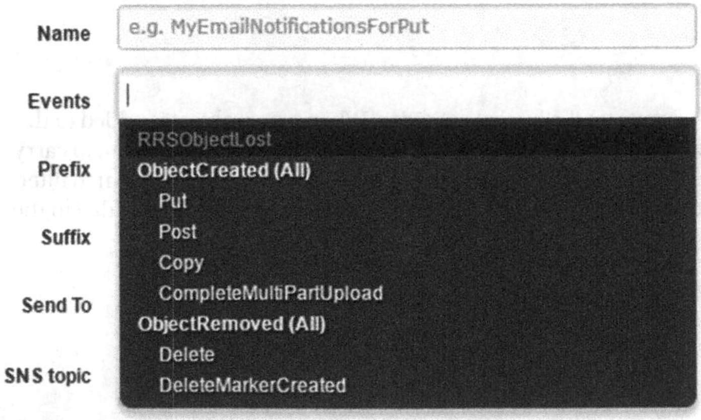

Name	e.g. MyEmailNotificationsForPut
Events		

RRSObjectLost
ObjectCreated (All)
   Put
   Post
   Copy
   CompleteMultiPartUpload
ObjectRemoved (All)
   Delete
   DeleteMarkerCreated

Prefix

Suffix

Send To

SNS topic

Figure 5-17. *Events types*

3. Select the destination where the event needs to be triggered:

- SNS topic

- SQS queue

- Lambda function

4. Once all details are filled in, click the Save button.

■ **Note** Please provide necessary permissions on SNS, SQS, or lambda function to be used by events configured on S3.

Versioning

Versioning helps to store every version of objects. Versioned objects can be used to recover the accidental override or expiration of an object. If bucket versioning is enabled, then it can't be disabled. It can only be suspended.

1. To enable versioning, click the Enable Versioning button, as shown in Figure 5-18.

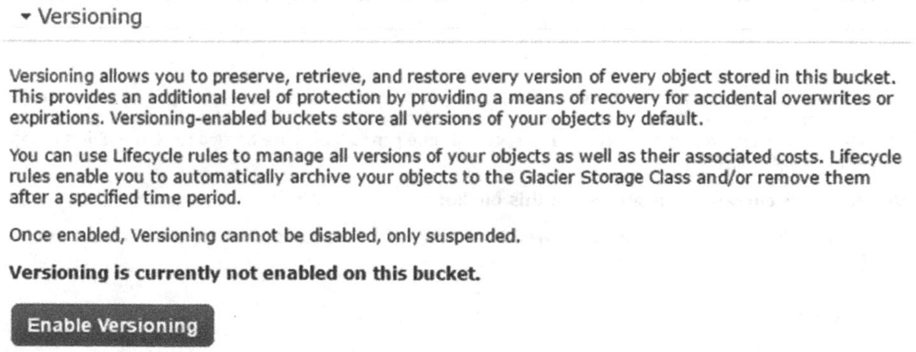

▾ Versioning

Versioning allows you to preserve, retrieve, and restore every version of every object stored in this bucket. This provides an additional level of protection by providing a means of recovery for accidental overwrites or expirations. Versioning-enabled buckets store all versions of your objects by default.

You can use Lifecycle rules to manage all versions of your objects as well as their associated costs. Lifecycle rules enable you to automatically archive your objects to the Glacier Storage Class and/or remove them after a specified time period.

Once enabled, Versioning cannot be disabled, only suspended.

Versioning is currently not enabled on this bucket.

Enable Versioning

Figure 5-18. Enable versioning

2. Now the bucket will store all versions of the object under the bucket. Maintaining every version of object is costly. To avoid this expense, you can have a life-cycle rule on the bucket that can help to archive objects to Glacier storage or delete them.

3. To suspend the versioning that is already enabled, click the Suspend Versioning button, as shown in Figure 5-19.

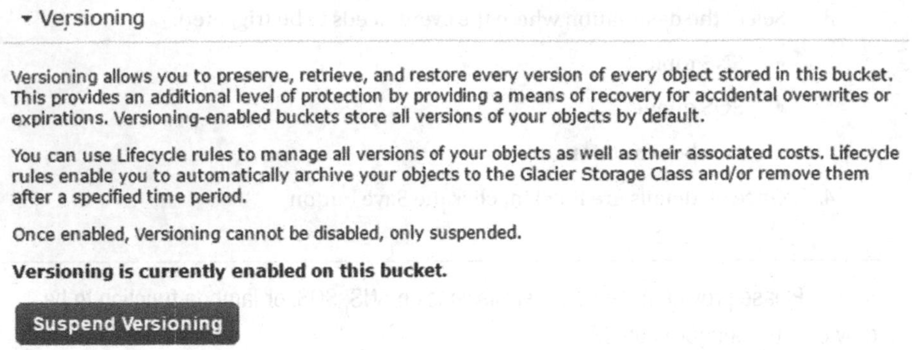

▾ Versioning

Versioning allows you to preserve, retrieve, and restore every version of every object stored in this bucket. This provides an additional level of protection by providing a means of recovery for accidental overwrites or expirations. Versioning-enabled buckets store all versions of your objects by default.

You can use Lifecycle rules to manage all versions of your objects as well as their associated costs. Lifecycle rules enable you to automatically archive your objects to the Glacier Storage Class and/or remove them after a specified time period.

Once enabled, Versioning cannot be disabled, only suspended.

Versioning is currently enabled on this bucket.

[Suspend Versioning]

Figure 5-19. *Suspend versioning*

Life Cycle

The life cycle of objects can be managed by creating life-cycle rules. You can create rules to move objects to other storage locations where objects are not accessed frequently, or you can move objects to Glacier storage or even set an expiry date for the object. (See Figure 5-20.)

■ **Note** Glacier is a service provided by Amazon for archiving and backup at a low cost.

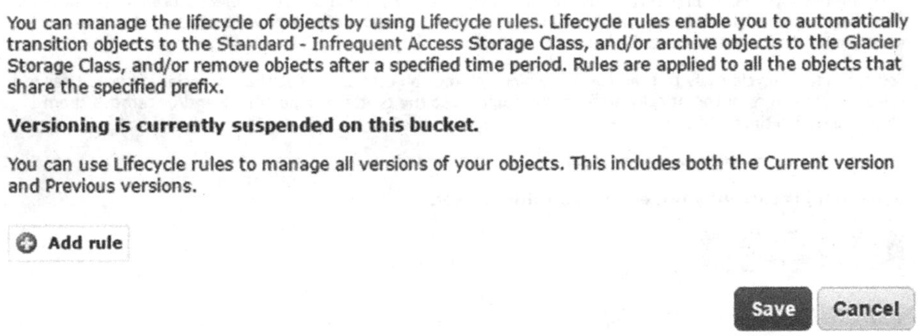

You can manage the lifecycle of objects by using Lifecycle rules. Lifecycle rules enable you to automatically transition objects to the Standard - Infrequent Access Storage Class, and/or archive objects to the Glacier Storage Class, and/or remove objects after a specified time period. Rules are applied to all the objects that share the specified prefix.

Versioning is currently suspended on this bucket.

You can use Lifecycle rules to manage all versions of your objects. This includes both the Current version and Previous versions.

⊕ **Add rule**

[Save] [Cancel]

Figure 5-20. *Life cycle configuration*

1. Clicking the Add rule button will open the Lifecycle Rules window, as shown in Figure 5-21.

Figure 5-21. *Lifecycle Rules screen*

> 2. Here you can select a rule that will be applicable on the
> bucket level or you can set the prefix of the objects. Click the
> Configure Rule button, as shown in Figure 5-22.

Figure 5-22. *Configure Rule button*

> 3. Select the check box based on the type of action you want to
> apply on objects. For this example, select Action on Current
> Version ➤ Expire in 365 days. This means the object will
> be deleted permanently after 365 days. Once the action is
> configured, click the Review button, as shown in Figure 5-23.

Figure 5-23. *Review rule*

4. Here you will provide the name to your rule (optional) and review the configuration. Once the configuration is verified, click the Create and Activate Rule button, as shown in Figure 5-24.

▾ Lifecycle

You can manage the lifecycle of objects by using Lifecycle rules. Lifecycle rules enable you to automatically transition objects to the Standard - Infrequent Access Storage Class, and/or archive objects to the Glacier Storage Class, and/or remove objects after a specified time period. Rules are applied to all the objects that share the specified prefix.

Versioning is currently suspended on this bucket.

You can use Lifecycle rules to manage all versions of your objects. This includes both the Current version and Previous versions.

Enabled	Name	Rule Target	
☑	Expire Rule 365	Whole Bucket	✎ ✕

⊕ **Add rule**

Save   Cancel

Figure 5-24. *Life cycle rule added*

5. To remove any rule, click the "x" icon and click the Save button.

Cross-Region Replication

Cross-region replication will replicate the bucket with objects to another region. To enable cross-region replication, you need to enable versioning. (See Figure 5-25.)

▾ Cross-Region Replication

Cross-Region Replication replicates every future upload of every object in this bucket to another bucket. Cross-Region Replication is designed for use in conjunction with Versioning. You will be required to enable Versioning on this bucket and the target bucket. Learn More

Versioning is currently enabled on this bucket.

Suspend Versioning

◉ | **Do Not Enable Cross-Region Replication** |

◯ | **Enable Cross-Region Replication** |

Save   Cancel

Figure 5-25. *Cross-region replication*

1. Click Enable Cross-Region Replication to replicate the bucket with objects to a different region, as shown in Figure 5-26.

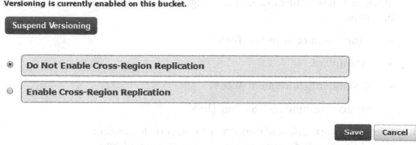

▾ Cross-Region Replication

Cross-Region Replication replicates every future upload of every object in this bucket to another bucket. Cross-Region Replication is designed for use in conjunction with Versioning. You will be required to enable Versioning on this bucket and the target bucket. Learn More

Versioning is currently enabled on this bucket.

Suspend Versioning

◯ | **Do Not Enable Cross-Region Replication** |

◉ | **Enable Cross-Region Replication** |

| Existing objects will not be replicated. Cross-Region Replication replicates every future upload of every object to another bucket. |

Source: ◉ This bucket (chapter5-s3-bucket) ❶
          ◯ A prefix in this bucket ❶

Destination Region: | Select a Destination Region ▾ | ❶

Destination Bucket: | Select a Destination Bucket ▾ | ❶

Destination Storage Class: | Same as source object (Default) ▾ | ❶

Create/Select IAM Role ❶

Selected IAM Role:

Save   Cancel

Figure 5-26. *Enable cross-region replication*

2. Select the source to replicate all objects or provide a prefix for the object. The destination region should be a different region from the source region where the objects will be replicated. The destination bucket will be used to store replicated objects of source bucket. The destination storage class can be any of the following:

- Same as source object (default)

- S3 Standard

- S3 Standard - Infrequent Access

- Reduced Redundancy Storage (RSS)

3. After selecting the destination storage class, create or select the IAM role that will have the required access to replicate objects. After all configurations are complete, click the Save button. (See Figure 5-27.)

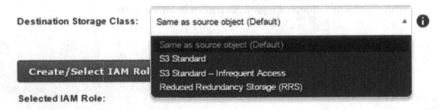

Figure 5-27. *Destination storage class*

Tags

Tags are used to provide a logical key value that will identify what a resource is being used for, who created the resource, or which project this resource belongs to. Also, tags are used to view aggregated billing. Cost allocation tagging helps to differentiate the cost of AWS S3 buckets used by specific projects. You can set 10 tags under each bucket. (See Figure 5-28.)

Figure 5-28. *Tags*

1. To add a tag, click "Add more tags." (See Figure 5-29.)

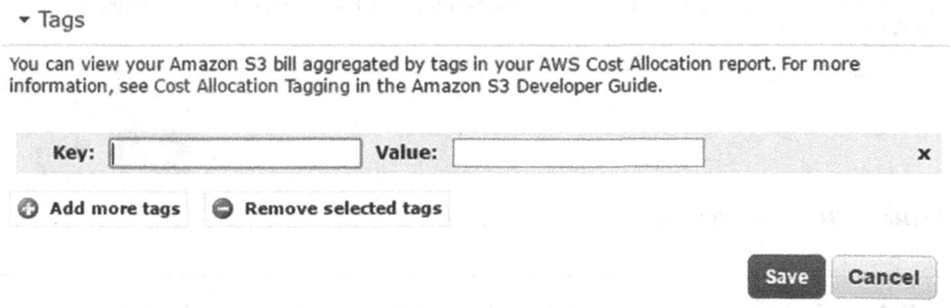

▾ Tags

You can view your Amazon S3 bill aggregated by tags in your AWS Cost Allocation report. For more information, see Cost Allocation Tagging in the Amazon S3 Developer Guide.

| Key: | | Value: | | x |

⊕ **Add more tags**   ⊖ **Remove selected tags**

Save   Cancel

Figure 5-29. Add more tags

2. Once the tag's key and value have been added, click the Save button, as shown in Figure 5-30.

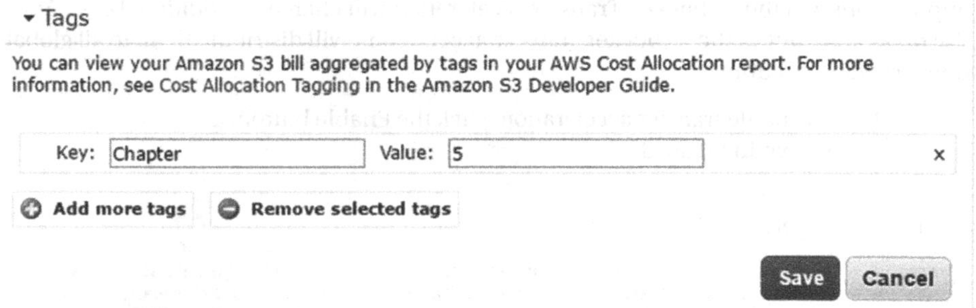

▾ Tags

You can view your Amazon S3 bill aggregated by tags in your AWS Cost Allocation report. For more information, see Cost Allocation Tagging in the Amazon S3 Developer Guide.

| Key: | Chapter | Value: | 5 | x |

⊕ **Add more tags**   ⊖ **Remove selected tags**

Save   Cancel

Figure 5-30. Tag added

3. To remove the tag, click "x" and then the Save button.

Requester Pays

Amazon S3 owners pay for the storage, data transfer, and requests made. If the AWS S3 bucket owner wants the requesters of the bucket to pay for data transfer and requests, the owner can configure the settings so this is possible. To enable the requester to pay, click the Enable check box and the Save button, as shown in Figure 5-31.

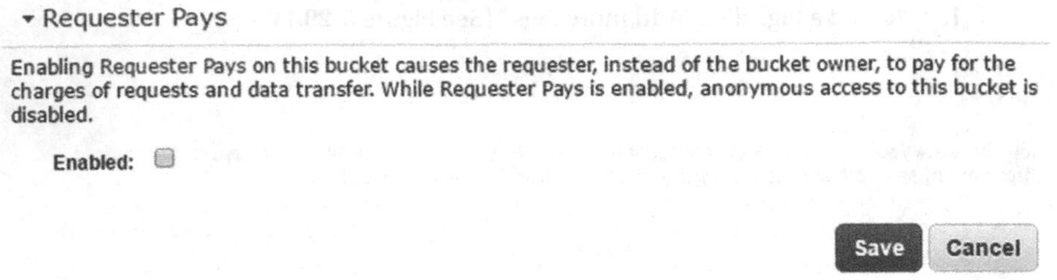

▾ Requester Pays

Enabling Requester Pays on this bucket causes the requester, instead of the bucket owner, to pay for the charges of requests and data transfer. While Requester Pays is enabled, anonymous access to this bucket is disabled.

Enabled: ☐

Save   Cancel

Figure 5-31. *Requester pays*

■ **Note**   Enabling requester pays will disable anonymous access to the bucket.

Transfer Acceleration

Transfer acceleration will help to transfer data fast, easily, and securely between the client applications and the S3 bucket. Transfer acceleration will charge an additional cost. As the objects are put in the S3 bucket, transfer acceleration will distribute them to all global delivery edge locations.

1. To enable transfer acceleration, click the Enable button, as shown in Figure 5-32.

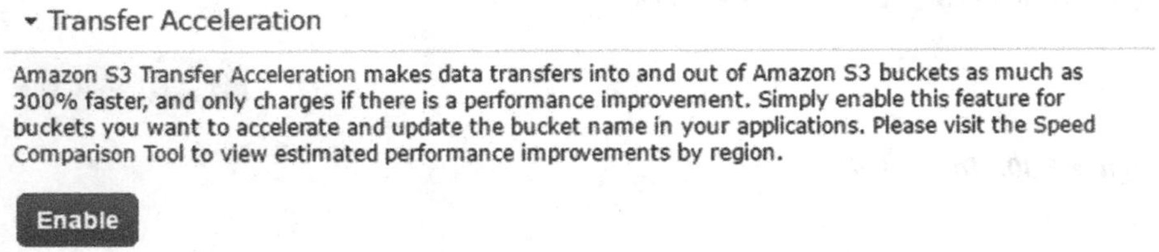

▾ Transfer Acceleration

Amazon S3 Transfer Acceleration makes data transfers into and out of Amazon S3 buckets as much as 300% faster, and only charges if there is a performance improvement. Simply enable this feature for buckets you want to accelerate and update the bucket name in your applications. Please visit the Speed Comparison Tool to view estimated performance improvements by region.

Figure 5-32. *Transfer acceleration*

Empty Bucket

When you want to delete all the objects from the bucket, you can use the Empty Bucket action.

1. To delete all objects from the bucket, select the bucket and click the Actions menu option, as shown in Figure 5-33.

Figure 5-33. *Action menu*

> 2. Click the Empty Bucket option, as shown in Figure 5-34. This will open the confirmation window to empty the bucket.

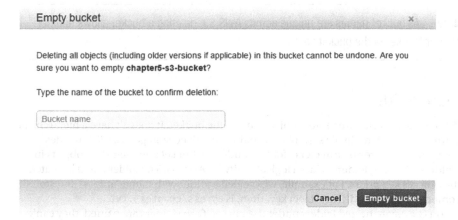

Figure 5-34. *Empty bucket*

Delete Bucket

To delete the bucket, select the bucket and click the Delete Bucket option under the Actions menu. (See Figure 5-35.)

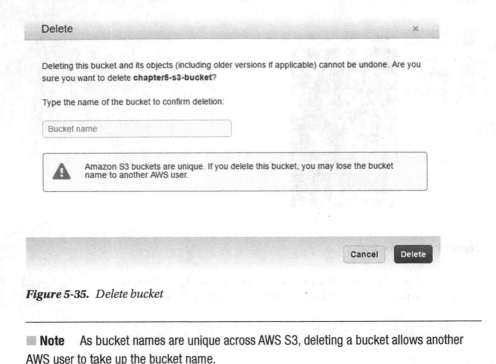

Figure 5-35. *Delete bucket*

Create Folder

AWS S3 has a flat structure to store objects under the bucket. It doesn't have a hierarchical structure that you have in file systems. To enable organized storage, AWS S3 provides folder creation where you can create folders under the bucket and then store objects in the folders. Creating folders is just a logical entity for AWS S3. The folder name is treated as the object's key prefix. For example, we created a folder with name "apress" and stored the object chapter5.txt. The object key, then, is apress/chapter5.txt.

You can create nested folders under the bucket. Once folders are named, they can't be renamed.

1. Click the Create Folder button that is available on the bar at the top of the screen, as shown on Figure 5-36.

Figure 5-36. *Create Folder top bar*

2. You can also click the Actions ➤ Create Folder... menu option, as shown in Figure 5-37.

Figure 5-37. *Create Folder in the Actions menu*

3. Open the Context (right-click) menu and click Create Folder..., as shown in Figure 5-38.

Figure 5-38. *Create Folder... in the Context menu*

4. We have created a folder with the name "apress," as shown in Figure 5-39.

Figure 5-39. Folder created

Public Folder

You can make the folder publicly available for viewing and downloading. Once the folder is made public, you cannot make it private. As a folder is just a logical entity, you need to update permissions of each object under that public folder to make it private.

You can make folder public by performing the following steps:

1. Select the folder and click the Actions ➤ Make Public menu option. OR

2. Select the folder, open the Context (right-click) menu, and click Make Public.

3. After you click Make Public, a confirmation dialog will pop up. Click the OK button, as shown in Figure 5-40.

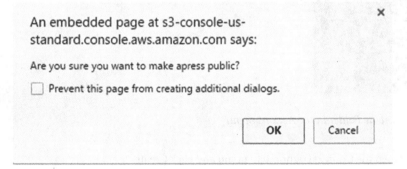

Figure 5-40. Making a folder public

Deleting Folders

Deleting a folder deletes all the objects automatically under it. Before deleting a folder, you may want to make a backup for the objects. If so, you can copy the objects to another bucket or folder. There are two ways to delete a folder:

Select the folder and click the Actions ➤ Delete menu option.

OR

Select the folder and open the Context (right-click) menu and click Delete.

After you click "Delete," a confirmation dialog box will pop up. Click the OK button, as shown in Figure 5-41.

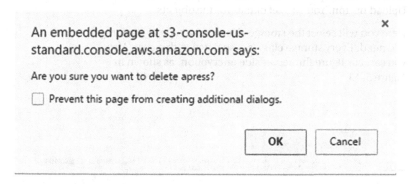

Figure 5-41. Delete folder

Uploading Objects

You can upload any type of files to AWS S3. All files are treated as objects in AWS S3. The object may be a text file, word document, audio or video files, photos, and so on. It is mandatory to store objects within a bucket or folder. You can store an object of a size up to 5TB, and you can have an unlimited number of objects.

1. To upload an object, click Upload from the "Actions" menu or Context (right-click) menu, as shown in Figure 5-42.

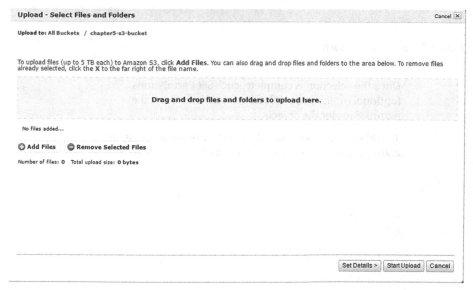

Figure 5-42. Upload - Select Files and Folder screen

2. Drag and drop files and folders or click Add Files. Here you can add multiple files and folders. Once the files and folders selection is complete, click Set Details (optional) or the Start Upload button. You will set details for the objects.

3. Here you will select the storage class for the type of S3 storage you need. Every storage class is associated with a cost. Also you can configure the server side encryption, as shown in Figure 5-43.

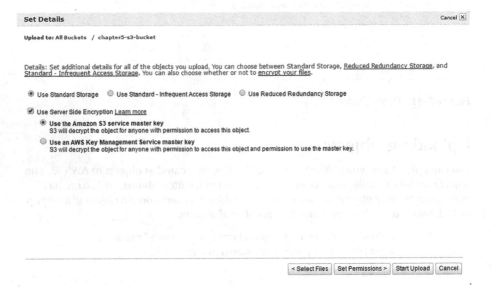

Figure 5-43. *Set Details screen*

4. Once the selection is complete, click Set Permissions (optional) or the Start Upload button. You will set the permissions for the objects.

5. To add more permissions, click Add more permissions and grant permissions, as shown in Figure 5-44.

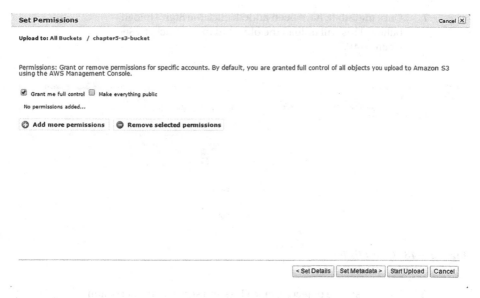

Figure 5-44. *Set Permissions screen*

6. Once permissions are granted, click Set Metadata (optional) or the Start Upload button. Next, you will set metadata. You can add metadata by clicking Add more metadata, as shown in Figure 5-45.

Figure 5-45. *Set Metadata screen*

7. Once metadata have been added, click the Start Upload button. This will upload the object to the S3 bucket. (See Figure 5-46.)

Figure 5-46. *Object listing*

8. You can set the object storage class and server side encryption from the Properties section under Details, as shown in Figure 5-47.

Figure 5-47. *Object's details*

9. You can configure permissions from the Properties section under Permissions, as shown in Figure 5-48.

▾ Permissions

You can control access to the bucket and its contents using access policies. Learn more.

Grantee: sunil.gulabani2   ☑ Open/Download ☑ View Permissions ☑ Edit Permissions   ×

⊕ **Add more permissions**

Save   Cancel

Figure 5-48. *Object permissions*

10. You can configure metadata from the Properties section under Metadata, as shown in Figure 5-49.

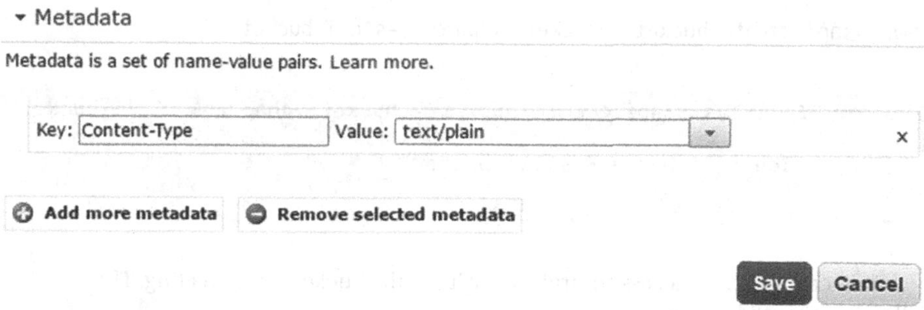

▾ Metadata

Metadata is a set of name-value pairs. Learn more.

Key: Content-Type   Value: text/plain ▾   ✕

⊕ Add more metadata   ⊖ Remove selected metadata

Save   Cancel

Figure 5-49. Object metadata

Deleting Objects

Deleting an object will remove the object from the bucket. There are two ways to delete an object:

1. Select the object, open the Context (right-click) menu, and click Delete. OR

2. Select the object and click Delete.

The screen in Figure 5-50 will appear, asking for confirmation to delete the object.

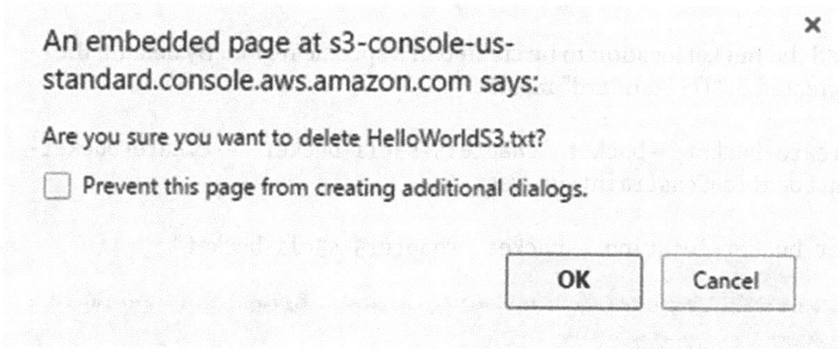

An embedded page at s3-console-us-standard.console.aws.amazon.com says: ✕

Are you sure you want to delete HelloWorldS3.txt?

☐ Prevent this page from creating additional dialogs.

OK   Cancel

Figure 5-50. Delete object

Using AWS CLI

In Chapter 1, you saw how to install AWS CLI. Now you will learn how to use AWS CLI to manage AWS S3.

Create Bucket

The create-bucket command helps to create a new bucket in AWS S3:

```
>aws s3api create-bucket --bucket "chapter5-s3cli-bucket"
```

```
C:\Users\Dell>aws s3api create-bucket --bucket "chapter5-s3cli-bucket"
{
    "Location": "/chapter5-s3cli-bucket"
}
```

You can assign an access control list (ACL) to the bucket while creating. The following are valid values:

- private
- public-read
- public-read-write
- authenticated-read

```
>aws s3api create-bucket --bucket "chapter5-s3cli-bucket" --acl
"public-read"
```

```
C:\Users\Dell>aws s3api create-bucket --bucket "chapter5-s3cli-bucket" --acl "public-read"
{
    "Location": "/chapter5-s3cli-bucket"
}
```

You can add the bucket location to be created in a specific region. By default, the bucket will be created in "US Standard" region:

```
>aws s3api create-bucket --bucket "chapter5-s3cli-bucket" --create-bucket-
configuration LocationConstraint=us-west-2
```

```
>aws s3api get-bucket-location --bucket "chapter5-s3cli-bucket"
```

```
C:\Users\Dell>aws s3api create-bucket --bucket "chapter5-s3cli-bucket" --create-bucket-configuration LocationConstraint=us-west-2
{
    "Location": "http://chapter5-s3cli-bucket.s3.amazonaws.com/"
}
C:\Users\Dell>aws s3api get-bucket-location --bucket "chapter5-s3cli-bucket"
{
    "LocationConstraint": "us-west-2"
}
```

The following are valid values for `LocationConstraint`:

- us-west-1
- us-west-2
- ca-central-1
- EU or eu-west-1
- eu-west-2
- eu-central-1
- ap-south-1
- ap-southeast-1
- ap-southeast-2
- ap-northeast-1
- ap-northeast-2
- sa-east-1
- " "empty string - US East region (N. Virginia)
- us-east-2

To grant access to grantee for `READ`, `WRITE`, `READ_ACP`, and `WRITE_ACP` on any objects in the bucket, we have the following:

- grant-full-control
- grant-read
- grant-read-acp
- grant-write
- grant-write-acp

The grantee can be provided in any of the following key-pair forms:

- emailAddress - Email address of AWS account
- id - AWS account's canonical ID
- uri - prefined group

```
>aws s3api create-bucket --bucket "chapter5-s3cli-bucket-full" --grant-full-
control emailAddress=sunil.gulabani1@gmail.com,emailAddress=sunil_gulabani@
yahoo.com
```

```
>aws s3api create-bucket --bucket "chapter5-s3cli-bucket-read" --grant-read
emailAddress=sunil.gulabani1@gmail.com,emailAddress=sunil_gulabani@yahoo.com
```

```
>aws s3api create-bucket --bucket "chapter5-s3cli-bucket-read-acp" --grant-
read-acp emailAddress=sunil.gulabani1@gmail.com,emailAddress=sunil_gulabani@
yahoo.com
```

```
>aws s3api create-bucket --bucket "chapter5-s3cli-bucket-write" --grant-
write emailAddress=sunil.gulabani1@gmail.com,emailAddress=sunil_gulabani@
yahoo.com
```

```
>aws s3api create-bucket --bucket "chapter5-s3cli-bucket-write-acp" --grant-
write-acp emailAddress=sunil.gulabani1@gmail.com,emailAddress=sunil_
gulabani@yahoo.com
```

To get the ACL for specific bucket, use get-bucket-acl:

```
>aws s3api get-bucket-acl --bucket "chapter5-s3cli-bucket-full"
```

Bucket Permissions

Bucket permission can also be added after the bucket is created. You can add bucket policy in multiple ways:

```
>aws s3api put-bucket-acl --bucket "chapter5-s3cli-bucket-full" --acl
private
```

Valid values for --acl are as follows:

- private

- public-read

- public-read-write

- authenticated-read

You can also provide the JSON format that has different grants to users:

```
>aws s3api put-bucket-acl --bucket "chapter5-s3cli-bucket-full" --access-
control-policy file://C:/Users/Dell/access-control-policy.json
```

```
access-control-policy.json
{
   "Grants": [
        {
        "Grantee": {
          "ID": "99r85d7ty258cf63e108d306ea1b4xxxxxxxxxxxxxxxxxxxxxx
                 AWSCanonicalUserID",
          "Type": "CanonicalUser"
        },
        "Permission": "FULL_CONTROL"
      }, {
        "Grantee": {
          "EmailAddress": "sunil.gulabani1@gmail.com",
          "Type": "AmazonCustomerByEmail"
        },
        "Permission": "WRITE"
      }
   ],
   "Owner": {
     "DisplayName": "sunil.gulabani2@gmail.com",
     "ID": "99r85d7ty258cf63e108d306ea1b4xxxxxxxxxxxxxxxxxxxxxx
            AWSCanonicalUserID"
   }
}
```

■ **Note**   To get the Canonical User ID, go to `https://console.aws.amazon.com/iam/home?#/security_credential`. Under the Account Identifiers section, you can get the Canonical User ID.

Valid values for grantee types are as follows:

- CanonicalUser

- AmazonCustomerByEmail

- Group

The following are valid values for permission:

- FULL_CONTROL

- WRITE

- WRITE_ACP

- READ

- READ_ACP

There are also specific grant commands that can have commas separating grantees. Grantees can be defined in key-value form. Keys can have the following forms:

- emailAddress

- id

- url

```
> aws s3api put-bucket-acl --bucket "chapter5-s3cli-bucket-full"
--grant-full-control emailaddress=sunil.gulabani1@gmail.com,emailAddress=
sunil_gulabani@yahoo.com

> aws s3api put-bucket-acl --bucket "chapter5-s3cli-bucket-read"
--grant-read emailaddress=sunil.gulabani1@gmail.com

> aws s3api put-bucket-acl --bucket "chapter5-s3cli-bucket-read-acp"
--grant-read-acp emailaddress=sunil.gulabani1@gmail.com

> aws s3api put-bucket-acl --bucket "chapter5-s3cli-bucket-write"
--grant-write emailaddress=sunil.gulabani1@gmail.com

> aws s3api put-bucket-acl --bucket "chapter5-s3cli-bucket-write-acp"
--grant-write-acp emailaddress=sunil.gulabani1@gmail.com
```

```
C:\Users\Dell>aws s3api put-bucket-acl --bucket "chapter5-s3cli-bucket-full" --acl private
C:\Users\Dell>aws s3api put-bucket-acl --bucket "chapter5-s3cli-bucket-full" --access-control-policy file://C:/Users/Dell/access-control-policy.json
C:\Users\Dell>aws s3api put-bucket-acl --bucket "chapter5-s3cli-bucket-full" --grant-full-control emailaddress=sunil.gulabani@gmail.com,emailAddress=sunil_gulabani@yah
oo.com
C:\Users\Dell>aws s3api put-bucket-acl --bucket "chapter5-s3cli-bucket-read" --grant-read emailaddress=sunil.gulabani@gmail.com
C:\Users\Dell>aws s3api put-bucket-acl --bucket "chapter5-s3cli-bucket-read-acp" --grant-read-acp emailaddress=sunil.gulabani@gmail.com
C:\Users\Dell>aws s3api put-bucket-acl --bucket "chapter5-s3cli-bucket-write" --grant-write emailaddress=sunil.gulabani@gmail.com
C:\Users\Dell>aws s3api put-bucket-acl --bucket "chapter5-s3cli-bucket-write-acp" --grant-write-acp emailaddress=sunil.gulabani@gmail.com
C:\Users\Dell>
```

The put-bucket-acl command doesn't provide any response.

Static Website Hosting

You can host static web sites on AWS S3. You need to create a bucket and then configure the bucket:

```
>aws s3api put-bucket-website --bucket "chapter5-s3cli-bucket"
--website-configuration file://C:/Users/Dell/website-configuration.json
```

website-configuration.json

```
{
  "ErrorDocument": {
    "Key": "error.html"
  },
  "IndexDocument": {
    "Suffix": "index.html"
  }
}
```

```
C:\Users\Dell>aws s3api put-bucket-website --bucket "chapter5-s3cli-bucket" --website-configuration file://C:/Users/Dell/website-configuration.json
C:\Users\Dell>
```

You can also add custom rules to redirect requests to other hosts or replace some keys:

```
>aws s3api put-bucket-website --bucket "chapter5-s3cli-bucket"
--website-configuration file://C:/Users/Dell/website-configuration-with-
routing-rules.json
```

website-configuration-with-routing-rules.json

```
{
  "ErrorDocument": {
    "Key": "error.html"
  },
  "IndexDocument": {
    "Suffix": "index.html"
  },
```

257

```
  "RoutingRules": [
    {
      "Condition": {
        "KeyPrefixEquals": "chapter5"
      },
      "Redirect": {
        "ReplaceKeyPrefixWith": "chapter"
      }
    }
  ]
}
```

C:\Users\Dell>aws s3api put-bucket-website --bucket "chapter5-s3cli-bucket" --website-configuration file://C:/Users/Dell/website-configuration-with-routing-rules.json
C:\Users\Dell>

The above-mentioned rules will replace the "chapter5" key with a "chapter" value. You can have other parameters that can be configured in routing rules:

```
"RoutingRules": [
    {
      "Condition": {
        "HttpErrorCodeReturnedEquals": "string",
        "KeyPrefixEquals": "string"
      },
      "Redirect": {
        "HostName": "string",
        "HttpRedirectCode": "string",
        "Protocol": "http"|"https",
        "ReplaceKeyPrefixWith": "string",
        "ReplaceKeyWith": "string"
      }
    }
  ]
```

You can also redirect all requests to a specific host:

```
>aws s3api put-bucket-website --bucket "chapter5-s3cli-bucket"
--website-configuration file://C:/Users/Dell/website-configuration-redirect-
all-request.json
```

```
website-configuration-redirect-all-request.json
```

```
{
  "RedirectAllRequestsTo": {
    "HostName": "sunilgulabani.com",
    "Protocol": "http"
  }
}
```

```
C:\Users\Dell>aws s3api put-bucket-website --bucket "chapter5-s3cli-bucket" --website-configuration file://C:/Users/Dell/website-configuration-redirect-all-request.json
C:\Users\Dell>
```

Valid values for "Protocol" are: HTTP and HTTPS.
To view the web site configuration, use the get-bucket-website command:

```
>aws s3api get-bucket-website --bucket "chapter5-s3cli-bucket"
```

```
C:\Users\Dell>aws s3api get-bucket-website --bucket "chapter5-s3cli-bucket"
{
    "RedirectAllRequestsTo": {
        "HostName": "sunilgulabani.com",
        "Protocol": "http"
    }
}
```

To delete the web site configuration, use the delete-bucket-website command:

```
>aws s3api delete-bucket-website --bucket "chapter5-s3cli-bucket"
```

```
C:\Users\Dell>aws s3api delete-bucket-website --bucket "chapter5-s3cli-bucket"
C:\Users\Dell>
```

Logging

You can enable the logging on bucket activities. Buckets need to have write and read acp ACL for LogDelivery system:

```
>aws s3api put-bucket-acl --bucket "chapter5-s3cli-bucket"
--grant-write URI=http://acs.amazonaws.com/groups/s3/LogDelivery
--grant-read-acp URI=http://acs.amazonaws.com/groups/s3/LogDelivery

>aws s3api put-bucket-logging --bucket "chapter5-s3cli-bucket"
--bucket-logging-status file://C:/Users/Dell/logging.json
```

logging.json

```
{
  "LoggingEnabled": {
    "TargetBucket": "chapter5-s3-bucket-log",
    "TargetPrefix": "logs",
    "TargetGrants": [
      {
        "Grantee": {
          "EmailAddress": "sunil.gulabani2@gmail.com",
```

```
        "Type": "AmazonCustomerByEmail"
      },
      "Permission": "FULL_CONTROL"
    }
  ]
}
}
```

C:\Users\Dell>aws s3api put-bucket-acl --bucket "chapter5-s3-bucket-log" --grant-write URI=http://acs.amazonaws.com/groups/s3/LogDelivery --grant-read-acp URI=http://a
cs.amazonaws.com/groups/s3/LogDelivery
C:\Users\Dell>aws s3api put-bucket-logging --bucket "chapter5-s3cli-bucket" --bucket-logging-status file://C:/Users/Dell/logging.json

The "TargetGrants" tag can have multiple combinations:

```
{
    "Grantee": {
      "DisplayName": "DISPLAY_NAME",
      "EmailAddress": "EMAIL_ADDRESS",
      "ID": "CANONICAL_USER_ID",
      "Type": "CanonicalUser"|"AmazonCustomerByEmail"|"Group",
      "URI": "GROUP_ID"
    },
      "Permission": "FULL_CONTROL"|"READ"|"WRITE"
}
```

To view the bucket logging status, use the following:

```
>aws s3api get-bucket-logging --bucket "chapter5-s3cli-bucket"
```

C:\Users\Dell>aws s3api get-bucket-logging --bucket "chapter5-s3cli-bucket"
{
    "LoggingEnabled": {
        "TargetPrefix": "logs",
        "TargetBucket": "chapter5-s3-bucket-log",
        "TargetGrants": [
            {
                "Grantee": {
                    "Type": "CanonicalUser",
                    "DisplayName": "sunil.gulabani2",
                    "ID": "
                },
                "Permission": "FULL_CONTROL"
            }
        ]
    }
}

To disable logging, you can use the same put-bucket-logging command, but the JSON structure will have no data:

```
>aws s3api put-bucket-logging --bucket "chapter5-s3cli-bucket"
--bucket-logging-status file://C:/Users/Dell/logging.json
```

Logging.json

```
{
}
```

Events

You can trigger notifications over certain events on buckets.

```
>aws s3api put-bucket-notification-configuration --bucket "chapter5-s3cli-
bucket" --notification-configuration file://C:/Users/Dell/notification.json
```

notification.json

```
{
    "TopicConfigurations": [{
        "TopicArn": "arn:aws:sns:us-east-1:298147259238:objectCreated
        SNSTopic",
        "Events": [
            "s3:ObjectCreated:*"
        ]
    }],
    "QueueConfigurations": [{
        "QueueArn": "arn:aws:sqs:us-east-1:298147259238:objectCreatedQueue",
        "Events": [
            "s3:ObjectRemoved:*"
        ],
        "Filter": {
            "Key": {
                "FilterRules": [{
                    "Name": "prefix",
                    "Value": "chapter5"
                }, {
                    "Name": "suffix",
                    "Value": "log"
                }
                }]
            }
        }
    }]
}
```

```
C:\Users\Dell>aws s3api put-bucket-notification-configuration --bucket "chapter5-s3cli-bucket" --notification-configuration file://C:/Users/Dell/notification.json
C:\Users\Dell>
```

You can also trigger events on SQS, SNS, and lambda function.
Valid values for events are the following:

- s3:ReducedRedundancyLostObject

- s3:ObjectCreated:*

- s3:ObjectCreated:Put

- s3:ObjectCreated:Post

- s3:ObjectCreated:Copy

- s3:ObjectCreated:CompleteMultipartUpload

- s3:ObjectRemoved:*

- s3:ObjectRemoved:Delete

- s3:ObjectRemoved:DeleteMarkerCreated

To add lambda function notification configuration, add the following tag:

```
"LambdaFunctionConfigurations": [{
    "LambdaFunctionArn": "arn:aws:lambda:us-east-1:298147259238:function:obj
    ectCreatedFunction",
    "Events": [
        "s3:ReducedRedundancyLostObject"
    ]
}]
```

■ **Note**   SQS, SNS, and lambda function should have an IAM policy so that S3 can publish events before creating notifications.

To view the bucket notification configurations, use the following:

```
>aws s3api get-bucket-notification-configuration
--bucket "chapter5-s3cli-bucket"
```

```
C:\Users\Dell>aws s3api get-bucket-notification-configuration --bucket "chapter5-s3cli-bucket"
{
    "TopicConfigurations": [
        {
            "Id": "ZTNkN2VhYzItOGY4NC000DA0LWJmOGUtODEwYzgyZmIzMDMx",
            "TopicArn": "arn:aws:sns:us-east-1:            :objectCreatedSNSTopic",
            "Events": [
                "s3:ObjectCreated:*"
            ]
        }
    ],
    "QueueConfigurations": [
        {
            "Filter": {
                "Key": {
                    "FilterRules": [
                        {
                            "Name": "Prefix",
                            "Value": "chapter5"
                        },
                        {
                            "Name": "Suffix",
                            "Value": "log"
                        }
                    ]
                }
            },
            "Id": "ZTRhZTM3OTEtNzg4Yy00MjM1LWFlZmUtMmQ2YTU0ZWYzNGYw",
            "QueueArn": "arn:aws:sqs:us-east-1:            :objectCreatedQueue",
            "Events": [
                "s3:ObjectRemoved:*"
            ]
        }
    ]
}
```

Versioning

Versioning is used to maintain multiple versions of objects. It is used to restore the older objects:

```
>aws s3api put-bucket-versioning --bucket "chapter5-s3cli-bucket"
--versioning-configuration Status=Enabled
```

```
C:\Users\Dell>aws s3api put-bucket-versioning --bucket "chapter5-s3cli-bucket" --versioning-configuration Status=Enabled
C:\Users\Dell>
```

To get the versioning state, use the get-bucket-versioning command:

```
>aws s3api get-bucket-versioning --bucket "chapter5-s3cli-bucket"
```

```
C:\Users\Dell>aws s3api get-bucket-versioning --bucket "chapter5-s3cli-bucket"
{
    "Status": "Enabled"
}
```

Versioning can't be disabled; it can only be enabled or suspended. To suspend the versioning, we will use the same put-bucket-configuration:

```
>aws s3api put-bucket-versioning --bucket "chapter5-s3cli-bucket"
--versioning-configuration Status=Suspended
```

```
>aws s3api get-bucket-versioning --bucket "chapter5-s3cli-bucket"
```

```
C:\Users\Dell>aws s3api put-bucket-versioning --bucket "chapter5-s3cli-bucket" --versioning-configuration Status=Suspended
C:\Users\Dell>aws s3api get-bucket-versioning --bucket "chapter5-s3cli-bucket"
{
    "Status": "Suspended"
}
```

Life Cycle

Object life cycle can be fined on the bucket level. Life-cycle management helps us to perform actions such as the following:

- Taking necessary steps for older versions of objects

- Applying specific rules on newly added objects

- Moving older objects to Glacier or Standard - Infrequent Access storage

```
>aws s3api put-bucket-lifecycle-configuration --bucket "chapter5-s3cli-
bucket" --lifecycle-configuration file://C:/Users/Dell/lifecycle-
configuration.json
```

lifecycle-configuration.json

```
{
    "Rules": [{
            "ID": "Expiration Action with Date",
            "Prefix": "chapter1",
            "Status": "Enabled",
            "Expiration": {
                    "Date": "2017-02-04T00:00:00.000Z"
            }
    }, {
            "ID": "Expiration Action with Days",
            "Prefix": "chapter2",
            "Status": "Enabled",
            "Expiration": {
                    "Days": 30
            }
    }, {
            "ID": "Move old objects to Glacier Action",
            "Prefix": "chapter3",
```

```
            "Status": "Enabled",
            "Transitions": [{
                    "Date": "2017-03-01T00:00:00.000Z",
                    "StorageClass": "GLACIER"
            }]
    }, {
            "ID": "Non-Current Versioned Object Actions",
            "Prefix": "chapter4",
            "Status": "Enabled",
            "NoncurrentVersionTransitions": [{
                    "NoncurrentDays": 30,
                    "StorageClass": "STANDARD_IA"
            }],
            "NoncurrentVersionExpiration": {
                    "NoncurrentDays": 40
            }
    }, {
            "ID": "Abort Incomplete Multipart Action",
            "Prefix": "chapter5",
            "Status": "Enabled",
            "AbortIncompleteMultipartUpload": {
                    "DaysAfterInitiation": 1
            }
    }]
}
```

```
C:\Users\Dell>aws s3api put-bucket-lifecycle-configuration --bucket "chapter5-s3cli-bucket" --lifecycle-configuration file://C:/Users/Dell/lifecycle-configuration.json
C:\Users\Dell>
```

The "Expiration" tag can contain the following:

- "Date": It signifies to activate action to expire objects starting from the specified date.

- "Day": It signifies to expire objects after the specified days of object creation.

The "Status" tag can have two values: Enabled or Disabled.
The "StorageClass" tag can have the following values:

- GLACIER

- STANDARD_IA

To view the bucket life-cycle configuration, use the get-bucket-lifecycle-configuration command:

```
>aws s3api get-bucket-lifecycle-configuration
--bucket "chapter5-s3cli-bucket"
```

```
C:\Users\Dell>aws s3api get-bucket-lifecycle-configuration --bucket "chapter5-s3cli-bucket"
{
    "Rules": [
        {
            "Status": "Enabled",
            "Prefix": "chapter1",
                    "Expiration": {
            "Date": "2017-02-04T00:00:00.000Z"
            },
            "ID": "Expiration Action with Date"
                },
        {
            "Status": "Enabled",
            "Prefix": "chapter2",
            "Expiration": {
                "Days": 30
            },
            "ID": "Expiration Action with Days"
        },
        {
            "Status": "Enabled",
            "Prefix": "chapter3",
            "Transitions": [
                {
                    "Date": "2017-03-01T00:00:00.000Z",
                    "StorageClass": "GLACIER"
                }
            ],
            "ID": "Move old objects to Glacier Action"
        },
        {
            "Status": "Enabled",
            "NoncurrentVersionExpiration": {
                        "NoncurrentDays": 40
            },
            "Prefix": "chapter4",
            "NoncurrentVersionTransitions": [
                {
                    "NoncurrentDays": 30,
                    "StorageClass": "STANDARD_IA"
                }
            ],
            "ID": "Non-Current Versioned Object Actions"
        },
        {
            "Status": "Enabled",
            "Prefix": "chapter5",
            "ID": "Abort Incomplete Multipart Action",
            "AbortIncompleteMultipartUpload": {
                "DaysAfterInitiation": 1
            }
        }
    ]
}
```

To delete the bucket life cycle configuration, use the delete-bucket-lifecycle command:

```
>aws s3api delete-bucket-lifecycle --bucket "chapter5-s3cli-bucket"
```

```
C:\Users\Dell>aws s3api delete-bucket-lifecycle --bucket "chapter5-s3cli-bucket"

C:\Users\Dell>
```

Cross-Region Replication

Buckets can be replicated to other regions for backup purposes or for faster availability to other regions' users. It is mandatory that versioning should be enabled on a bucket:

```
>aws s3api put-bucket-replication --bucket "chapter5-s3cli-bucket"
--replication-configuration file://C:/Users/Dell/replication.json
```

replication.json

```
{
    "Role": "arn:aws:iam::298147259238:role/s3-bucket-replication",
    "Rules": [
        {
            "ID": "S3 bucket replication",
            "Prefix": "",
            "Status": "Enabled",
            "Destination": {
                "Bucket": "arn:aws:s3:::chapter5-s3cli-bucket-backup",
                "StorageClass": "STANDARD"
            }
        }
    ]
}
```

```
C:\Users\Dell>aws s3api put-bucket-replication --bucket "chapter5-s3cli-bucket" --replication-configuration file://C:/Users/Dell/replication.json
C:\Users\Dell>
```

"Role" should have a policy to access S3 with all operations and a trust relationship for role should have the following:

Service Policy

```
{
    "Version": "2012-10-17",
    "Statement": [
        {
            "Effect": "Allow",
            "Action": "s3:*",
            "Resource": "*"
        }
    ]
}
```

Trust Relationships

```
{
    "Version": "2012-10-17",
    "Statement": [
        {
            "Effect": "Allow",
            "Principal": {
                "Service": "s3.amazonaws.com"
            },
            "Action": "sts:AssumeRole"
        }
    ]
}
```

"Status" can have value: Enabled or Disabled.
"StorageClass" can have the following values:

- STANDARD

- REDUCED_REDUNDANCY

- STANDARD_IA

■ **Note**   Versioning needs to be enabled for source and destination buckets.

To get the replication configuration, use the get-bucket-replication command:

```
>aws s3api get-bucket-replication --bucket "chapter5-s3cli-bucket"
```

```
C:\Users\Dell>aws s3api get-bucket-replication --bucket "chapter5-s3cli-bucket"
{
    "ReplicationConfiguration": {
        "Rules": [
            {
                "Status": "Enabled",
                "Prefix": "",
                "Destination": {
                    "Bucket": "arn:aws:s3:::chapter5-s3cli-bucket-backup",
                    "StorageClass": "STANDARD"
                },
                "ID": "S3 bucket replication"
            }
        ],
        "Role": "arn:aws:iam:: ▓▓▓▓▓▓▓▓ :role/s3-bucket-replication"
    }
}
```

To delete the bucket replication configuration, use the delete-bucket-replication command:

```
>aws s3api delete-bucket-replication --bucket "chapter5-s3cli-bucket"
```

```
C:\Users\Dell>aws s3api delete-bucket-replication --bucket "chapter5-s3cli-bucket"
C:\Users\Dell>
```

Tags

Tagging can be set on buckets. Tags can have a key-value format:

```
>aws s3api put-bucket-tagging --bucket "chapter5-s3cli-bucket" --tagging
file://C:/Users/Dell/tagging.json
```

tagging.json

```
{
    "TagSet": [{
            "Key": "Chapter",
            "Value": "5"
    }, {
            "Key": "Name",
            "Value": "S3"
    }]
}
```

```
C:\Users\Dell>aws s3api put-bucket-tagging --bucket "chapter5-s3cli-bucket" --tagging file://C:/Users/Dell/tagging.json
C:\Users\Dell>
```

To get the tags associated with the bucket, use the get-bucket-tagging command:

```
>aws s3api get-bucket-tagging --bucket "chapter5-s3cli-bucket"
```

```
C:\Users\Dell>aws s3api get-bucket-tagging --bucket "chapter5-s3cli-bucket"
{
    "TagSet": [
        {
            "Value": "5",
            "Key": "Chapter"
        },
        {
            "Value": "S3",
            "Key": "Name"
        }
    ]
}
```

To delete the bucket tagging, use the delete-bucket-tagging command:

```
> aws s3api delete-bucket-tagging --bucket "chapter5-s3cli-bucket"
```

```
C:\Users\Dell>aws s3api delete-bucket-tagging --bucket "chapter5-s3cli-bucket"
C:\Users\Dell>aws s3api get-bucket-tagging --bucket "chapter5-s3cli-bucket"
An error occurred (NoSuchTagSet) when calling the GetBucketTagging operation: The TagSet does not exist
```

Requester Pays

The Requester Pays feature enables the bucket requestor to pay for the download of the objects instead of the bucket owner:

```
>aws s3api put-bucket-request-payment --bucket "chapter5-s3cli-bucket"
--request-payment-configuration file://C:/Users/Dell/requester-payment.json
```

requester-payment.json

```
{
    "Payer": "Requester"
}
```

```
C:\Users\Dell>aws s3api put-bucket-request-payment --bucket "chapter5-s3cli-bucket" --request-payment-configuration file://C:/Users/Dell/requester-payment.json
C:\Users\Dell>
```

The "Payer" can have value: Requester or BucketOwner.
To get the requester's payment, use the following command:

```
>aws s3api get-bucket-request-payment --bucket "chapter5-s3cli-bucket"
```

```
C:\Users\Dell>aws s3api get-bucket-request-payment --bucket "chapter5-s3cli-bucket"
{
    "Payer": "Requester"
}
```

Transferring Acceleration

Transferring acceleration makes retrieving the bucket objects much faster:

```
>aws s3api put-bucket-accelerate-configuration --bucket "chapter5-s3cli-
bucket" --accelerate-configuration file://C:/Users/Dell/accelerate.json
accelerate.json
{
    "Status": "Enabled"
}
```

```
C:\Users\Dell>aws s3api put-bucket-accelerate-configuration --bucket "chapter5-s3cli-bucket" --accelerate-configuration file://C:/Users/Dell/accelerate.json
C:\Users\Dell>
```

"Status" can have value: Enabled or Suspended.

To get the transfer accelerate configuration, use the following command:

```
>aws s3api get-bucket-accelerate-configuration --bucket "chapter5-s3cli-
bucket"
```

```
C:\Users\Dell>aws s3api get-bucket-accelerate-configuration --bucket "chapter5-s3cli-bucket"
{
    "Status": "Enabled"
}
```

Emptying Buckets

To delete all objects from the S3 bucket, use the high-level S3 command:

```
>aws s3 rm s3://chapter5-s3cli-bucket --recursive
```

```
C:\Users\Dell>aws s3 rm s3://chapter5-s3cli-bucket --recursive
delete: s3://chapter5-s3cli-bucket/chapter.txt
delete: s3://chapter5-s3cli-bucket/HelloWorldS3.txt
delete: s3://chapter5-s3cli-bucket/index.html
```

Deleting Buckets

To delete a bucket permanently, use the delete-bucket command:

```
>aws s3api delete-bucket --bucket "chapter5-s3cli-bucket"
```

```
C:\Users\Dell>aws s3api delete-bucket --bucket "chapter5-s3cli-bucket"

C:\Users\Dell>
```

To verify that the bucket has been deleted, use the list-buckets command:

```
>aws s3api list-buckets
```

```
C:\Users\Dell>aws s3api list-buckets
{
    "Owner": {
        "DisplayName": "sunil.gulabani2",
        "ID": "▮▮▮▮▮▮▮▮▮▮▮▮▮▮▮▮▮▮▮▮▮▮▮▮▮▮▮▮▮▮▮▮"
    },
    "Buckets": [
        {
            "CreationDate": "2017-01-31T14:47:14.000Z",
            "Name": "cf-templates-t9hoikys420l-us-west-2"
        }
    ]
}
```

Creating Folders

You can create folders under the bucket using the put-object command:

```
>aws s3api put-object --bucket "chapter5-s3cli-bucket" --key apress/
```

```
C:\Users\Dell>aws s3api put-object --bucket "chapter5-s3cli-bucket" --key apress/
{
    "ETag": "\"d41d8cd98f00b204e9800998ecf8427e\""
}
```

You can check that the folder has been created by using the list-objects command:

```
>aws s3api list-objects --bucket "chapter5-s3cli-bucket"
```

```
C:\Users\Dell>aws s3api list-objects --bucket "chapter5-s3cli-bucket"
{
    "Contents": [
        {
            "LastModified": "2017-02-05T08:56:54.000Z",
            "ETag": "\"d41d8cd98f00b204e9800998ecf8427e\"",
            "StorageClass": "STANDARD",
            "Key": "apress/",
            "Owner": {
                "DisplayName": "sunil.gulabani2",
                "ID": "▮▮▮▮▮▮▮▮▮▮▮▮▮▮▮▮▮▮▮▮▮▮▮▮▮▮▮▮▮▮▮▮"
            },
            "Size": 0
        }
    ]
}
```

Deleting Folders

To delete a folder, use the delete-object command:

```
>aws s3api delete-object --bucket "chapter5-s3cli-bucket" --key apress/
```

```
C:\Users\Dell>aws s3api delete-object --bucket "chapter5-s3cli-bucket" --key apress/
C:\Users\Dell>
```

Uploading Objects

Uploading an object will add an object to the S3 bucket:

```
>aws s3api put-object --bucket "chapter5-s3cli-bucket" --key "apress/
chapter.txt" --body C:/Users/Dell/chapter.txt
```

```
C:\Users\Dell>aws s3api put-object --bucket "chapter5-s3cli-bucket" --key "apress/chapter.txt" --body C:/Users/Dell/chapter.txt
{
    "ETag": "\"236bf30c70dc03f69175f030afbe38f3\""
}
```

You can assign permissions and other object metadata while uploading the object. To assign server-side encryption and storage class, use the following command:

```
>aws s3api put-object --bucket "chapter5-s3cli-bucket" --key "apress/
chapter1.txt" --body file://C:/Users/Dell/chapter.txt --server-side-
encryption AES256 --storage-class "STANDARD"
```

```
C:\Users\Dell>aws s3api put-object --bucket "chapter5-s3cli-bucket" --key "apress/chapter1.txt" --body C:/Users/Dell/chapter.txt --server-side-encryption AES256 --stora
ge-class "STANDARD"
{
    "ETag": "\"236bf30c70dc03f69175f030afbe38f3\"",
    "ServerSideEncryption": "AES256"
}
```

Following are possible values for server-side encryption:

- AES256

- aws:kms

Possible values for storage class are as follows:

- STANDARD

- REDUCED_REDUNDANCY

- STANDARD_IA

273

To assign canned ACL to an object, use the following command:

```
>aws s3api put-object --bucket "chapter5-s3cli-bucket" --key "apress/
chapter2.txt" --body C:/Users/Dell/chapter.txt --acl public-read
```

```
C:\Users\Dell>aws s3api put-object --bucket "chapter5-s3cli-bucket" --key "apress/chapter2.txt" --body C:/Users/Dell/chapter.txt --acl public-read
    "ETag": "\"236bf30c70dc03f69175f030afbe38f3\""
}
```

Following are possible canned ACL values:

- private
- public-read
- public-read-write
- authenticated-read
- aws-exec-read
- bucket-owner-read
- bucket-owner-full-control

To grant object permissions to individual users, use the following command:

```
>aws s3api put-object --bucket "chapter5-s3cli-bucket" --key "apress/
chapter3.txt" --body C:/Users/Dell/chapter.txt --grant-full-control
emailaddress=sunil.gulabani2@gmail.com --grant-read emailaddress=sunil.
gulabani1@gmail.com --grant-read-acp emailaddress=sunil.gulabani1@gmail.
com --grant-write emailaddress=sunil.gulabani1@gmail.com --grant-write-acp
emailaddress=sunil.gulabani1@gmail.com
```

```
C:\Users\Dell>aws s3api put-object --bucket "chapter5-s3cli-bucket" --key "apress/chapter3.txt" --body C:/Users/Dell/chapter.txt --grant-full-control emailaddress=sunil
.gulabani2@gmail.com --grant-read emailaddress=sunil.gulabani1@gmail.com --grant-read-acp emailaddress=sunil.gulabani1@gmail.com --grant-write emailaddress=sunil.gulaba
ni1@gmail.com --grant-write-acp emailaddress=sunil.gulabani1@gmail.com
    "ETag": "\"236bf30c70dc03f60175f030afbe38f3\""
}
```

To add metadata to objects, use the following command:

```
>aws s3api put-object --bucket "chapter5-s3cli-bucket" --key "apress/
chapter4.txt" --body C:/Users/Dell/chapter.txt --content-type "text/plain"
--metadata Chapter=4,Name=AWS
```

```
C:\Users\Dell>aws s3api put-object --bucket "chapter5-s3cli-bucket" --key "apress/chapter4.txt" --body C:/Users/Dell/chapter.txt --content-type "text/plain" --metadata
Chapter=4,Name=AWS
    "ETag": "\"236bf30c70dc03f60175f030afbe38f3\""
}
```

Metadata will have a key-value form that will be associated with objects. This
metadata will have the prefix key "x-amz-meta-".

■ **Note** For more metadata keys, see `http://docs.aws.amazon.com/cli/latest/`
`reference/s3api/put-object.html`.

Deleting Objects

To delete object from an S3 bucket, use the following command:

```
>aws s3api delete-object --bucket "chapter5-s3cli-bucket"
--key apress/chapter.txt
```

```
C:\Users\Dell>aws s3api delete-object --bucket "chapter5-s3cli-bucket" --key apress/chapter.txt
C:\Users\Dell>
```

Using AWS SDK - Java

In this section, you will learn to use AWS Java SDK to manage AWS S3.

Creating Amazon S3 Client

To create AmazonS3Client, first create the AWSCredentials using either of the credential
provider mechanisms. In our case, we will use ProfileCredentialsProvider:

```
AWSCredentials credentials =
    new ProfileCredentialsProvider("sunilgulabani").getCredentials();

AmazonS3Client amazonS3Client = new AmazonS3Client(credentials);
```

This will load the "sunilgulabani" profile's access key and secret key via the
credentials file.

Also you need to set the region, which tells the Amazon S3 Client to perform
operations on a specific region:

```
amazonS3Client.setRegion(Region.getRegion(Regions.US_WEST_2));
```

Creating Buckets

To create a bucket, invoke the createBucket method:

```
String BUCKET_NAME = "chapter5-s3sdk-bucket";

createBucket(BUCKET_NAME);
```

```java
public void createBucket(String bucketName) {
    Bucket bucket = amazonS3Client.createBucket(bucketName);
}
```

```
{
  "name": "chapter5-s3sdk-bucket"
}
```

You can also create buckets along with access control limit (ACL) and canned ACL:

```java
String BUCKET_NAME_2 = "chapter5-s3sdk-bucket-new";

String AWS_CANONICAL_ID =
    "87d32d7bd285c6f3e01d8360ae4b1ceaa8656b0a0e42e3b237c5be90c9ce487a";

String EMAIL_ID = "sunil.gulabani1@gmail.com";

AccessControlList accessControlList =
    createAccessControlList(AWS_CANONICAL_ID, EMAIL_ID);

createBucket(BUCKET_NAME_2,
                        accessControlList,
                        CannedAccessControlList.BucketOwnerFullControl);

public AccessControlList createAccessControlList(
                                        String awsMemberCanonicalId,
                                        String emailId) {
    AccessControlList accessControlList = new AccessControlList();

    accessControlList.grantPermission(GroupGrantee.AllUsers, Permission.Read);

    accessControlList.grantPermission(GroupGrantee.LogDelivery,
                                                    Permission.ReadAcp);

    accessControlList.grantPermission(GroupGrantee.LogDelivery,
                                                    Permission.Write);

    CanonicalGrantee canonicalGrantee =
        new CanonicalGrantee(awsMemberCanonicalId);

    accessControlList.grantPermission(canonicalGrantee,
                                                    Permission.FullControl);

    EmailAddressGrantee emailAddressGrantee =
        new EmailAddressGrantee(emailId);

    accessControlList.grantPermission(emailAddressGrantee, Permission.Write);
```

```
Owner owner = new Owner();

owner.setDisplayName("sunil.gulabani2@gmail.com");

owner.setId(awsMemberCanonicalId);

accessControlList.setOwner(owner);

return accessControlList;
}

public void createBucket(String bucketName,
                                 AccessControlList accessControlList,
                                 CannedAccessControlList cannedAcl) {
    CreateBucketRequest request = new CreateBucketRequest(bucketName);

    request.setRegion(region.getName());

    if(accessControlList != null) {
        request.setAccessControlList(accessControlList);
    }

    if(cannedAcl != null) {
        request.setCannedAcl(cannedAcl);
    }

    Bucket bucket = amazonS3Client.createBucket(request);
}

{
  "name": "chapter5-s3sdk-bucket-new"
}
```

Listing Buckets

To get a list of all buckets for which current the AWS account user is owner, invoke the listBuckets method:

```
listBuckets();

public void listBuckets() {
    List<Bucket> response = amazonS3Client.listBuckets();
}
```

```
[
    {
        "name": "chapter5-s3sdk-bucket",
        "owner": {
            "displayName": "sunil.gulabani2",
            "id": "█████████████████████████████████████████"
        },
        "creationDate": "Feb 10, 2017 8:38:14 PM"
    },
    {
        "name": "chapter5-s3sdk-bucket-new",
        "owner": {
            "displayName": "sunil.gulabani2",
            "id": "█████████████████████████████████████████"
        },
        "creationDate": "Feb 10, 2017 8:38:20 PM"
    }
]
```

Configuring Bucket ACL

To configure the bucket access control limit (ACL) after the bucket has been created, invoke the setBucketAcl method:

```
setBucketAcl(BUCKET_NAME,
                AWS_CANONICAL_ID,
                GroupGrantee.AllUsers,
                Permission.Read);

public void setBucketAcl(String bucketName,
                                String awsMemberCanonicalId,
                                Grantee grantee,
                                Permission permission) {
    AccessControlList acl = new AccessControlList();

    acl.grantPermission(grantee, permission);

    Owner owner = new Owner();

    owner.setDisplayName("sunil.gulabani2@gmail.com");

    owner.setId(awsMemberCanonicalId);

    acl.setOwner(owner);

    amazonS3Client.setBucketAcl(bucketName, acl);
}
```

To check that the bucket ACL has been configured, invoke the getBucketAcl
method:

```
getBucketAcl(BUCKET_NAME);

public void getBucketAcl(String bucketName) {
    AccessControlList response = amazonS3Client.getBucketAcl(bucketName);
}
```

```
{
  "grantList": [
    {
      "grantee": "AllUsers",
      "permission": "Read"
    }
  ],
  "owner": {
    "displayName": "sunil.gulabani2",
    "id": "███████████████████████████████████████████████"
  },
  "isRequesterCharged": false
}
```

Bucket Web Site Configuration

To configure the web site hosting configuration in the bucket, invoke the
setBucketWebsiteConfiguration method:

```
setBucketWebsiteConfiguration(BUCKET_NAME, "sunilgulabani.com");

public void setBucketWebsiteConfiguration(String bucketName,
                                                 String hostName) {
    BucketWebsiteConfiguration configuration =
        new BucketWebsiteConfiguration();

    RedirectRule redirectRule = new RedirectRule();

    redirectRule.setHostName(hostName);

    redirectRule.setProtocol("http");

    configuration.setRedirectAllRequestsTo(redirectRule);

    amazonS3Client.setBucketWebsiteConfiguration(bucketName, configuration);
}
```

The previous code will redirect all requests to a specific host when the bucket URL is
executed. To check that the bucket web site configuration has been properly set, invoke
the getBucketWebsiteConfiguration:

```
getBucketWebsiteConfiguration(BUCKET_NAME);

public void getBucketWebsiteConfiguration(String bucketName) {
    BucketWebsiteConfiguration response =
        amazonS3Client.getBucketWebsiteConfiguration(bucketName);
}
```

```
{
  "redirectAllRequestsTo": {
    "protocol": "http",
    "hostName": "sunilgulabani.com"
  },
  "routingRules": []
}
```

You can have an index.html and error.html page in your bucket and configure your bucket to display pages accordingly:

```
setBucketWebsiteConfiguration(BUCKET_NAME, "index.html", "error.html");

public void setBucketWebsiteConfiguration(String bucketName,
                                                String indexDocument,
                                                String errorDocument) {
    BucketWebsiteConfiguration configuration =
        new BucketWebsiteConfiguration();

    configuration.setIndexDocumentSuffix(indexDocument);

    configuration.setErrorDocument(errorDocument);

    amazonS3Client.setBucketWebsiteConfiguration(bucketName, configuration);
}
```

To check that the bucket web site configuration has been properly set, invoke the getBucketWebsiteConfiguration:

```
getBucketWebsiteConfiguration(BUCKET_NAME);
```

```
{
  "indexDocumentSuffix": "index.html",
  "errorDocument": "error.html",
  "routingRules": []
}
```

Additionally, you can also have routing rules on request coming in.

Bucket Logging Configuration

To log the bucket activities, invoke the setBucketLoggingConfiguration method:

```
String LOG_FILE_PREFIX = "logs";

setBucketLoggingConfiguration(BUCKET_NAME, BUCKET_NAME_2, LOG_FILE_PREFIX);

public void setBucketLoggingConfiguration(String bucketName,
                                          String destinationBucketName,
                                          String logFilePrefix) {
    BucketLoggingConfiguration loggingConfiguration =
        new BucketLoggingConfiguration();

    loggingConfiguration.setDestinationBucketName(destinationBucketName);

    loggingConfiguration.setLogFilePrefix(logFilePrefix);

    SetBucketLoggingConfigurationRequest request =
        new SetBucketLoggingConfigurationRequest(
                                          bucketName,
                                          loggingConfiguration);

    amazonS3Client.setBucketLoggingConfiguration(request);
}
```

To check if the bucket logging configuration has been set properly, invoke the getBucketLoggingConfiguration method:

```
getBucketLoggingConfiguration(BUCKET_NAME);

public void getBucketLoggingConfiguration(String bucketName) {
    BucketLoggingConfiguration response =
        amazonS3Client.getBucketLoggingConfiguration(bucketName);
}
```

```
{
  "destinationBucketName": "chapter5-s3sdk-bucket-new",
  "logFilePrefix": "logs"
}
```

Bucket Event Notification Configuration

You can trigger event notification to SNS, SQS, and lambda on bucket activities. To do that, invoke the setBucketNotificationConfiguration method:

```
setBucketNotificationConfiguration_SNS(
                                       BUCKET_NAME,
                                       S3Event.ObjectCreated,
                                       SNS_TOPIC_ARN,
                                       null,
                                       null);
public void setBucketNotificationConfiguration_SNS(
                                       String bucketName,
                                       S3Event s3Event,
                                       String topicARN,
                                       String prefixValue,
                                       String suffixValue) {

   BucketNotificationConfiguration bucketNotificationConfiguration =

   getBucketNotificationConfiguration(bucketName);

   TopicConfiguration topicConfiguration = new TopicConfiguration();

   topicConfiguration.addEvent(s3Event);

   topicConfiguration.setTopicARN(topicARN);

   topicConfiguration.setFilter(createFilters(prefixValue, suffixValue));

   bucketNotificationConfiguration.addConfiguration(
       "SNSS3Notification", topicConfiguration);

   amazonS3Client.setBucketNotificationConfiguration(
       bucketName, bucketNotificationConfiguration);
}
```

Here we will first get the bucket notification configuration in order to add new events using:

```
BucketNotificationConfiguration bucketNotificationConfiguration =
   getBucketNotificationConfiguration(bucketName);
```

Next is we will set the SQS event notification on bucket as:

```
setBucketNotificationConfiguration_SQS(
                                       BUCKET_NAME,
                                       S3Event.ObjectRemoved,
                                       SQS_ARN,
                                       null,
                                       null);
```

```
public void setBucketNotificationConfiguration_SQS(
                                    String bucketName,
                                    S3Event s3Event,
                                    String queueARN,
                                    String prefixValue,
                                    String suffixValue) {

    BucketNotificationConfiguration bucketNotificationConfiguration =
        getBucketNotificationConfiguration(bucketName);

    QueueConfiguration queueConfiguration = new QueueConfiguration();

    queueConfiguration.setQueueARN(queueARN);

    queueConfiguration.addEvent(s3Event);

    queueConfiguration.setFilter(createFilters(prefixValue, suffixValue));

    bucketNotificationConfiguration.addConfiguration(
                            "SQSS3Notification", queueConfiguration);

    amazonS3Client.setBucketNotificationConfiguration(
                            bucketName, bucketNotificationConfiguration);
}
```

Next, you will set the lambda event notification on the bucket:

```
setBucketNotificationConfiguration_Lambda(
                            BUCKET_NAME,
                            S3Event.ReducedRedundancyLostObject,
                            LAMBDA_TOPIC_ARN,
                            "chapter5",
                            "log");

public void setBucketNotificationConfiguration_Lambda(
                            String bucketName,
                            S3Event s3Event,
                            String lambdaFunctionARN,
                            String prefixValue,
                            String suffixValue) {

    BucketNotificationConfiguration bucketNotificationConfiguration =
        getBucketNotificationConfiguration(bucketName);

    LambdaConfiguration lambdaConfiguration =
        new LambdaConfiguration(lambdaFunctionARN);
```

```java
        lambdaConfiguration.addEvent(s3Event);

        lambdaConfiguration.setFilter(createFilters(prefixValue, suffixValue));

        bucketNotificationConfiguration.addConfiguration(
                "LambdaFunctionS3Notification", lambdaConfiguration);

        amazonS3Client.setBucketNotificationConfiguration(
                bucketName, bucketNotificationConfiguration);
    }

    private Filter createFilters(String prefixValue, String suffixValue) {
        Filter filter = null;

        if(!StringUtils.isNullOrEmpty(prefixValue) &&
            !StringUtils.isNullOrEmpty(suffixValue)) {
            List<FilterRule> filterRules = new ArrayList<>();
            if(!StringUtils.isNullOrEmpty(prefixValue)) {
                FilterRule prefixFilterRule = new FilterRule();

                prefixFilterRule.setName("prefix");

                prefixFilterRule.setValue(prefixValue);

                filterRules.add(prefixFilterRule);
            }

            if(!StringUtils.isNullOrEmpty(suffixValue)) {
                FilterRule suffixFilterRule = new FilterRule();

                suffixFilterRule.setName("suffix");

                suffixFilterRule.setValue(suffixValue);

                filterRules.add(suffixFilterRule);
            }

            S3KeyFilter s3KeyFilter = new S3KeyFilter();

            s3KeyFilter.setFilterRules(filterRules);

            filter = new Filter();

            filter.setS3KeyFilter(s3KeyFilter);
        }

        return filter;
    }
```

In the lambda event notification, we added filters for events to be triggered where we provided prefix and suffix to the configuration.

To check if event notifications have been properly set, invoke the getBucketNotificationConfiguration method:

```
getBucketNotificationConfiguration(BUCKET_NAME);
```

```
public BucketNotificationConfiguration getBucketNotificationConfiguration(
                                                String bucketName) {
    BucketNotificationConfiguration response =
        amazonS3Client.getBucketNotificationConfiguration(bucketName);
    return response;
}
```

```
{
  "configurations": {
    "SNSS3Notification": {
      "topicARN": "arn:aws:sns:us-west-2:          :objectCreatedSNSTopic",
      "events": [
        "s3:ObjectCreated:*"
      ],
      "objectPrefixes": []
    },
    "LambdaFunctionS3Notification": {
      "functionARN": "arn:aws:lambda:us-west-2:          :function:reducedRedundancyLostObjectLambda",
      "events": [
        "s3:ReducedRedundancyLostObject"
      ],
      "objectPrefixes": [],
      "filter": {
        "s3KeyFilter": {
          "filterRules": [
            {
              "name": "Prefix",
              "value": "chapter5"
            },
            {
              "name": "Suffix",
              "value": "log"
            }
          ]
        }
      }
    },
    "SQSS3Notification": {
      "queueARN": "arn:aws:sqs:us-west-2:          :objectRemovedQueue",
      "events": [
        "s3:ObjectRemoved:*"
      ],
      "objectPrefixes": []
    }
  }
}
```

Bucket Versioning Configuration

You can maintain the object's version available under the bucket so that you can see the older versions for restoration or tracking purpose. To do so, invoke the setBucketVersioningConfiguration method:

```
setBucketVersioningConfiguration(BUCKET_NAME,
                                 BucketVersioningConfiguration.ENABLED);

public void setBucketVersioningConfiguration(
                                    String bucketName, String status) {

    BucketVersioningConfiguration configuration =
        new BucketVersioningConfiguration();

    configuration.setStatus(status);

    SetBucketVersioningConfigurationRequest request =
        new SetBucketVersioningConfigurationRequest(bucketName, configuration);

    amazonS3Client.setBucketVersioningConfiguration(request);
}
```

To check if versioning has been enabled, invoke the getBucketVersioningConfiguration method:

```
getBucketVersioningConfiguration(BUCKET_NAME);
```

```
{
  "status": "Enabled"
}
```

To suspend the versioning, invoke the same setBucketVersioningConfiguration method with status:

```
setBucketVersioningConfiguration(BUCKET_NAME,
                                 BucketVersioningConfiguration.SUSPENDED);
```

To check if the versioning has been suspended, invoke the getBucketVersioningConfiguration method:

```
getBucketVersioningConfiguration(BUCKET_NAME);
```

```
{
  "status": "Suspended"
}
```

Bucket Life Cycle Configuration

You can configure the bucket life cycle, which is applicable on objects. You can also configure what actions need to be performed when specific criteria is met on an object. To do so, invoke the setBucketLifecycleConfiguration method:

```
setBucketLifecycleConfiguration(BUCKET_NAME);

public void setBucketLifecycleConfiguration(String bucketName) {
    BucketLifecycleConfiguration configuration =
        new BucketLifecycleConfiguration();

    List<BucketLifecycleConfiguration.Rule> rules = new ArrayList<>();

    rules.add(expirationRuleWithDate());

    rules.add(expirationRuleWithDays());

    rules.add(moveOldObjectsToGlacierRule());

    rules.add(nonCurrentVersionTransitionsAndExpirationRule());

    rules.add(abortIncompleteMultipartUploadRule());

    configuration.setRules(rules);

    SetBucketLifecycleConfigurationRequest request =
        new SetBucketLifecycleConfigurationRequest(bucketName, configuration);

    amazonS3Client.setBucketLifecycleConfiguration(request);
}
```

To add a rule with an expiration based on date, use the following code:

```
private BucketLifecycleConfiguration.Rule expirationRuleWithDate() {
    BucketLifecycleConfiguration.Rule rule =
        new BucketLifecycleConfiguration.Rule();

    rule.setId("Expiration Action with Date");

    rule.setPrefix("chapter1");

    rule.setStatus(BucketLifecycleConfiguration.ENABLED);

    rule.setExpirationDate(getDate());

    return rule;
}
```

To add a rule with an expiration based on days, use the following code:

```java
private BucketLifecycleConfiguration.Rule expirationRuleWithDays() {
    BucketLifecycleConfiguration.Rule rule =
        new BucketLifecycleConfiguration.Rule();

    rule.setId("Expiration Action with Days");

    rule.setPrefix("chapter2");

    rule.setStatus(BucketLifecycleConfiguration.ENABLED);

    rule.setExpirationInDays(30);

    return rule;
}
```

The following code will allow you to add a rule with moving old objects to Glacier:,

```java
private BucketLifecycleConfiguration.Rule moveOldObjectsToGlacierRule() {
    BucketLifecycleConfiguration.Rule rule =
        new BucketLifecycleConfiguration.Rule();

    rule.setId("Move old objects to Glacier Action");

    rule.setPrefix("chapter3");

    rule.setStatus(BucketLifecycleConfiguration.ENABLED);

    List<BucketLifecycleConfiguration.Transition> transitionList =
        new ArrayList<>();

    BucketLifecycleConfiguration.Transition transition =
        new BucketLifecycleConfiguration.Transition();

    transition.setDate(getDate());

    transition.setStorageClass(StorageClass.Glacier);

    transitionList.add(transition);

    rule.setTransitions(transitionList);

    return rule;
}
```

To add a rule for noncurrent versioned objects along with expiration of objects based on object creation days, use the following code:

```
private BucketLifecycleConfiguration.Rule
    nonCurrentVersionTransitionsAndExpirationRule() {

    BucketLifecycleConfiguration.Rule rule =
        new BucketLifecycleConfiguration.Rule();

    rule.setId("Non-Current Versioned Object Actions");

    rule.setPrefix("chapter4");

    rule.setStatus(BucketLifecycleConfiguration.ENABLED);

    BucketLifecycleConfiguration.NoncurrentVersionTransition
        nonCurrentVersionTransition =
            new BucketLifecycleConfiguration.NoncurrentVersionTransition();

    nonCurrentVersionTransition.setDays(30);

    nonCurrentVersionTransition.setStorageClass(
                            StorageClass.StandardInfrequentAccess);

    List<BucketLifecycleConfiguration.NoncurrentVersionTransition>
        nonCurrentVersionTransitionList = new ArrayList<>();

    nonCurrentVersionTransitionList.add(nonCurrentVersionTransition);

    rule.setNoncurrentVersionTransitions(nonCurrentVersionTransitionList);

    rule.setNoncurrentVersionExpirationInDays(40);

    return rule;
}
```

To add a rule to abort an incomplete multipart upload of objects, use the following code:

```
private BucketLifecycleConfiguration.Rule abortIncompleteMultipartUploadRule() {
    BucketLifecycleConfiguration.Rule rule =
        new BucketLifecycleConfiguration.Rule();

    rule.setId("Abort Incomplete Multipart Action");

    rule.setPrefix("chapter5");
```

```
    rule.setStatus(BucketLifecycleConfiguration.ENABLED);

    AbortIncompleteMultipartUpload abortIncompleteMultipartUpload =
        new AbortIncompleteMultipartUpload();

    abortIncompleteMultipartUpload.setDaysAfterInitiation(1);

    rule.setAbortIncompleteMultipartUpload(abortIncompleteMultipartUpload);

    return rule;
}
```

For adding dates in a rule, follow the GMT with only the date (without hours, minutes, seconds and milliseconds):

```
private Date getDate() {
    TimeZone.setDefault(TimeZone.getTimeZone("GMT"));
    Calendar gmt = Calendar.getInstance(TimeZone.getTimeZone("GMT"));
    gmt.set(Calendar.HOUR_OF_DAY, 0);
    gmt.set(Calendar.MINUTE, 0);
    gmt.set(Calendar.SECOND, 0);
    gmt.set(Calendar.MILLISECOND, 0);
    long millis = gmt.getTimeInMillis();
    return new Date(millis);
}
```

To check that the bucket life cycle has been configured, invoke the getBucketLifecycleConfiguration method:

```
getBucketLifecycleConfiguration(BUCKET_NAME);
```

```
{
  "rules": [{
      "id": "Expiration Action with Date",
      "prefix": "chapter1",          "status": "Enabled",
      "expirationInDays": -1,         "expiredObjectDeleteMarker": false,
      "noncurrentVersionExpirationInDays": -1,
      "expirationDate": "Feb 10, 2017 12:00:00 AM"
  }, {
      "id": "Expiration Action with Days",
      "prefix": "chapter2",          "status": "Enabled",
      "expirationInDays": 30,         "expiredObjectDeleteMarker": false,
      "noncurrentVersionExpirationInDays": -1
  }, {
      "id": "Move old objects to Glacier Action",
      "prefix": "chapter3",          "status": "Enabled",
      "expirationInDays": -1,         "expiredObjectDeleteMarker": false,
      "noncurrentVersionExpirationInDays": -1,
      "transitions": [{"days": -1,  "date": "Feb 10, 2017 12:00:00 AM", "storageClass": "GLACIER"}]
  }, {
      "id": "Non-Current Versioned Object Actions",
      "prefix": "chapter4",          "status": "Enabled",
      "expirationInDays": -1,         "expiredObjectDeleteMarker": false,
      "noncurrentVersionExpirationInDays": 40,
      "noncurrentVersionTransitions": [{"days": 30, "storageClass": "STANDARD_IA"}]
  }, {
      "id": "Abort Incomplete Multipart Action",
      "prefix": "chapter5",          "status": "Enabled",
      "expirationInDays": -1,         "expiredObjectDeleteMarker": false,
      "noncurrentVersionExpirationInDays": -1,
      "abortIncompleteMultipartUpload": {"daysAfterInitiation": 1}
  }
  ]
}
```

To delete the bucket life cycle configuration, invoke the deleteBucketLifecycleConfiguration method:

```
deleteBucketLifecycleConfiguration(BUCKET_NAME);
```

```
public void deleteBucketLifecycleConfiguration(String bucketName) {
    amazonS3Client.deleteBucketLifecycleConfiguration(bucketName);
}
```

Bucket Replication Configuration

To have a backup of a bucket's objects, you can replicate all objects to another bucket that should be created in a region other than the source bucket's region.

Use the following code to create a bucket in another region (Regions.AP_SOUTHEAST_1):

```
String BUCKET_NAME_BACKUP = "chapter5-s3cli-buckets-backups";
createBucket(BUCKET_NAME_BACKUP);
```

You also need the bucket versioning for the source and destination bucket enabled:

```
setBucketVersioningConfiguration(
                            BUCKET_NAME,
                            BucketVersioningConfiguration.ENABLED);
```

```
setBucketVersioningConfiguration(
                                BUCKET_NAME_BACKUP,
                                BucketVersioningConfiguration.ENABLED);
```

Next, invoke the setBucketReplicationConfiguration method:

```
String ROLE_ARN = "arn:aws:iam::298147259238:role/s3BucketReplicationRole";
String DESTINATION_BUCKET_ARN = "arn:aws:s3:::" + BUCKET_NAME_BACKUP;

setBucketReplicationConfiguration(
                                BUCKET_NAME,
                                ROLE_ARN,
                                DESTINATION_BUCKET_ARN);

public void setBucketReplicationConfiguration(
                                String bucketName,
                                String roleARN,
                                String destinationBucketARN) {

    BucketReplicationConfiguration configuration =
        new BucketReplicationConfiguration();

    configuration.setRoleARN(roleARN);
    ReplicationDestinationConfig destination =
        new ReplicationDestinationConfig();

    destination.setBucketARN(destinationBucketARN);

    destination.setStorageClass(StorageClass.Standard);

    ReplicationRule replicationRule = new ReplicationRule();

    replicationRule.setPrefix("");

    replicationRule.setStatus(ReplicationRuleStatus.Enabled);

    replicationRule.setDestinationConfig(destination);

    Map<String, ReplicationRule> rules = new HashMap<>();

    rules.put("S3 bucket replication", replicationRule);

    configuration.setRules(rules);

    amazonS3Client.setBucketReplicationConfiguration(bucketName, configuration);
}
```

Here Role ARN plays important role in providing access to S3 to replicate a bucket in another region. To get the bucket replication configuration, invoke the getBucketReplicationConfiguration method:

```
getBucketReplicationConfiguration(BUCKET_NAME);

public void getBucketReplicationConfiguration(String bucketName) {
    BucketReplicationConfiguration response =
        amazonS3Client.getBucketReplicationConfiguration(bucketName);
}
```

```
{
  "roleARN": "arn:aws:iam::▓▓▓▓▓▓▓:role/s3BucketReplicationRole",
  "rules": {
    "S3 bucket replication": {
      "prefix": "",
      "status": "Enabled",
      "destinationConfig": {
        "bucketARN": "arn:aws:s3:::chapter5-s3cli-buckets-backups",
        "storageClass": "STANDARD"
      }
    }
  }
}
```

To delete the bucket replication configuration, invoke the deleteBucketReplicationConfiguration method:

```
deleteBucketReplicationConfiguration(BUCKET_NAME);
public void deleteBucketReplicationConfiguration(String bucketName) {
    amazonS3Client.deleteBucketReplicationConfiguration(bucketName);
}
```

Bucket Tagging Configuration

You can add tags to the bucket, which can be used for report purposes. To do so, invoke the setBucketTaggingConfiguration method:

```
setBucketTaggingConfiguration(BUCKET_NAME);

public void setBucketTaggingConfiguration(String bucketName) {
    BucketTaggingConfiguration configuration =
        new BucketTaggingConfiguration();

    TagSet tagSet1 = new TagSet();

    tagSet1.setTag("Chapter", "5");

    tagSet1.setTag("Name", "AWSS3");
```

```
    List<TagSet> tagSets = new ArrayList<>();

    tagSets.add(tagSet1);

    configuration.setTagSets(tagSets);

    amazonS3Client.setBucketTaggingConfiguration(bucketName, configuration);
}
```

To get the bucket tagging configuration, invoke the getBucketTaggingConfiguration method:

```
getBucketTaggingConfiguration(BUCKET_NAME);

public void getBucketTaggingConfiguration(String bucketName) {
    BucketTaggingConfiguration response =
        amazonS3Client.getBucketTaggingConfiguration(bucketName);
}
```

```
{
  "tagSets": [
    {
      "tags": {
        "Chapter": "5",
        "Name": "AWSS3"
      }
    }
  ]
}
```

Configuring Requester Pay

Bucket owners can configure that the requester needs to pay for accessing the bucket. The requester only needs to pay for the reading and downloading portion of the bucket's object price; the bucket owner will pay the storage price. To make this possible, invoke the enableRequesterPays method:

```
enableRequesterPays(BUCKET_NAME);

public void enableRequesterPays(String bucketName) {
    amazonS3Client.enableRequesterPays(bucketName);
}
```

To check that Requester Pays has been enabled, invoke the isRequesterPaysEnabled method:

```
isRequesterPaysEnabled(BUCKET_NAME);

public void isRequesterPaysEnabled(String bucketName) {
    boolean isRequesterPaysEnabled =
        amazonS3Client.isRequesterPaysEnabled(bucketName);
}
```

true

To disable Requester Pays, invoke the disableRequesterPays method:

```
disableRequesterPays(BUCKET_NAME);

public void disableRequesterPays(String bucketName) {
    amazonS3Client.disableRequesterPays(bucketName);
}
```

To check that Requester Pays has been enabled, invoke the isRequesterPaysEnabled method:

```
isRequesterPaysEnabled(BUCKET_NAME);
```

false

Bucket Transfer Accelerate Configuration

You can configure the bucket to perform quickly in terms of read and write. To do so, invoke the setBucketAccelerateConfiguration method:

```
setBucketAccelerateConfiguration(
                        BUCKET_NAME,
                        BucketAccelerateStatus.Enabled);

public void setBucketAccelerateConfiguration(
                        String bucketName,
                        BucketAccelerateStatus bucketAccelerateStatus) {
    BucketAccelerateConfiguration configuration =
        new BucketAccelerateConfiguration(bucketAccelerateStatus);

    amazonS3Client.setBucketAccelerateConfiguration(bucketName, configuration);
}
```

To get the bucket accelerate configuration, invoke the getBucketAccelerate Configuration method:

```
getBucketAccelerateConfiguration(BUCKET_NAME);

public void getBucketAccelerateConfiguration(String bucketName) {
    BucketAccelerateConfiguration response =
        amazonS3Client.getBucketAccelerateConfiguration(bucketName);
}
```

```
{
  "status": "Enabled"
}
```

To suspend the bucket transfer accelerate configuration, invoke the same setBucketAccelerateConfiguration method with "Suspend" status:

```
setBucketAccelerateConfiguration(BUCKET_NAME,
                                 BucketAccelerateStatus.Suspended);
```

To check that the bucket transfer accelerate configuration has been suspended, will invoke the getBucketAccelerateConfiguration method:

```
{
  "status": "Suspended"
}
```

Creating Folders

In S3, all data are considered in terms of bucket and objects. You can create logical folders that can ease your storage model. To do so, invoke the " " method:

```
String FOLDER_NAME = "apress";

createFolder(BUCKET_NAME, FOLDER_NAME);

public void createFolder(String bucketName, String folderName) {
    ObjectMetadata metadata = new ObjectMetadata();

    metadata.setContentLength(0);

    InputStream emptyContent = new ByteArrayInputStream(new byte[0]);

    PutObjectRequest request = new PutObjectRequest(
                                                bucketName,
                                                folderName + "/",
                                                emptyContent,
                                                metadata);

    PutObjectResult response = amazonS3Client.putObject(request);
}
```

To create a folder in a bucket, you need to set the object's metadata length to 0, empty content as part of InputStream, and follow the folder name with "/":

```
{
  "eTag": "d41d8cd98f00b204e9800998ecf8427e",
  "contentMd5": "1B2M2Y8AsgTpgAmY7PhCfg\u003d\u003d",
  "metadata": {
    "userMetadata": {},
    "metadata": {
      "Content-Length": 0,
      "ETag": "d41d8cd98f00b204e9800998ecf8427e"
    }
  },
  "isRequesterCharged": false
}
```

To delete a folder, invoke the deleteObject method:

```
deleteFolder(BUCKET_NAME, FOLDER_NAME);

public void deleteFolder(String bucketName, String folderName) {
    DeleteObjectRequest request =
        new DeleteObjectRequest(bucketName, folderName + "/");

    amazonS3Client.deleteObject(request);
}
```

Uploading Objects

To upload objects under a specific bucket, invoke the putObject method:

```
Path tempFile = Files.createTempFile("chapter", ".tmp");

List<String> lines = Arrays.asList("Hello World!!!", "AWS S3");

Files.write(tempFile, lines,
            Charset.defaultCharset(), StandardOpenOption.WRITE);

putObject(BUCKET_NAME, "chapter.txt", tempFile.toFile());

public void putObject(String bucketName, String keyName, File file)
    throws IOException {

    PutObjectRequest request = new PutObjectRequest(bucketName, keyName, file);

    PutObjectResult response = amazonS3Client.putObject(request);
}
```

We have created a temporary file that we can upload in the bucket. The object's key name will be set to "chapter.txt":

```
{
  "eTag": "bd2edff2b61bf7a30835ec01e30aaf43",
  "contentMd5": "vS7f8rYb96MINewB4wqvQw\u003d\u003d",
  "metadata": {
    "userMetadata": {},
    "metadata": {
      "Content-Length": 0,
      "ETag": "bd2edff2b61bf7a30835ec01e30aaf43"
    }
  },
  "isRequesterCharged": false
}
```

Listing Objects

To get a list of objects under the bucket, invoke the listObjects method:

```
listObjects(BUCKET_NAME);
public void listObjects(String bucketName) {
    ObjectListing response = amazonS3Client.listObjects(bucketName);
}
```

```
{
  "objectSummaries": [
    {
      "bucketName": "chapter5-s3sdk-bucket",
      "key": "chapter.txt",
      "eTag": "bd2edff2b61bf7a30835ec01e30aaf43",
      "size": 24,
      "lastModified": "Feb 10, 2017 3:09:37 PM",
      "storageClass": "STANDARD",
      "owner": {
        "displayName": "sunil.gulabani2",
        "id": "                                    "
      }
    }
  ],
  "commonPrefixes": [],
  "bucketName": "chapter5-s3sdk-bucket",
  "isTruncated": false,
  "maxKeys": 1000
}
```

Deleting Objects

To delete an object from the bucket permanently, invoke the deleteObject method:

```
deleteObject(BUCKET_NAME, "chapter.txt");

public void deleteObject(String bucketName, String keyName) {
    DeleteObjectRequest request = new DeleteObjectRequest(bucketName, keyName);

    amazonS3Client.deleteObject(request);
}
```

Emptying Buckets

To delete all objects from a bucket permanently, invoke the same deleteObject method after you fetched all objects:

```
deleteObjects(BUCKET_NAME);

public void deleteObjects(String bucketName) {
    S3Objects s3ObjectSummaries =
        S3Objects.inBucket(amazonS3Client, bucketName);

    s3ObjectSummaries.forEach(objectSummary -> {
        deleteObject(bucketName, objectSummary.getKey());
    });
}
```

Deleting Buckets

To delete a bucket permanently, invoke the deleteBucket method:

```
deleteBucket(BUCKET_NAME);

public void deleteBucket(String bucketName) {
    for (S3VersionSummary version :
            S3Versions.inBucket(amazonS3Client, bucketName)) {
        String key = version.getKey();

        String versionId = version.getVersionId();

        amazonS3Client.deleteVersion(bucketName, key, versionId);
    }

    DeleteBucketRequest request = new DeleteBucketRequest(bucketName);

    amazonS3Client.deleteBucket(request);
}
```

Before deleting a bucket, make sure the bucket is empty (including versioned objects). To check that the bucket has been deleted, invoke the listBuckets method:

```
listBuckets();
public void listBuckets() {
    List<Bucket> response = amazonS3Client.listBuckets();
}
```

[]

Monitoring Using CloudWatch

CloudWatch allows you to monitor the S3 having different metrics. It will trigger an alarm when a threshold is exceeded on specific metrics. The following steps are used to create an alarm:

1. Go to the CloudWatch Management Console and click Alarm from left navigation, as shown in Figure 5-51.

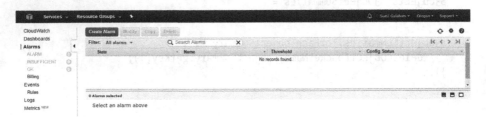

Figure 5-51. *CloudWatch alarm*

2. Click Create Alarm.

3. The Create Alarm screen shown in Figure 5-52 will be displayed, which has two steps:

   • Select Metric

   • Define Alarm

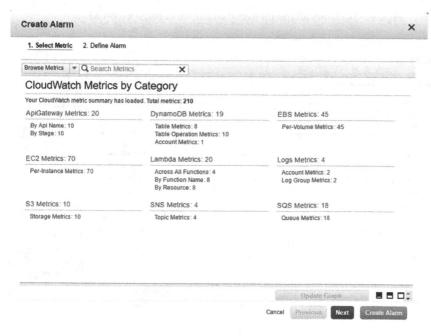

Figure 5-52. *Create Alarm screen*

4. First, select the metric for S3. Click Browse Metrics and select "S3," as shown in Figure 5-53.

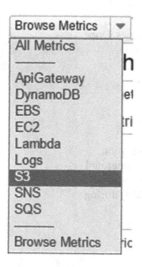

Figure 5-53. *Browse Metrics screen*

5. Figure 5-54 shows all the metrics that can be configured on S3.

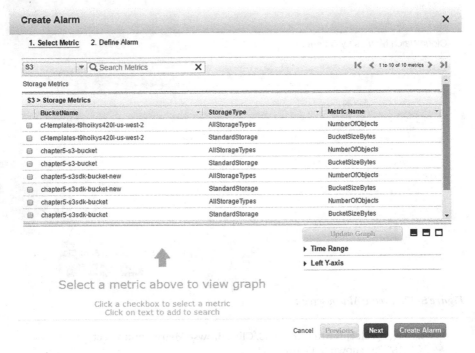

Figure 5-54. S3 metrics listing

6. For our case, we will select the "BucketSizeBytes" metrics. Once you select, click the Next button, as shown in Figure 5-55.

Figure 5-55. Metrics Selected

7. Define the alarm settings by providing a name, description, and threshold values on which the alarm should be generated. You will use the average of the objects' size, which should be greater than or equal to operation1048576 bytes (1MB) during one day of interval. (See Figure 5-56.)

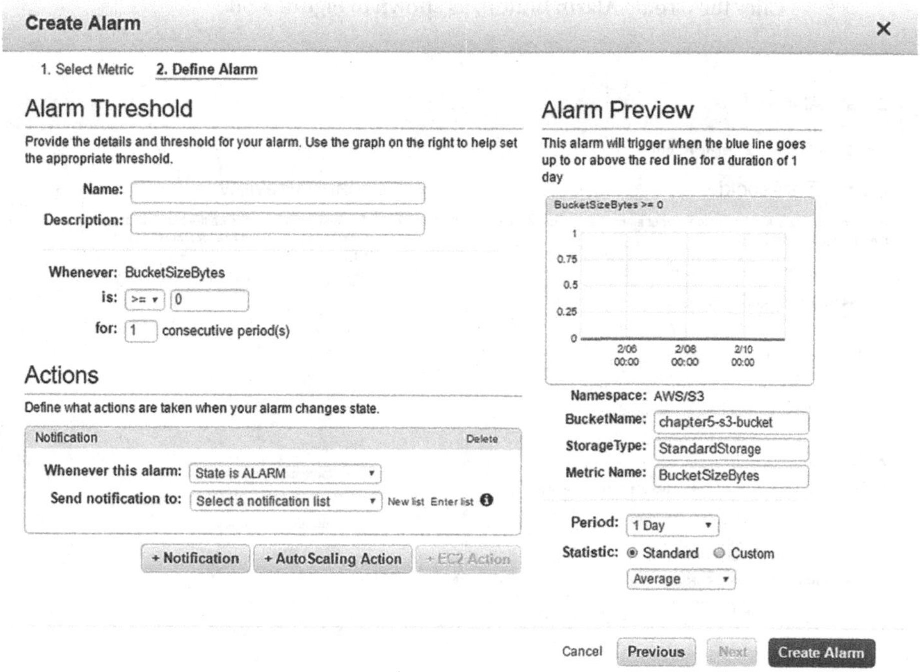

Create Alarm ✕

1. Select Metric   **2. Define Alarm**

Alarm Threshold

Provide the details and threshold for your alarm. Use the graph on the right to help set the appropriate threshold.

Name: [   ]

Description: [   ]

Whenever: BucketSizeBytes

is: [>= ▾] [0]

for: [1] consecutive period(s)

Actions

Define what actions are taken when your alarm changes state.

Notification	Delete

Whenever this alarm: [State is ALARM ▾]

Send notification to: [Select a notification list ▾] New list Enter list ❶

[+ Notification] [+ Auto Scaling Action] [+ EC2 Action]

Alarm Preview

This alarm will trigger when the blue line goes up to or above the red line for a duration of 1 day

BucketSizeBytes >= 0

Namespace: AWS/S3
BucketName: [chapter5-s3-bucket]
StorageType: [StandardStorage]
Metric Name: [BucketSizeBytes]

Period: [1 Day ▾]
Statistic: ◉ Standard ○ Custom
[Average ▾]

Cancel **Previous** Next **Create Alarm**

Figure 5-56. Define Alarm screen

8. You will also configure Actions to trigger a notification when the alarm state is "ALARM." To configure this setting, select from the drop-down list the value "Send notification to" or create a new notification by clicking New List. Enter the topic's name and the e-mail address where notifications need to be sent. (See Figure 5-57.)

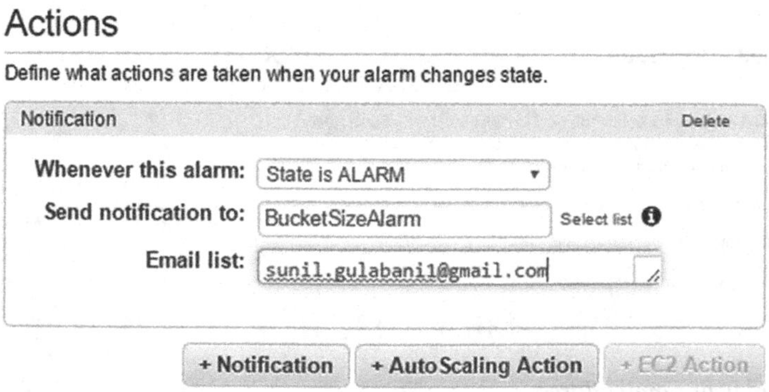

Actions

Define what actions are taken when your alarm changes state.

Notification	Delete

Whenever this alarm: [State is ALARM ▾]

Send notification to: [BucketSizeAlarm] Select list ❶

Email list: [sunil.gulabani1@gmail.com]

[+ Notification] [+ Auto Scaling Action] [+ EC2 Action]

Figure 5-57. Define actions

303

9. Click the Create Alarm button, as shown in Figure 5-58.

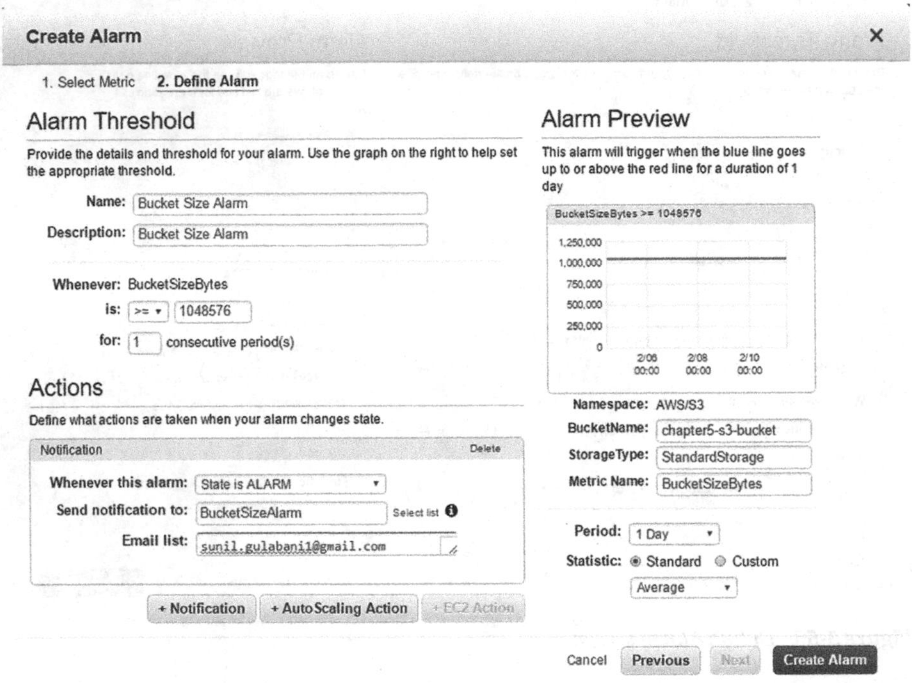

Create Alarm ✕

1. Select Metric   **2. Define Alarm**

Alarm Threshold

Provide the details and threshold for your alarm. Use the graph on the right to help set the appropriate threshold.

Name: Bucket Size Alarm

Description: Bucket Size Alarm

Whenever: BucketSizeBytes

is: >= ▾   1048576

for: 1   consecutive period(s)

Actions

Define what actions are taken when your alarm changes state.

Notification   Delete

Whenever this alarm: State is ALARM ▾

Send notification to: BucketSizeAlarm   Select list ❶

Email list: sunil.gulabani1@gmail.com

+ Notification   + Auto Scaling Action   + EC2 Action

Alarm Preview

This alarm will trigger when the blue line goes up to or above the red line for a duration of 1 day

BucketSizeBytes >= 1048576

1,250,000
1,000,000
750,000
500,000
250,000
0
   2/06   2/08   2/10
   00:00   00:00   00:00

Namespace: AWS/S3
BucketName: chapter5-s3-bucket
StorageType: StandardStorage
Metric Name: BucketSizeBytes

Period: 1 Day ▾
Statistic: ⦿ Standard ◯ Custom
Average ▾

Cancel   Previous   Next   Create Alarm

Figure 5-58. Create Alarm screen

10. If you have added a new e-mail that is not subscribed to SNS, you will be asked to confirm the e-mail address by opening the link sent in the e-mail, as shown in Figure 5-59.

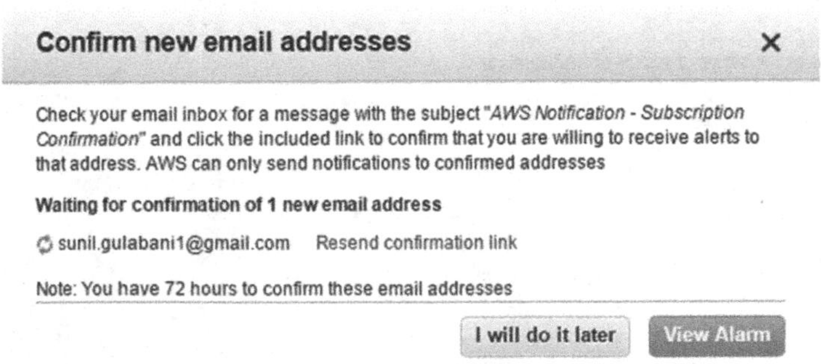

Confirm new email addresses ✕

Check your email inbox for a message with the subject "*AWS Notification - Subscription Confirmation*" and click the included link to confirm that you are willing to receive alerts to that address. AWS can only send notifications to confirmed addresses

Waiting for confirmation of 1 new email address

↻ sunil.gulabani1@gmail.com   Resend confirmation link

Note: You have 72 hours to confirm these email addresses

I will do it later   View Alarm

Figure 5-59. Confirm new e-mail address

11.   Once you confirm the subscription, you will be able to get
       e-mails when the alarm is triggered. (See Figure 5-60.)

Figure 5-60. *Confirm new e-mail address - 2*

You can see that the alarm has been created in Figure 5-61.

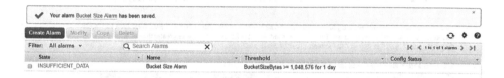

Figure 5-61. *Alarm listing*

12.   To test that the alarm has being generated, uploaded multiple
       objects to the bucket whose average size exceeded 1MB.

13.   You can see that the alarm state has been changed to
       "ALARM" in Figure 5-62.

305

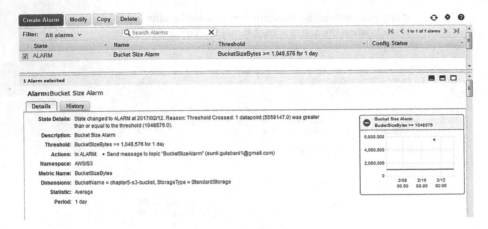

Figure 5-62. Alarm status changed

An e-mail has also been triggered in Figure 5-63.

AWS Notifications no-reply@sns.amazonaws.com via amazonses.com   13:25 (23 hours ago) ☆ ↰ ▾
to me ▾

You are receiving this email because your Amazon CloudWatch Alarm "Bucket Size Alarm" in the US West - Oregon region
has entered the ALARM state, because "Threshold Crossed: 1 datapoint (5569147.0) was greater than or equal to the
threshold (1048576.0)." at "Sunday 12 February, 2017 07:55:43 UTC".

View this alarm in the AWS Management Console:
https://console.aws.amazon.com/cloudwatch/home?region=us-west-2#s=Alarms&alarm=Bucket%20Size%20Alarm

Alarm Details:
- Name: Bucket Size Alarm
- Description: Bucket Size Alarm
- State Change: INSUFFICIENT_DATA -> ALARM
- Reason for State Change: Threshold Crossed: 1 datapoint (5569147.0) was greater than or equal to the threshold
(1048576.0).
- Timestamp: Sunday 12 February, 2017 07:55:43 UTC
- AWS Account: ▆▆▆▆▆▆▆

Threshold:
- The alarm is in the ALARM state when the metric is GreaterThanOrEqualToThreshold 1048576.0 for 86400 seconds.

Monitored Metric:
- MetricNamespace: AWS/S3
- MetricName: BucketSizeBytes
- Dimensions: [BucketName = chapter5-s3-bucket] [StorageType = StandardStorage]
- Period: 86400 seconds
- Statistic: Average
- Unit: not specified

State Change Actions:
- OK:
- ALARM: [arn:aws:sns:us-west-2:▆▆▆▆▆▆:BucketSizeAlarm]
- INSUFFICIENT_DATA:

--
If you wish to stop receiving notifications from this topic, please click or visit the link below to unsubscribe:
https://sns.us-west-2.amazonaws.com/unsubscribe.html?SubscriptionArn=arn:aws:sns:us-west-2:▆▆▆▆▆▆:
BucketSizeAlarm▆▆▆▆▆▆▆▆▆▆▆&Endpoint=sunil.gulabani1@gmail.com

Please do not reply directly to this email. If you have any questions or comments regarding this email, please contact us at
https://aws.amazon.com/support

Figure 5-63. Alarm e-mail

14. After objects are deleted or moved to another location from the bucket, the alarm state will be back to "OK" or "INSUFFICIENT_DATA," as shown in Figure 5-64.

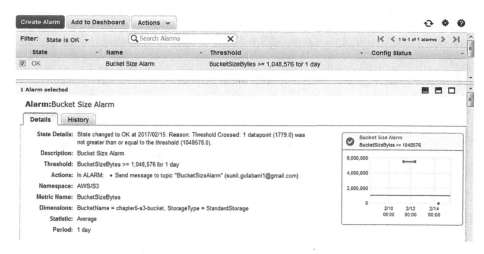

Figure 5-64. *Alarm status changed - OK*

Summary

In this chapter, you have learned how to create a bucket and how to configure a bucket for versioning. You have also learned about the life cycle management of objects and how to host a static web site. Finally, you have learned how to create folders and upload objects using AWS Management Console, AWS CLI, and AWS Java SDK.

Index

© Sunil Gulabani 2017
S. Gulabani, *Practical Amazon EC2, SQS, Kinesis, and S3*,
DOI 10.1007/978-1-4842-2841-8

Get the eBook for only $5!

Why limit yourself?

With most of our titles available in both PDF and ePUB format, you can access your content wherever and however you wish—on your PC, phone, tablet, or reader.

Since you've purchased this print book, we are happy to offer you the eBook for just $5.

To learn more, go to http://www.apress.com/companion or contact support@apress.com.

Apress®

Printed in the United States
By Bookmasters